The International Sourcebook
on Capital Punishment

The International Sourcebook on Capital Punishment

1997 EDITION

Center for Capital Punishment Studies, London

EDITED BY *William A. Schabas*

ASSOCIATE EDITORS: *Hugo Adam Bedau*
Peter Hodgkinson
Michael Radelet
Andrew Rutherford

Northeastern University Press
BOSTON

Northeastern University Press

ISBN   1-55553-299-3
ISSN   1090-0373

Designed by Ann Twombly

Composed in Plantin by Graphic Composition, Inc., Athens,
Georgia. Printed and bound by Thomson-Shore, Dexter, Michigan.
The paper is Glatfelter Supple Opaque Recycled, an acid-free stock.

MANUFACTURED IN THE UNITED STATES OF AMERICA
00 99 98 97   3 2 1

Contents

Editor's Preface

The death penalty is being abolished at a rate that few of us ever expected. The news, in January 1996, that the Russian Federation will impose a moratorium on capital punishment and, within a year, ratify an international treaty prohibiting its use in peacetime, is the latest in a number of recent and encouraging developments. It is now possible to speak of a zone north of the fiftieth parallel that is, for all intents and purposes, free of the death penalty.

In order to keep pace with these developments, the Center for Capital Punishment Studies of the University of Westminster, London, has undertaken the regular publication of a yearbook on capital punishment, of which this volume is the first. Contributions for the next edition may be sent to the center directly or to the undersigned (Département des sciences juridiques, Université du Québec à Montréal, C.P. 8888, Succursale Centre-Ville, Montréal, Canada H3C 3P8; Telephone: (514) 987 6547; Fax: (514) 987-4784; schabas.william@uqam.ca).

I would like to thank the associate editors, Hugo Adam Bedau, Peter Hodgkinson, Michael Radelet, and Andrew Rutherford, for their assistance and their contributions. I also wish to express my appreciation to the publishers for agreeing to undertake this ambitious project, and specifically to Bill Frohlich and Scott Brassart.

William A. Schabas
Université du Québec à Montréal
March 1996

Center for Capital Punishment Studies

VISITING PROFESSORS

Hugo Adam Bedau (appointed April 1994). Dr. Bedau, Austin Fletcher Professor of Philosophy at Tufts University, Massachusetts, joined the faculty at Tufts, having taught previously at Dartmouth College, Reed College, and Princeton University. He is best known for his writings on civil disobedience and on the death penalty. His definitive book *The Death Penalty in America* was first published in 1964, and the fourth edition is currently with the publishers. His most recent death penalty publication, *In Spite of Innocence* (1992), is jointly authored with Constance Putnam and Professor Michael Radelet. He is past chair of the National Coalition to Abolish the Death Penalty.

Andrew Rutherford (appointed April 1994). Andrew Rutherford is Professor of Law, University of Southampton, United Kingdom. After studying criminology at Cambridge University, he joined the Prison Service in 1962, where he worked at three Borstals as Assistant and later Deputy Governor. He was a Harkness Fellow in the United States of America between 1968 and 1970 and left the prison service in 1973 to return to the United States, where he taught and researched at a number of institutions, including Ohio State University, University of Minnesota, and Yale University. He has been actively involved in the Howard League for Penal Reform for many years and has served as chair since 1984. His publications include *Prisons and the Process of Justice* (1984), *Growing Out of Crime* (1986), and *Criminal Justice and the Pursuit of Decency* (1993). His most recent publication, *Capital Punishment: Global Issues and Prospects*, is edited with Peter Hodgkinson.

Michael Radelet (appointed December 1994). Dr. Radelet, Professor of Sociology, University of Florida at Gainesville, was educated at Michigan State University and received his Ph.D. at Purdue University, in Indiana. Professor Radelet is widely published, and his works include *Capital Punishment in America: An Annotated Bibliography* (1988), *Facing the Death Penalty: Essays on a Cruel and Unusual Punishment* (1989), *In Spite of Innocence: Erroneous Convictions in Capital Cases* (1992; with Hugo Adam Bedau and Constance Putnam), and *Executing the Mentally Ill* (1993; with Dr. Kent

Miller). He is regularly invited to give testimony before legislative bodies of both state and federal governments and has been an expert witness at over forty capital trials.

For further information about the Center for Capital Punishment Studies, please contact

Peter Hodgkinson
Director—Center for Capital Punishment Studies
School of Law
University of Westminster
Red Lion Square
London WC1R 4SR, U.K.

Telephone: (0171) 911 5000, ext. 2501
Fax: (0171) 911 5152
hodgkinsonp@wmin.ac.uk

ARTICLES

STEPHEN B. BRIGHT

Legalized Lynching: Race, the Death Penalty and the United States Courts

July of 1996 marks the twentieth anniversary of *Gregg* v. *Georgia*, in which the United States Supreme Court allowed Georgia and other states to resume capital punishment. The Supreme Court handed down its decision in *Gregg* on July 2, 1976.[1] On the same day, the Court upheld the capital punishment statutes of Florida and Texas.[2] The Court held that new statutes that had been adopted by the states would prevent the discrimination against racial minorities and the poor and the arbitrariness that had resulted in the Court's striking down the death penalty just four years earlier.[3]

The Court's assumption that the death penalty could be imposed fairly and without discrimination has not been borne out by experience. Nevertheless, Georgia will not have reassessed its use of the death penalty in 1996 but rather will have devoted its energy to the Olympic Games, which will be held in Atlanta in July. There is no likelihood of a decision in 1996 from the courts of Georgia or the United States Supreme Court even remotely similar to the decision of the Constitutional Court of South Africa unanimously concluding that the punishment of death is cruel, unusual, and degrading.[4] Although South Africa suffers from far more violent crime than does the United States, the Constitutional Court, after reviewing the history of capital punishment, concluded, as did Justice Harry A. Blackmun of the U.S. Supreme Court, that "the death penalty experiment has failed" because "no combination of procedural rules or substantive regulations ever can save the death penalty from its inherent constitutional deficiencies."[5]

South Africa, like Georgia, has had capital punishment as part of its "harsh legal heritage."[6] South Africa's past, like Georgia's, included "repression not freedom," "apartheid and prejudice not equality,"[7] and "too much savagery."[8] South Africa's enlightening includes a changing outlook, from "vengeance to an appreciation of the need for understanding."[9]

However, Georgia and other states in the United States, unlike South Africa, are not moving to a new day, but instead cling to an outdated, racist, and discredited form of punishment. Not long after the Olympic visitors leave the state, Georgia hopes to carry out the execution of Wilburn Dobbs, an African-American man, who was referred to at his trial as "colored" and "colored boy" by the judge and the defense lawyer and called by his first name by the prosecutor.[10] Two of the jurors who sentenced Dobbs to death admitted after trial to using the slur "nigger."[11] Dobbs was tried only two weeks after being indicted for murder and four other offenses. He was assigned a court-appointed lawyer who did not even know for certain until the day of trial that he was going to represent Dobbs. Trial counsel testified "[t]here was uncertainty all the way up until the trial began as to whether or not I would represent him"[12] and "didn't know for sure what he was going to be tried for."[13] The lawyer filed only one motion, a demand for a copy of the accusation and a list of witnesses,[14] and asked for a postponement on the morning of trial,[15] stating to the trial court that he was "not prepared to go to trial"[16] and that he was "in a better position to prosecute the case than defend it."[17] Nevertheless, the trial court denied the motion, and the case proceeded to trial.[18] A federal court described the defense lawyer's attitude towards African Americans as follows:

> Dobbs' trial attorney was outspoken about his views. He said that many blacks are uneducated and would not make good teachers, but do make good basketball players. He opined that blacks are less educated and less intelligent than whites either because of their nature or because "my granddaddy had slaves." He said that integration has led to deteriorating neighborhoods and schools and referred to the black community in Chattanooga as "black boy jungle." He strongly implied that blacks have inferior morals by relating a story about sex in a classroom. He also said that when he was young, a maid was hired with the understanding that she would steal some items. He said that blacks in Chattanooga are more troublesome

than blacks in Walker County [Georgia]. The attorney stated that he uses the word "nigger" jokingly.[19]

During the penalty phase of Dobbs's trial, when the jury could have heard anything about his life and background and any reasons Dobbs should not have been sentenced to death,[20] the lawyer presented no evidence.[21] For a closing argument he read part of Justice Brennan's concurring opinion in *Furman v. Georgia*,[22] which expressed the view that the death penalty was unconstitutional and could not be carried out.[23] Thus, rather than emphasizing to the jury the enormous decision that it had to make about whether Dobbs was going to live or die, the lawyer suggested that because the death penalty would never be carried out, the jury's decision was not important. A prosecutor is not allowed to make an argument that would diminish the jury's sense of responsibility for its life and death decision.[24]

The case of Wilburn Dobbs starkly illustrates the indifference of the courts of Georgia and the United States to racial discrimination and incompetent legal representation in capital cases. Dobbs's death sentence has been upheld despite the racial prejudice of the judge, the prosecutor, the defense lawyer, and the jurors in his case. The United States Court of Appeals concluded that "[a]lthough certain of the jurors' statements revealed racial prejudice, no juror stated that they viewed blacks as more prone to violence than whites . . . ."[25] Similarly, because neither the trial judge nor the defense lawyer decided the penalty, the Court held that "apart from the trial judge's and defense lawyer's references to Dobbs as 'colored' and 'colored boy,' it cannot be said that the trial judge's or the defense lawyer's racial attitudes affected the jurors' sentencing determination."[26]

Dobbs is not an isolated example. In at least five capital cases tried in Georgia in the last twenty years, the accused were subject to racial slurs by *their own lawyers* during court proceedings. Charlie Young, Curfew Davis, George Dungee, Terry Lee Goodwin, and Eddie Lee Ross were all referred to as "niggers" by their defense lawyers at some point in the trials at which they were sentenced to death. No court even held a hearing on the racial prejudice that infected the sentencing of William Henry Hance before he was executed by Georgia in

1994, even though jurors admitted in affidavits that racial slurs had been used during deliberations.[27] The Georgia Supreme Court upheld the death sentence in another case in which racial slurs were used by jurors during their deliberations.[28] The court reasoned that the evidence "shows only that two of the twelve jurors possessed some racial prejudice and does not establish that racial prejudice caused those two jurors to vote to convict [the defendant] and sentence him to die."[29]

Wilburn Dobbs, William Henry Hance, and most other African Americans sentenced to death in Georgia were tried before a white judge sitting in front of the Confederate battle flag. Georgia adopted the Confederate battle flag as part of its state flag in 1956[30] to symbolize its rejection of the federal Constitution and the Supreme Court's decision in *Brown* v. *Board of Education.*[31] The flag was described as follows by a federal judge: "The predominant part of the 1956 flag is the Confederate battle flag, which is historically associated with the Ku Klux Klan. The legislators who voted for the 1956 bill knew that the new flag would be interpreted as a statement of defiance against federal desegregation mandates and an expression of anti-black feelings."[32] The new flag was to carry the message that Georgia "intend[s] to uphold what [it] stood for, will stand for, and will fight for"—state-sponsored commitment to black subordination and denial of equal protection of the laws to Georgia's African-American school children.[33] Governor Marvin Griffin delivered the same message of defiance during his State of the State address in 1956, saying "[a]ll attempts to mix the races whether they be in the classrooms, on the playgrounds, in public conveyances, or in any other area of close contact, imperil the mores of the South."[34] Although it is well recognized that the flag serves as "a visual focal point for racial tensions,"[35] and symbolizes defiance of the principle of equal protection under law, it is displayed in most Georgia courtrooms.

Since *Gregg* in 1976, Georgia had carried out twenty executions by March 31, 1996.[36] Twelve of those executed were African Americans.[37] Six of the African Americans executed were sentenced to death by all-white juries.[38] In eighteen of the cases the victim was white.[39] These patterns are not limited to Georgia. Nine of the first twelve persons executed in Alabama were African American.[40] Although African Americans are the victims in half of the murders that occur each year in the United States,[41] over 80 percent of the executions that have been carried out have been for the murders of white persons.[42] An analysis of twenty-eight studies by the U.S. General Accounting Office found a pattern of racial disparities in capital sentencing throughout the country: "In 82 percent of the studies, race of the victim was found to influence the likelihood of being charged with capital murder or receiving the death penalty, *i.e.*, those who murdered whites were found to be more likely to be sentenced to death than those who murdered blacks. This finding was remarkably consistent across data sets, states, data collection methods, and analytic techniques."[43]

A study in 1994 of death sentences in Houston, Harris County, Texas, which has carried out more executions and sent more people to death than most states, found that "Harris County has sent blacks to death row nearly twice as often as whites during the last ten years, a growing imbalance that eclipses the pre–civil rights days of 'Old Sparky' the notorious Texas electric chair."[44] Thirty-seven people sentenced to death in Houston had been executed by the end of February 1995, more executions than any state except Texas. Harris County accounts for 113 persons on Texas's death row awaiting execution.[45] Only eleven states besides Texas have over one hundred persons under death sentence.[46] In Florida, which has the nation's third largest death row,[47] the Racial and Ethnic Bias Commission of the Florida Supreme Court found that "the application of the death penalty in Florida is not colorblind."[48] A congressional study found stark racial disparities in the use of the federal death penalty.[49] Racial disparities have been documented by other observers.[50]

Thus, the death penalty statutes approved by the Supreme Court in 1976 have failed to end the historic relationship between racial discrimination and the death penalty. Racial prejudice continues to influence every stage of the process leading to imposition of the death penalty. This article will first review briefly the historic relationship between racial violence and the death penalty in the United States.

It will then examine the ways in which racial biases continue to influence who is sentenced to death. Finally, it will describe the failure of courts and legislatures in the United States to deal with racial discrimination in capital cases.

Legal Lynchings

The death penalty is a direct descendant of lynching and other forms of racial violence and racial oppression in the United States. From colonial times until the Civil War, the criminal law in many states expressly differentiated between crimes committed by and against blacks and whites.[51] For example, Georgia law provided that the rape of a free white female by a black man "shall be" punishable by death, while the rape by anyone else of a free white female was punishable by a prison term of not less than two or more than twenty years.[52] The rape of a black woman was punishable "by fine and imprisonment, at the discretion of the court."[53] Disparate punishments—exacted both by the courts and by the mob—based upon both the race of the victim and the race of the defendant continued in practice after the abolition of slavery. At least 4,743 people were killed by lynch mobs.[54] More than 90 percent of the lynchings took place in the South, and three-fourths of the victims were African Americans.[55] The threat that Congress might pass an antilynching statute in the early 1920s led Southern states to "replace lynchings with a more '[humane] . . . method of racial control'—the judgment and imposition of capital sentences by all-white juries."[56] As one historian observed,

> Southerners . . . discovered that lynchings were untidy and created a bad press . . . . [L]ynchings were increasingly replaced by situations in which the Southern legal system prostituted itself to the mobs' demand. Responsible officials begged would-be lynchers to "let the law take its course," thus tacitly promising that there would be a quick trial and the death penalty . . . . [S]uch proceedings retained the essence of mob murder, shedding only its outward forms.[57]

The process of "legal lynchings" was so successful that in the 1930s, two-thirds of the people being executed were black.[58] As racial violence was achieved increasingly through the criminal courts, Georgia carried out more executions than any other state in the twentieth century. Between 1900 and the end of 1994, Georgia carried out 673 executions, the most of any state during this period.[59] Between 1924 and 1972, Georgia executed 337 black people and 75 white people.[60] After adopting electrocution as a means of execution in 1924, Georgia put more people to death than any other state and "set national records for executions over a twenty-year period in the 1940s and 1950s."[61]

There were particularly pronounced racial disparities throughout the United States in the infliction of the death penalty for rape. Of the 455 persons executed for rape after the Justice Department began compiling statistics, 405 were African Americans.[62] In part because of this history of discrimination, the Supreme Court held in *Furman v. Georgia*[63] that the death penalty as it had been used in the United States was unconstitutional. The five justices who made up the majority in Furman concluded that because the death penalty was being imposed discriminatorily,[64] arbitrarily,[65] and infrequently,[66] and was unnecessary for law enforcement purposes,[67] it constituted cruel and unusual punishment. Justice Marshall found the death penalty "morally unacceptable" to contemporary society,[68] and Justice Brennan concluded that because "the deliberate extinguishment of human life by the State is uniquely degrading to human dignity" it is inconsistent with "the evolving standards of decency that mark the progress of a maturing society."[69]

But the stop at what Justice Marshall called "a major milestone in the long road up from barbarism,"[70] was only temporary. New death penalty statutes were enacted almost immediately by a number of states,[71] and, as previously mentioned, some of those statutes were upheld in 1976. The Supreme Court upheld the statutes enacted by Georgia, Florida, and Texas.[72] It struck down the statutes adopted by North Carolina and Louisiana.[73] The first execution in the United States after the Supreme Court allowed the resumption of capital punishment was in 1977, when Gary Gilmore was killed by a firing squad in Utah. The practice of condemning people to die was resumed, and, despite assurances to the contrary by state legislatures and the courts, race once again plays a prominent role in determining who dies.

Racial Discrimination under the New Statutes

The breadth of the death penalty statutes approved in 1976 and the unfettered discretion given to prosecutors and juries provide ample room for racial prejudice to influence whether the death penalty is sought or imposed. The United States Supreme Court has observed that "because of the range of discretion entrusted to a jury in a capital sentencing hearing, there is a unique opportunity for racial prejudice to operate."[74] Even greater discretion is provided to prosecutors. However, the Court has refused to require procedures and remedies adequate to identify and prevent the influence of race. The majority of death penalty schemes adopted by the states after *Furman* v. *Georgia* provide for the death penalty for most first degree and felony murders. Any murder involving a robbery, burglary, rape, or kidnapping may be prosecuted as a capital case.[75] In addition, death may be imposed for any other "heinous, atrocious or cruel"[76] or "horrible"[77] murders. Of course, these terms describe almost all murders. Whether death or a term of imprisonment is imposed is determined by means of an imprecise and wholly subjective consideration of aggravating and mitigating factors or a guess as to whether the defendant poses a future danger to society.[78] The Supreme Court upheld the admission of expert testimony on future dangerousness despite the opinion of the American Psychiatric Association and others that the evidence is unreliable.[79]

People of color may have no voice in the discretionary decisions authorized by these statutes. The criminal justice systems are the institutions least affected by the Civil Rights Movement, which brought changes to many institutions in the United States in the last forty years. Judges and prosecutors are still elected in many states in judicial circuits drawn to dilute the voting strength of racial minorities.[80] Thus, even in many areas where a substantial part of the population is made up of people of color, all of the judges and prosecutors are white.[81] In Georgia, for example, all of the elected district attorneys are white.[82] Many other states also have no or very few African Americans as prosecutors.[83] People of color are often underrepresented in jury pools and excluded in the jury selection process.[84] Often the only person of color who participates in the process is the accused.

Thus, the critical decisions about whether the death penalty will be sought or imposed are often made by persons who may have overt or unconscious racial biases. The perfunctory capital trial—the legal lynching—is not a thing of the past. The poor are frequently represented by inept court-appointed lawyers, who often fail to protect the rights of their clients and fail to provide juries with critical information needed for the sentencing decision, leaving the accused virtually defenseless.[85] Capital cases are often tried before judges who are more interested in winning the next election than in enforcing the protections of the Bill of Rights.[86]

Discretion Exercised by Law Enforcement Officials and Prosecutors

The most important decisions that may determine whether the accused is sentenced to die are those made by the prosecutor regarding whether to seek the death penalty and whether to resolve the case with a plea bargain for a sentence less than death. In many jurisdictions, these critical decisions are made by a single white man, the elected district attorney, with no input from the community. There are no statewide standards that govern when the death penalty is sought. Each local district attorney sets his or her own policy in deciding which cases will be prosecuted as death cases.

From among the many cases in which death could be sought, the district attorney decides which few will actually be prosecuted as capital cases. For the white men who usually make these decisions, the crime may seem more heinous if the victim is a prominent white citizen. As one scholar has observed, "The life-and-death decision is made on trivial grounds, and tends to reflect the community's prejudices."[87] Race may also influence the decision to seek the death sentence in more subtle ways. Prosecutors make the decision whether to seek the death penalty based in part on the strength of the evidence brought to them by law enforcement in each case. Often the amount of evidence available differs because the local sheriffs and police departments investigate crime in the white community much more aggressively than crime in the black community.[88] Even before the beating of Rodney King and the discovery of tapes of racial slurs by Detective Mark Furhman, there was concern about the racial attitudes of the police department in Los Angeles.[89] While massive searches involving the police, army units, and local citizens may occur when there is a crime against a white person, often nothing more than a missing person report is completed when a black citizen disappears. This disparity in the investigative treatment of cases results in a disparity of evidence available to prosecute the cases. Thus, racial discrimination against crime victims by police officers results in the prosecutor's having stronger evidence with which to justify seeking the death penalty in white victim cases and not seeking it in cases where the victim is a person of color.

As a result of these influences, many cases in which prosecutors decide to seek the death penalty are not distinguishable from hundreds of other murder cases in which the death penalty is not sought. An investigation into why some cases are being treated as capital cases when other similar cases are not will almost always reveal the influence of race, class, and politics. Often there is more publicity and greater outrage in the community over an interracial crime than other crimes. The community outrage, the need to avenge the murder because of the prominence of the victim in the community, the insistence of the victim's family on the death penalty, the social and political clout of the family in the community, and the amount of publicity regarding the crime may be far more important in determining whether death is sought than the facts of the crime or the defendant's record and background.

For example, an investigation of all of the murder cases prosecuted in Georgia's Chattahoochee Judicial Circuit from 1973 to 1990 revealed that in cases involving the murder of a white person, prosecutors often met with the victim's family and discussed whether to seek the death penalty.[90] In a case involving the murder of the daughter of a prominent white contractor, the prosecutor contacted the contractor and asked him if he wanted to seek the death penalty.[91] When the contractor replied in the affirmative, the prosecutor said that was all he needed to know.[92] He obtained the death penalty at trial.[93] Later he was rewarded with a contribution of $5,000 from the contractor when he ran successfully for judge in the next election.[94] The contribution was the largest received by the district attorney. There were other cases in which the district attorney issued press releases announcing that he was seeking the death penalty after meeting with the family of a white victim.[95] However, prosecutors did not meet with African Americans whose family members had been murdered to determine what sentence they wanted. Most were not even notified that the case had been resolved.[96] As a result of these practices, although African Americans were the victims of 65 percent of the homicides in the Chattahoochee Judicial Circuit, 85 percent of the capital cases in that circuit were white victim cases.[97]

EXCLUSION OF PERSONS OF COLOR FROM JURIES

The prosecutor's decision to seek the death penalty may never be reviewed by a person of color as a juror. Many capital cases are tried in white-flight suburban communities where there are so few persons of color that there is little likelihood that they will be represented on the jury. Counties like Baltimore County, Maryland, and Cobb County, Georgia, account for a disproportionately high number of persons sentenced to death in those states.[98] I am aware of seventeen death sentences imposed in Cobb County, Georgia, under the death penalty statute adopted by Georgia in 1973. This is among the highest number of death sentences for a Georgia county. Yet even in communities where there is a substantial number of people of color in the population, prosecutors are often successful in preventing or minimizing participation by minorities.

During jury selection for a capital trial, the judge or the prosecutor asks potential jurors if they are conscientiously opposed to the death penalty. If they are and cannot put their views aside, the state is entitled to have those people removed for cause.[99] Although this process results in a more conviction-prone jury, it has been upheld by the Supreme Court.[100] This "death qualification" process often results in the removal of prospective jurors who are more often persons of color than white persons. People of color may have reservations about the death penalty because it has been used in a racially discriminatory manner. This process is one of many ways in which the history of racial discrimination in the infliction of the death penalty perpetuates continued discrimination. Often the death qualification process reduces the number of people of color in the jury venire to few enough that those remaining can be eliminated by the prosecutor with peremptory strikes.

It is the publicly announced policy of Ed Peters, the district attorney of Hinds County, Mississippi, to "get rid of as many" black citizens as possible when exercising his peremptory strikes to select a jury.[101] As a result of this "policy" by a government official, Leo Edwards, an African American, was sentenced to death by an all-white jury even though he was tried in a community that is 34 percent African American.[102] The federal courts rejected Edwards's challenge to Peters's discrimination,[103] and Leo Edwards was executed in 1989.[104] A prosecutor in Chambers County, Alabama, used twenty-six jury strikes against twenty-six African Americans who had been qualified for jury duty to get three all-white juries in a case involving Albert Jefferson, a mentally retarded African American accused of a crime against a white victim.[105] One jury was for a hearing on Jefferson's mental competence to stand trial, another was for guilt, and the third was for sentencing. At the time of Jefferson's trial, marriage records at the courthouse in Chambers County were kept in books engraved "white" and "colored."[106] During state postconviction proceedings, lawyers representing Jefferson discovered lists that had been made by the prosecutor prior to jury selection in which the prosecutor divided prospective jurors into four lists—"strong," "medium," "weak," and "black."[107] A state circuit judge in Chambers County ruled that no racial discrimination occurred in the selection of the juries.[108] The court held there were race-neutral reasons for each of the strikes of African Americans.

A federal court in Alabama found that the "standard operating procedure of the Tuscaloosa County District Attorney's Office," was "to use the peremptory challenges to strike as many blacks as possible from the venires in cases involving serious crimes."[109] The district court also found that prosecutors manipulated the trial docket in their effort to preserve the racial purity of criminal juries. Inasmuch as they actually set the criminal trial dockets until 1982, they implemented a scheme in which juries with fewer black venirepersons would be called for the serious cases.[110] Joseph Briley, the prosecutor in Georgia's Ocmulgee Judicial Circuit, tried thirty-three death penalty cases in his tenure as district attorney in the circuit between 1974 and his resignation in 1994. Of those thirty-three cases, twenty-four were against African-American defendants.[111] It was discovered that Briley instructed jury commissioners in one county in the circuit to underrepresent black citizens on the master jury lists from which grand and trial juries were selected.[112] Additionally, the African Americans who were summoned for jury duty in the circuit were often sent back home after Briley used his peremptory jury strikes against them. In the cases in which the defendants were black and the victims were white, Briley used 93 percent of his jury challenges—96 out of 103—against black citizens.[113] When a prosecutor uses the overwhelming majority of his jury strikes against a racial minority, that part of the community is prohibited from participating in the process. A jury does not represent "the conscience of the community on the ultimate question of life or death,"[114] when one-fourth or more of the community is not represented on the jury.

African Americans and other people of color continue to be excluded from jury service, even after the Supreme Court's decision in *Batson* v. *Kentucky*,[115] which modified the almost insurmountable burden of establishing that a prosecutor had discriminated by striking people of one race from the jury. Before the *Batson* decision, the burden of establishing discimination in the use of jury strikes was proof that the prosecutor struck black citizens "in case after case, whatever the circumstances, whatever the crime and whoever the defendant or the victim may be . . . with the result that no Negroes ever serve on petit juries."[116] It was usually impossible for poor defendants to gather the evidence to prove such claims. And even if the prosecutor discriminated in an individual case, the courts could deny relief if discrimination had not occurred in "case after case." The Supreme Court in *Batson* v. *Kentucky* held that a showing of disparate strikes against minority jurors in a particular case shifted the burden to the prosecution to provide race-neutral reasons for those strikes.

Batson requires elected trial judges to assess reasons given by the district attorney to determine whether the prosecutor intended to discriminate.[117] Many judges are former prosecutors who may have hired the district attorneys appearing before them.[118] Even if the judge is not personally close to the prosecutor, he or she may be dependent upon the prosecutor's support in elections to remain in office.[119] Thus, in the many jurisdictions where judges are elected, it may be politically impossible and personally difficult for the judge to reject a reason proffered by the prosecutor for striking a person of color. Courts routinely uphold convictions and death sentences in which a grossly disproportionate number of African Americans have been excluded from jury service by the prosecutor's peremptory jury strikes.[120]

Racial Diversity on Juries Makes a Difference in Capital Trials

Juries selected through discriminatory practices often bring to the jury box, either consciously or subconsciously, "racial stereotypes and assumptions" that influence them "in the direction of findings of black culpability and white victimization, . . . black immorality and white virtue, . . . blacks as social problems and whites as valued citizens."[121] Experience has taught that the death penalty is much more likely to be imposed in cases tried to all-white juries than in cases tried to more racially diverse juries.[122] The effect is particularly pronounced and results in the most severe sentences when the victim is of the same race and the defendant is of a different race from that of the jurors.[123] More diverse juries bring to their decision making a broader perspective gained through varied life experiences. An African-American member of the Georgia Supreme Court has observed that "[w]hen it comes to grappling with racial issues in the criminal justice system today, often white Americans find one reality while African-Americans see another."[124] Yet despite the fact that the criminal justice system is usually determining whether an African American will lose his or her life or freedom, the decision is often based only on the version of "reality" seen by white people.

Disparities in Imposition of Death Sentences in the State Courts

Racial disparities occur in all types of sentencing in the courts of the United States,[125] but they are particularly evident in death penalty cases. Although African Americans make up only 12 percent of the total population of the United States, they have been the victims in about half of the total homicides in the country in the last twenty-five years.[126] In some states in the South, where capital punishment is most often imposed, African Americans are the victims of over 60 percent of the murders. Yet over 80 percent of the cases in which the death penalty has been carried out have involved white victims.[127] In Georgia, for example, although African Americans were the victims of 63.5 percent of the murders between 1976 and 1980, 85 percent of the cases in which death was imposed during that period involved murders of whites.[128] Professor David Baldus and his associates conducted two studies of the influence of race in the infliction of the death penalty, examining over 2,000 murder cases that occurred in Georgia during the 1970s.[129] They found that prosecutors are more likely to seek the death penalty where the victim is white and that juries are more likely to impose the death penalty in such cases.[130] Defendants charged with killing white victims were 4.3 times more likely to receive a death sentence than defendants charged with killing blacks.[131]

Disparities in Federal Death Prosecutions

The federal government, in pursuing death sentences authorized by the Anti–Drug Abuse Act of 1988,[132] has an even worse record of discrimination than the states have. The act authorizes the death penalty for murders committed by "kingpins" involved in drug trafficking "enterprises."[133] Federal prosecutors are given wide discretion in deciding whether to seek the death penalty. As observed by one congressional committee, "The drug trafficking 'enterprise' can consist of as few as five individuals, and even a low-ranking 'foot soldier' in the organization can be charged with the death penalty if involved in a killing."[134] Although three-fourths of those convicted of participating in a drug enterprise under the general provisions of 21 U.S.C. 848 are white,[135] the death penalty provisions of the act have been used almost exclusively against minorities. Of the first thirty-seven federal death penalty prosecutions, all but four were against people of color.[136] Nevertheless, Congress provided for the death penalty for sixty additional crimes in the Violent Crime Control and Law Enforcement Act of 1994 and refused to enact the Racial Justice Act.[137] There is no reason to expect that the federal government will be more successful in preventing discrimination under the Violent Crime Control Act than it has been with the Anti–Drug Abuse Act.

Those accused of federal capital crimes are supposedly protected from racial discrimination by the requirement that juries be instructed not to discriminate and that all jurors sign certificates that they did not discriminate.[138] But this provision is hardly any protection against racial discrimination. By the time the jury is selected, racial prejudice may have already influenced the prosecutor's decision to seek the death penalty or the striking of people of color from the jury. Moreover, the most pernicious racial discrimination that occurs today is that perpetrated by those who have the sophistication not to admit their biases. Those who live in racially exclusive neighborhoods, are members of racially exclusive social organizations, send their children to segregation academies, and refuse to rent to black citizens may be more than happy to listen to jury instructions and sign the certificate before sending some black person off to her or his death.

Failure of the United States Supreme Court to Remedy Racial Discrimination in Capital Cases

The United States Supreme Court, by a five-four vote, held in *McCleskey* v. *Kemp*[139] that Georgia could carry out its death penalty law despite racial disparities that would not be tolerated in any other area of the law. The Court accepted the racial disparities in infliction of the death penalty as "an inevitable part of our criminal justice system."[140] The Court found that the studies by Baldus and his associates established "at most . . . a discrepancy that appears to correlate with race" and declined "to assume that that which is unexplained is invidious,"[141] thus holding the disparities insufficient even to raise a prima facie case of racial discrimination. The Court also found that "McCleskey's claim, taken to its logical conclusion, throws into serious question the principles that underlie our entire criminal justice system."[142] Justice Brennan, in dissent, characterized this concern as "a fear of too much justice."[143]

The Court's fear of too much justice may result in no justice at all. The decision in *McCleskey* v. *Kemp* has been employed to avoid dealing with issues of racial discrimination by lower federal and state courts. *McCleskey* v. *Kemp* demonstrates the indifference of the Supreme Court to the overwhelming evidence that racial prejudice influences the vast discretion exercised in making the highly charged, emotional decision about who is to die.

Failure of Congress to Pass the Racial Justice Act

Despite the pronounced racial disparities in the infliction of the death penalty in both state and federal capital cases, Congress refused to include the Racial Justice Act as part of the crime bill in 1994, just as it has refused to enact the act in previous years. The Racial Justice Act was adopted in a version of the crime bill that passed the House of Representatives in April 1994,[144] but because of opposition in the Senate it was not included in the final bill reported out of the conference committee and adopted by both the Senate and the House later in the summer. The Racial Justice Act was a modest proposal that would have required courts to have hearings on racial disparities in infliction of the death penalty and to look behind the disparities to determine whether they are related to race or some other factor.[145] Nevertheless, the Racial Justice Act presented the threat of too much justice to the United States Senate and was defeated.

It is not surprising that Congress failed to pass the Racial Justice Act. Congress steadfastly refused to pass an antilynching law when African Americans and other minorities were being lynched in the 1920s and 1930s.[146] Instead, the federal government put its law enforcement efforts into pursuing moonshiners. Today, the government of the United States commits ample resources for questionable and expensive efforts to demonstrate it is "tough on crime"—the war on drugs, the pursuit of federal death sentences for crimes that can be prosecuted in the state courts, and the housing of ever increasing numbers of people in federal prisons for longer periods of time. Few resources, though, are devoted to the constitutional commitment of equality for racial minorities and the poor.

Conclusion

In *McCleskey* v. *Kemp,* the Supreme Court said that evidence of racial discrimination should be taken to the legislatures.[147] Legislators in the United States, however, respond to powerful, monied interests. The poor person accused of a crime has no political action committee, no lobby, and often no effective advocate even in the court where his life is at stake. The crime debate in the United States has become increasingly demagogic and irresponsible. There is little reason for hope in the legislatures.

But, most unfortunately, neither the state nor the federal courts appear likely to address racial discrimination in the infliction of the death penalty in the near future. The courts, bowing to enormous political pressures to get on with executions, have substituted a notion of what the criminal justice should be for what it is. As Justice Thurgood Marshall said in another context, "constitutionalizing wishful thinking" that "racial discrimination is largely a phenomenon of the past" does a "grave disservice . . . to those victims of past and present racial discrimination."[148]

There is a long history of racial violence in the United States, and the criminal justice systems have been a part of that history. In addition, the criminal justice systems in many parts of the United States have suffered both from years of neglect and from inadequate funding, and have often been entrusted to persons without the ability or the inclination to carry out their high functions. It should not surprise anyone that the problems of racial exclusion and racial discrimination are greater there than in other parts of society. One must hope that the courts of the United States will eventually come to the same recognition as that made by the Constitutional Court of South Africa: it is impossible to devise a system that will fairly determine who should die. The courts of the United States must also realize that they cannot deliver justice when they tolerate racial prejudice and racial exclusion. Responding to the public clamor for executions is no justification for ignoring racial discrimination in the court system. Courts of vengeance are not courts of justice.

Notes

Stephen B. Bright is Director, Southern Center for Human Rights, Atlanta, Georgia, and J. Skelly Wright Fellow and Visiting Lecturer in Law, Yale Law School. B.A. 1971, J.D. 1975, University of Kentucky. The author has represented persons facing the death penalty at trials, on appeals, and in post-conviction proceedings since 1979. This article draws upon those experiences as well as the authorities cited.

1. 428 U.S. 153, 96 S.Ct. 2909, 49 L.Ed.2d 859 (1976).

2. *Proffitt* v. *Florida*, 428 U.S. 242, 96 S.Ct. 2960, 49 L.Ed.2d 913 (1976); *Jurek* v. *Texas*, 428 U.S. 262, 96 S.Ct. 2950, 49 L.Ed.2d 929 (1976).

3. *Furman* v. *Georgia*, 408 U.S. 238, 92 S.Ct. 2726, 33 L.Ed.2d 346 (1972).

4. *Makwanyane and Mchunu* v. *The State* (1995), 16 *H.R.L.J.* 154 (Constitutional Court of South Africa).

5. *Callins* v. *Collins*, 114 S.Ct. 1127, 127 L.Ed 435 (1994) (Blackmun, J., dissenting from the denial of certiorari).

6. *Makwanyane and Mchunu* v. *The State*, *supra* note 4, at p. 200 (*per* Mokgoro, J.).

7. *Ibid.*, at p. 201 (*per* O'Regan, J.).

8. *Ibid.*, at p. 185 (*per* Didcott, J.).

9. *Ibid.*, at p. 190 (*per* Langa, J.).

10. *Dobbs* v. *Zant*, 720 F. Supp. 1566, 1578 (N.D. Ga. 1989), *aff'd*, 963 F.2d 1519, 1523 (11th Cir. 1991), *remanded*, 113 S.Ct. 835 (1993).

11. *Ibid.*, at pp. 1576–1578, 1576 n. 22.

12. Transcript of State Habeas Corpus Hearing of September 28, 1977, at p. 55, included in Record on Appeal, *Dobbs* v. *Zant*, 963 F.2d 1403 (11th Cir.1991), *rev'd and remanded*, 113 S.Ct. 835 (1993).

13. Testimony of the lawyer in federal court hearing of October 6, 1982, at p. 85, included as part of the Record on Appeal in *Dobbs*, *supra* note 12.

14. Record on Appeal to Georgia Supreme Court, at p. 24, included in the Record on Appeal in *Dobbs*, *supra* note 12.

15. Transcript of trial, at p. 2, included in the Record on Appeal in *Dobbs*, *supra* note 12.

16. *Ibid.*, at p. 7.

17. *Ibid.*, at p. 5.

18. *Ibid.*, at p. 10.

19. *Dobbs* v. *Zant*, *supra* note 10, at p. 1577.

20. Any aspect of the life and background of the accused may be considered by the sentencer as a reason to impose a sentence less than death. *Penry* v. *Lynaugh*, 492 U.S. 302, 109 S.Ct. 2934, 106 L.Ed.2d 256 (1989); *Eddings* v. *Oklahoma*, 455 U.S. 104, 110 (1982); *Lockett* v. *Ohio*, 438 U.S. 586, 604, 98 S.Ct. 2954, 57 L.Ed.2d 973 (1978).

21. Transcript of trial, at pp. 503–505, included as part of the Record on Appeal in *Dobbs* v. *Zant, supra* note 12.

22. 408 U.S. 238, pp. 257–306 (1972).

23. Transcript of Closing Argument, included as part of the Record on Appeal in *Dobbs* v. *Zant, supra* note 12.

24. *Caldwell* v. *Mississippi*, 472 U.S. 320 (1985).

25. *Dobbs* v. *Zant*, 946 F.2d, at p. 1523.

26. *Ibid.*

27. *Hance* v. *Zant*, Super.Ct. of Butts Co., Ga., No. 93-V-172 (affidavits of jurors Patricia LeMay and Gayle Lewis Daniels). See also *Hance* v. *Zant*, 696 F.2d 940 (11th Cir.1983), *cert. denied*, 463 U.S. 1210 (1994) (Blackmun, J., dissenting from denial of certiorari); Bob HERBERT, "Mr. Hance's 'Perfect Punishment,' " *New York Times*, March 27, 1994, at p. D17; Bob HERBERT, "Jury Room Injustice," *New York Times*, March 30, 1994, at p. A15.

28. *Spencer* v. *State*, 398 S.E.2d 179 (Ga. 1990).

29. *Ibid.*, at p. 185.

30. Off. Code Ga. Ann. 50-3-1 (Michie 1994).

31. 347 U.S. 483 (1954) (holding that racial segregation in the public schools violates the equal protection clause of the Constitution); *Brown* v. *Board of Education*, 349 U.S. 294, 300 (1955) (requiring that desegregation of the public schools proceed "with all deliberate speed").

32. *Coleman* v. *Miller*, 885 F. Supp. 1561, 1569 (M.D. Ga. 1995). See also Julius CHAMBERS, "Protection of Civil Rights: A Constitutional Mandate for the Federal Government" (1989), 87 *Mich. L. Rev.* 1599, 1601 n.9.

33. Jim AUCHMUTEY, "Unraveling the Flag: A Guide to Rebel Colors," *Atlanta Journal & Constitution*, September 29, 1991, at p. M8 (statement by state representative Denmark Groover).

34. Mark SHERMAN, "Pledging Allegiances at Flag Forum," *Atlanta Journal & Constitution*, January 29, 1993, at p. G6.

35. *Augustus* v. *School Board of Escambia County*, 507 F.2d 152, 155 (5th Cir. 1975).

36. *Death Row U.S.A.*, published by the NAACP Legal Defense and Education Fund, Inc., at p. 9 (Summer 1995).

37. *Ibid.*, at pp. 4–9.

38. The author has made this determination from the trial judge's reports to the Georgia Supreme Court in the six cases which indicate that no member of the defendant's race was on the jury that sentenced him to death.

39. *Death Row U.S.A.*, *supra* note 36, at pp. 4–9.

40. *Ibid.*, at pp. 4–7.

41. Bureau of Justice Statistics, U.S. Dep't of Justice, *Sourcebook of Criminal Justice Statistics 1993* (Kathleen Maguire and Ann L. Pastore, eds., 1993), at p. 384, table 3.128.

42. *Death Row U.S.A.*, *supra* note 36, at p. 3 (reporting that in 82 percent of the cases in which executions have been carried out, the victims were white).

43. U.S. General Accounting Office, *Death Penalty Sentencing: Research Indicates Pattern of Racial Disparities*, (February 1990) p. 5.

44. Bryan DENSON, "Death Penalty: Equal Justice?" *The Houston Post*, October 16, 1994, at p. A1.

45. Tamar LEWIN, "Who Decides Who Will Die? Even Within the States It Varies," *New York Times*, February 23, 1995, at pp. A1, A13.

46. *Death Row U.S.A. supra* note 36.

47. Ibid., at p. 18 (341 people on Florida's death row).

48. Report and Recommendation of the Florida Supreme Court Racial and Ethnic Bias Study Commission, at xvi (December 11, 1991). See also Michael L. RADELET, Glenn L. PIERCE, "Choosing Those Who Will Die: Race and the Death Penalty in Florida" (1991), 43 *U. Fla. L. Rev.* 1.

49. Staff Report by the Subcommittee on Civil and Constitutional Rights of the Committee of the Judiciary, U.S. House of Representatives, *Racial Disparities in Federal Death Penalty Prosecutions 1984-1994* (103d Cong. 2d Sess. March, 1994), at 2 [hereinafter cited as House Subcommittee, *Racial Disparities in Federal Death Penalty Prosecutions*].

50. In addition to the studies cited by the General Accounting Office in its report, see: David C. BALDUS *et al.*, *Equal Justice and the Death Penalty* (1990); Samuel R. GROSS, Robert MAURO, *Death & Discrimination: Racial Disparities in Capital Sentencing* (1989); David MARGOLICK, "In the Land of Death Penalty, Accusations of Racial Bias," *New York Times*, July 10, 1991, at p. A1 (describing racial disparities in the infliction of the death penalty in Georgia's Chattahoochee Judicial Circuit, which includes the city of Columbus); Thomas J. Keil and Gennaro F. Vito, "Race and the Death Penalty in Kentucky Murder Trials: 1976–1991," paper presented to the Academy of Criminal Justice Sciences, Chicago (1994) (finding that blacks accused of killing whites had a higher than average probability of being charged with a capital crime by the prosecutor and being sentenced to death by the jury); Bob LEVENSON, Debbie SALAMORE, "Prosecutors see death penalty in black and white," *Orlando Sentinel*, May 24, 1992, at p. A-1 (reporting that "[j]ustice . . . is not colorblind in Central Florida when it comes to the prosecution of first degree murder cases"); Paul PINKHAM and Robin LOWENTHAL, "The Color of Justice in Jacksonville: Killers of Blacks Get Off Easier than Killers of Whites," *Florida Times Union*, Jacksonville, December 8, 1991, at p. D1; Jim HENDERSON, Jack TAYLOR, "Killers of Dallas blacks escape the death penalty," *Dallas Times Herald*, November 17, 1985, at p. 1 (accompanied by other stories and charts demonstrating relationship between race and imposition of the death sentence).

51. Leon HIGGINBOTHAM, Jr., *In the Matter of Color: Race in the American Legal Process* 256 (1978).

52. *Ibid.*

53. *Ibid.* See also *McCleskey v. Kemp*, 481 U.S. 279, pp. 329–332, 107 S.Ct. 1756, 95 L.Ed.2d 262 (1987) (Brennan, J., dissenting).

54. These numbers come from the archives at Tuskegee University, where lynchings have been documented since 1882. Mark CURRIDEN, "The Legacy of Lynching," *Atlanta Journal and Constitution*, January 15, 1995, at p. M1.

55. *Ibid.*

56. Douglas L. COLBERT, "Challenging the Challenge: Thirteenth Amendment as a Prohibition Against the Racial Use of Peremptory Challenges" (1990), 76 *Cornell L. Rev.* 1, p. 79 (quoting Michael Belknap, federal law, and Southern Order 22–26 (1987)).

57. Dan T. CARTER, *Scottsboro: A Tragedy of the American South* (rev. ed. 1979), at p. 115.

58. Douglas L. COLBERT, *supra* note 56, at p. 80. For other descriptions of the evolution from lynching to perfunctory capital trials, see, for example, Eric W. RISE, *The Martinsville Seven: Race, Rape, and Capital Punishment* (1995); W. Fitzhugh BRUNDAGE, *Lynching in the New South: Georgia and Virginia, 1880–1930* (1993); George C. WRIGHT, *Racial Violence in Kentucky, 1865–1940: Lynchings, Mob Rule, and "Legal Lynchings"* (1990).

59. "The Pace of Executions: Since 1976 and Through History," *New York Times*, December 4, 1994, at p. 3.

60. Prentice PALMER, Jim GALLOWAY, "Georgia Electric Chair Spans Five Decades," *Atlanta Journal*, December 15, 1983, at p. 15A.

61. *Ibid.*

62. *Furman v. Georgia, supra* note 3, at p. 364 n.149 (1972) (Marshall, J., concurring).

63. *Ibid.*

64. *Ibid.*, 408 U.S., at pp. 249–252 (Douglas, J., concurring), *ibid.*, at p. 310 (Stewart, J., concurring), *ibid.*, at pp. 364–366 (Marshall, J., concurring).

65. *Ibid.*, at pp. 291–295 (Brennan, J., concurring), *ibid.*, at p. 306 (Stewart, J., concurring), *ibid.*, at p. 313 (White, concurring) ("there is no meaningful basis for distinguishing the few cases in which it is imposed from the many cases in which it is not").

66. *Ibid.*, at p. 310 (White, J., concurring).

67. *Ibid.*, at p. 359 (Marshall, J., concurring).

68. *Ibid.*, at pp. 360–369 (Marshall, J., concurring).

69. *Ibid.*, at pp. 270, 291 (Brennan, J., concurring).

70. *Ibid.*, at p. 371 (Marshall, J., concurring) quoting Ramsey CLARK, *Crime in America*, at p. 336 (1970).

71. *Gregg v. Georgia, supra* note 1, at pp. 179–180 and n.23 (1976) (noting that at least thirty-five states passed death penalty statutes).

72. *Ibid.*; *Proffitt v. Florida, supra* note 2; *Jurek v. Texas, supra* note 2.

73. *Woodson v. North Carolina*, 428 U.S. 280, 96 S.Ct. 2978, 49 L.Ed.2d 944 (1976); *Roberts (Stanislaus) v. Louisiana*, 428 U.S. 325, 96 S.Ct. 3001, 49 L.Ed.2d 974 (1976).

74. *Turner v. Murray*, 476 U.S. 28, 35 (1985).

75. See, *e.g.*, Off. Code Ga. Ann. 16-5-1, 17-10-30; Fla. Stat. 921.141; Ala. Code 13A-5-40.

76. Fla. Stat. 921.141(5)(h).

77. Off. Code Ga. Ann. 17-10-30(b)(7).

78. Tex. Code Crim. Pro. 37.071.

79. *Barefoot* v. *Estelle*, 463 U.S. 880 (1983).

80. *Nipper* v. *Smith*, 39 F.3d 1484, pp. 1537–1541 (11th Cir.1994) (en banc); *League of United Latin American Citizens, Counsel No. 434* v. *Clements*, 999 F.2d 831, pp. 904–918 (5th Cir.1993) (en banc) (King, J., dissenting), *cert. denied*, 114 S.Ct. 878 (1994). Ruth MARCUS, "Does Voting Rights Law Cover Judicial Elections?" *Washington Post*, April 21, 1991, at p. A4.

81. Mark CURRIDEN, "Racism Mars Justice in U.S. Panel Reports," *Atlanta Journal and Constitution*, Aug. 11, 1991, at pp. D1, D3 (observing that only six of Georgia's 134 Superior Court judges were African-American, and those six were in three judicial circuits); Associated Press, "Second Black Alabama Supreme Court Justice Sworn In," *Columbus (Ga.) Ledger-Enquirer*, November 2, 1993, at p. B2 (noting that there was only one African American among Alabama's seventeen appellate court judges, and only twelve blacks among the state's 255 circuit and district court judges); Rorie SHERMAN, "Is Mississippi Turning?" *National Law Journal*, February 20, 1989, at pp. 1, 24 (only 2.6 percent of all state court judges in the United States are black).

82. Mark CURRIDEN, "Racism Mars Justice in U.S. Panel Reports," *supra* note 81, at pp. D1, D3.

83. Jesse SMITH, Robert JOHNS, eds., *Statistical Record of Black America*, at pp. 774–775 (3d ed. 1995) (listing the African Americans serving as judges, magistrates, and justices of the peace, and showing no African Americans as "other judicial officials" in Arkansas, Connecticut, Florida, Illinois, Indiana, Michigan, Oklahoma, South Carolina, and Texas).

84. American Bar Association Task Force on Minorities and the Justice System, *Achieving Justice in a Diverse America*, at p. 15 (1992).

85. For a discussion of the impact of poverty on the imposition of the death penalty due to the quality of representation provided by court-appointed counsel see, Stephen B. BRIGHT, "Counsel for the Poor: The Death Sentence Not for the Worst Crime but for the Worst Lawyer" (1994), 103 *Yale L. J.* 1835.

86. For a discussion of the political pressures that often affect state court judges, see Stephen B. BRIGHT, Patrick J. KEENAN, "Judges and the Politics of Death: Deciding Between the Bill of Rights and the Next Election in Capital Cases" (1995), 75 *Boston U. L. Rev.* 759.

87. Rick BRAGG, "Two Crimes, Two Punishments," *New York Times*, January 22, 1995, at p. 1 (quoting Franklin Zimring, Director of the Earl Warren Legal Institute at the University of California at Berkeley).

88. Studies and cases documenting discriminatory practices by police against racial minorities are collected and discussed by Prof. Charles J. OGLE-

TREE in "Does Race Matter in Criminal Prosecutions," *Champion*, July 1991, at pp. 7, 112.

89. See *Los Angeles* v. *Lyons*, 461 U.S. 95, p. 116 n. 3 (1983) (Marshall, J., dissenting) (noting that although only 9 percent of the residents of Los Angeles are black males, they have accounted for 75 percent of the deaths resulting from chokeholds by police).

90. The evidence was gathered and presented in the case of *State* v. *Brooks*, Super. Ct. of Muscogee Co., Ga., Indictment Nos. 3888, 54606 (1991) [cited hereinafter as "Hearing on Racial Discrimination"]. The evidence is collected in *Chattahoochee Judicial District: The Buckle of the Death Belt*, published by the Death Penalty Information Center, Washington, D.C., 1991.

91. Transcript of Hearing, at p. 38, *Davis* v. *Kemp*, Super. Ct. of Butts Co., Ga. (1988) (No. 86-V-865) (testimony of James Isham, father of the victim).

92. *Ibid.*

93. *Davis* v. *State*, 340 S.E.2d 869 (Ga. 1986), *cert. denied*, 479 U.S. 871 (1986).

94. Clint CLAYBROOK, "Slain girl's father top campaign contributor," *Columbus (Ga.) Ledger-Enquirer*, August 7, 1988, at p. B-1.

95. See, *e.g.*, Phil GAST, "District Attorney Criticizes Court for Rejecting Sentence," *Columbus (Ga.) Enquirer*, September 17, 1983, at pp. A1, A2.

96. Hearing on Racial Discrimination, *supra* note 90, at pp. 178, 184–185, 192–193, 197, 199–200 (testimony of African Americans about failure of prosecutor to contact them about cases involving the murder of a family member).

97. See Defense Exhibit 1A, admitted at Hearing on Racial Discrimination, *supra* note 90.

98. See *Report of the Governor's Commission on the Death Penalty: An Analysis of Capital Punishment in Maryland: 1978 to 1993*, at pp. 91, 92, 119 (November 1993) (although Baltimore City has well over ten times as many murders as Baltimore County each year, of forty-one death sentences imposed in Maryland under its current death penalty statute, twenty-two were imposed in Baltimore County; of the fifteen death sentences in effect on June 30, 1993, all but four were from Baltimore County; only five death sentences were imposed in Baltimore City and only two of the sentences in effect on June 30, 1993, were from Baltimore City).

99. *Wainwright* v. *Witt*, 469 U.S. 810 (1985); *Witherspoon* v. *Illinois*, 391 U.S. 510, 88 S.Ct. 1770, 20 L.Ed.2d 776 (1968).

100. *Lockhart* v. *McCree*, 476 U.S. 162 (1986).

101. *Edwards* v. *Scroggy*, 849 F.2d 204, 207 (5th Cir. 1988).

102. *Ibid.*

103. *Ibid.*

104. *Death Row U.S.A.*, *supra* note 36, at p. 6.

105. *Jefferson* v. *Alabama*, Cir. Court Chambers Co., No. 81–77.

106. "Alabama County Still Records Marriages by Race," *Atlanta Journal and Constitution*, July 21, 1991, at p. A2.

107. *Alabama* v. *Jefferson*, Cir. Ct. Chambers Co. No. CC-81-77, Order of October 2, 1992.

108. *Ibid.*

109. *Jackson* v. *Thigpen*, 752 F. Supp. 1551, 1554 (N.D. Ala. 1990), *aff'd in part and rev'd in part, sub nom. Jackson* v. *Herring*, 42 F.3d 1350 (11th Cir. 1995).

110. *Ibid.*, 752 F. Supp. at p. 1555.

111. Charts showing most of the prosecutor's capital trials are included in *Horton* v. *Zant*, 941 F.2d 1449, pp. 1468–1470 (11th Cir.1991), *cert. denied*, 117 L.Ed.2d 652 (1992).Two other capital cases were tried against white defendants before the prosecutor left office: *Tharpe* v. *State*, 416 S.E.2d 78 (Ga.1992); *Fugate* v. *State*, 431 S.E.2d 104 (Ga.1993).

112. *Amadeo* v. *Zant*, 486 U.S. 214 (1988).

113. *Horton* v. *Zant*, 941 F.2d at p. 1458.

114. *Witherspoon* v. *Illinois*, 391 U.S. 510, 519 (1968).

115. 476 U.S. 79 (1986).

116. *Swain* v. *Alabama*, 380 U.S. 202, 223 (1965).

117. *Batson* v. *Kentucky*, 476 U.S. at p. 98.

118. Stephen B. BRIGHT, Patrick J. KEENAN, "Judges and the Politics of Death," *supra* note 86, at pp. 781–784.

119. See, *e.g.*, Mark BALLARD, "Gunning for a Judge; Houston's Lanford Blames DA's Office for His Downfall," *Texas Lawyer*, April 13, 1992, at p. 1 (describing how Houston District Attorney John B. Holmes, unhappy with rulings by a Republican judge in two murder cases, helped cause the judge's defeat by running one of his assistants against the judge and creating congestion in his docket).

120. See, *e.g.*, *Purkett* v. *Elem*, 115 S.Ct. 1769 (1995) (holding that prosecutor's explanation that black juror was struck because he had long, unkempt hair, a mustache, and a beard was a "race-neutral" reason and deferring to state court's finding that prosecutor was not motivated by discriminatory intent); *United States* v. *Clemmons*, 892 F.2d 1153, 1159–1163 (8th Cir. 1989) (Higginbotham, concurring) (citing cases and articles to demonstrate that in cases since Batson "superficial or almost frivolous excuses for peremptory challenges with racial overtones have been proffered and accepted," including "reasons that are clearly, but subtly, racial in nature"); Kenneth B. NUNN, "Rights Held Hostage: Race, Ideology and the Peremptory Challenge" (1993), 28 *Harv. Civil Rights–Civil Liberties L. Rev.* 63; Michael J. RAPHAEL, Edward J. UNGVARSKY, "Excuses, Excuses: Neutral Explanations Under *Batson* v. *Kentucky* (1993), 27 *U. Mich. J.L. Ref.* 229.

121. Peggy C. DAVIS, "Popular Legal Culture: Law as Microaggression" (1989), 98 *Yale L. J.* 1559, p. 1571. See also Sheri Lynn JOHNSON, "Black Innocence and the White Jury" (1985), 83 *Mich. L. Rev.* 1611 (documenting tendency among white jurors to convict black defendants in instances where white defendants would be acquitted).

122. The psychological tendency of predominantly white decision makers to sympathize more with whites than blacks is described in Samuel J. PILLSBURY, "Emotional Justice: Moralizing the Passions of Criminal Punishment" (1989), 74 *Cornell L. Rev.* 655, p. 708; Francis C. DANE, Laurence S. WRIGHTSMAN, "Effects of Defendants' and Victims' Characteristics on Jurors' Verdicts," in *The Psychology of the Courtroom*, pp. 104–106 (1982).

123. Francis C. DANE, Laurence S. WRIGHTSMAN, *ibid.*, at p. 106.

124. *Lingo* v. *State*, 437 S.E.2d 463, 468 (Ga.1993) (Sears-Collins, J., dissenting).

125. See, *e.g.*, *State* v. *Russell*, 477 N.W. 2d 866 (Minn.1991) (more severe sentences imposed for possession of crack cocaine, a crime for which 96.6 percent of those charged are black, than for powdered cocaine, a crime for which 79.6 percent of those charged are white); *Stephens* v. *State*, 456 S.E.2d 560 (Ga. 1995) (of 375 persons serving a life sentence for a second conviction for sale or possession with intent to distribute certain narcotics, 98.4 percent are African Americans); Ruth MARCUS, "Racial Bias Widely Seen in Criminal Justice System," *Washington Post*, May 12, 1992, at p. A4; Tracy THOMPSON, "Justice in Toombs circuit not colorblind, some say," *Atlanta Journal and Constitution*, December 13, 1987, at p. 1A (three other articles appeared on the following days); Tracy THOMPSON, "Blacks Sent to Jail More Than Whites for Same Crimes," *Atlanta Journal and Constitution*, April 30, 1989, at p. 1A (with related stories and charts).

126. Erik ECKHOLM, "Studies Find Death Penalty Often Tied to Victim's Race," *New York Times*, February 24, 1995, at p. A1; see also Bureau of Justice Statistics, *Sourcebook of Criminal Justice Statistics 1993*, *supra* note 41, at p. 384, table 3.128.

127. *Death Row U.S.A.*, *supra* note 36, at p. 3.

128. Samuel R. GROSS, Robert MAURO, *supra* note 50, at pp. 43–44 (1989).

129. The studies are discussed extensively in Baldus et al., *supra* note 50, and in the Supreme Court's decision in *McCleskey* v. *Kemp*, *supra* note 53, at pp. 286–287; *ibid.*, at pp. 325–328 (Brennan, J., dissenting).

130. Baldus et al., *supra* note 50, at pp. 149–157, 160–178, 311–340; *McCleskey* v. *Kemp*, *supra* note 53, at p. 287.

131. Baldus et al., *supra* note 50, at p. 316; *McCleskey* v. *Kemp*, *supra* note 53, at p. 287.

132. 21 U.S.C. 848 (1988).

133. House Subcommittee, *Racial Disparities in Federal Death Penalty Prosecutions*, *supra* note 49, at p. 2.

134. *Ibid.*

135. *Ibid.*

136. *Ibid.*, at p. 3.

137. See *The Violent Crime Control and Law Enforcement Act of 1994*, Pub. L. No. 103–322, 108 Stat. 1796 (1994).

138. 18 U.S.C. 848(o)(1).

139. 481 U.S. 279 (1987).

140. *Ibid.*, at p. 312.

141. *Ibid.*, at p. 313.

142. *Ibid.*, at pp. 314–315.

143. *Ibid.*, at p. 339 (Brennan, J., dissenting).

144. See David COLE, "Fear of Too Much Justice," *Legal Times,* Washington, D.C., May 9, 1994, at p. 26.

145. See *ibid.*

146. See W. Fitzhugh BRUNDAGE, *Lynchings in the New South: Georgia and Virginia, 1881–1930* (1993).

147. 481 U.S., at p. 319.

148. *Richmond* v. *J.A. Croson Co.*, 488 U.S. 469, 552–553 (1989) (Marshall, J., dissenting).

WILLIAM A. SCHABAS

African Perspectives on
Abolition of the Death Penalty

Two important events focused attention on the death penalty within
Africa in the year 1995: the June 6 judgment of the South African
Constitutional Court, finding the death penalty to be contrary to the
interim constitution's provisions protecting the right to life and prohibiting cruel, inhuman, and degrading punishments,[1] and the November 10 execution of Ken Saro-Wiwa and several of his associates
by the Nigerian government, despite massive international protest
and an appeal from the Commonwealth heads of state.[2] The two developments demonstrate the best and the worst that the troubled
continent has to offer with respect to the protection of human rights
in general: on the one hand, a marvelous and eloquent decision that
will serve as a precedent for courts throughout the world, and on the
other, a gruesome flashback to the dark ages of kangaroo courts and
politically directed executions.

From the standpoint of abolition of the death penalty, Africa is
surely the most dynamic continent. At the close of the 1980s, nine
African countries could be classified as abolitionist de jure or de
facto. Now, midway through the next decade, more than twice that
number belong to the abolitionist camp.

This article will focus both on the status of the death penalty within
Africa and on some of the important developments on the subject in
recent years.

Overview of the Death Penalty in Africa

Africa is a continent of regions with important historical, ethnic, and
cultural distinctions that must be taken into account in any serious

analysis. Perhaps the most exciting of the regions at the current time, at least from the standpoint of human rights, is southern Africa, recently freed from the yoke of apartheid. The South African judgment of June 1995 fits squarely within a trend in that region. Already, two southern African states, Mozambique and Namibia, have not only abolished the death penalty but also ratified the Second Optional Protocol to the International Covenant on Civil and Political Rights,[3] becoming the first African states to be parties to that abolitionist treaty, which has been in force only since July 1991. In the north are the Arab states, influenced by so-called Islamic legal theories proclaiming the eternity of the death penalty because its use is allegedly prescribed by sacred texts. Yet there are important distinctions within this subregion, with enthusiastic supporters of the death penalty, such as Sudan, bordering on states like Tunisia, where it has almost fallen into disuse. Between these two extremes, northern and southern Africa, lie some of the poorest countries, and some of the worst human rights situations, in the world. Yet even here, there is ambivalence on the subject, and, while few have taken the step of outright abolition, many states in central Africa can now be qualified as de facto abolitionist.

Within the African continent, twenty-five states may be classified as abolitionist. Of these, only nine are abolitionist de jure: Angola, Cape Verde, Guinea-Bissau, Mauritius, Mozambique, Namibia, São Tomé and Principe, Seychelles, and South Africa. Of the nine de jure abolitionist states, all but one have abolished the death penalty since 1990. Of the sixteen de facto abolitionist states, only four qualified for this category prior to 1990. Thus, of the twenty-five abolitionist states in Africa, twenty have abolished the death penlty in the past five years. Abolitionism in Africa is thus a very recent phenomenon. An example of where Africa sat on the death penalty issue at the dawn of the 1990s can be seen from the recorded vote in the United Nations General Assembly, when the Second Optional Protocol was adopted in December 1989. Of thirty-five African states that participated in the vote, only two, Cape Verde and Togo, voted in favor of the Protocol.[4] Nine African states opposed the Protocol.[5] But the fact that twenty-four abstained may have manifested an ambivalence that signaled important developments in years to come.[6]

Cape Verde, a former Portuguese colony lying several hundred kilometers off the coast of Senegal, abolished the death penalty in 1981 and dates its last execution to the year 1835. Seychelles has never imposed the death penalty since independence. Mozambique, Namibia, and São Tomé and Principe abolished the death penalty in 1990, Angola in 1992, Guinea-Bissau in 1993, and South Africa and Mauritius in 1995. In the case of South Africa, abolition was effected by judgment of the Constitutional Court declaring a provision of the country's criminal law to be unconstitutional. Elimination of the death penalty has generally been associated with major social changes, a period of national reconciliation, and a desire to break with an oppressive and troubled past.

Sixteen African states, most of them in the center of the continent, are considered de facto abolitionist, meaning that they have not conducted executions for at least ten years. Of these, at least half have joined the list within the past decade, because their last executions date to the early 1980s. In many cases, courts continue to pronounce the death penalty in accordance with existing criminal legislation, but rulers systematically decline to carry it out. Frequently, there are growing death row populations as a result of this reticence to impose capital punishment. Abolition of the death penalty is more fragile in these states, yet the reluctance to use the extreme sanction must be taken as evidence of an important social consensus. The significance of this development for Africa was underscored in the recent quinquennial report of the secretary-general of the United Nations on capital punishment, covering the years 1989–1993. The secretary-general noted that five countries had become abolitionist de facto over the period under study, all five of them African.[7] The de facto abolitionist states in Africa are Burundi, Central African Republic, Comoros, Congo, Djibouti, Gambia, Guinea, Ivory Coast, Lesotho, Madagascar, Mali, Niger, Rwanda, Senegal, Swaziland, and Togo.

Twenty-eight African states are classified as retentionist. They are Algeria, Benin, Botswana, Burkina Faso, Cameroon, Chad, Egypt, Equatorial Guinea, Eritrea, Ethiopia, Gabon, Ghana, Kenya, Liberia, Libya, Malawi, Mauritania, Morocco, Nigeria, Sierra Leone, Somalia, Sudan, Tanzania, Tunisia, Uganda, Zaire, Zambia, and Zimbabwe. Thus, retentionist states are in the majority, although a change in status of only two states would even the balance. Nine of the twenty-eight have not conducted an execution in the 1990s and are therefore well on their way to de facto abolitionist status. We have already noted that most of the African states classified in the abolitionist camp are relative newcomers, having abolished the death penalty since 1990. It seems completely realistic to expect this trend to continue. Developments such as the June 1995 judgment of the South African Constitutional Court, which enjoys immense prestige throughout the continent, can only reinforce it.

It is interesting to examine the situation from a regional perspective. Clearly, all of the Arab countries in northern Africa continue to employ the death penalty, although with varying degrees of enthusiasm. If they are eliminated from the calculation, abolitionist states are in the majority, with twenty states still using the death penalty to twenty-five having abolished it. This balance in favor of abolition can be seen also within some of the subregions of the continent. Within francophone Africa, excluding the Arab states, abolitionist states are in a clear majority. The same is true of southern Africa, where, with the exceptions of Zimbabwe, Zambia, and Malawi, the death penalty has been for all intents and purposes eliminated. On the other hand, the anglophone states of eastern Africa are more consistently retentionist, although even in this subregion there are important manifestations of abolitionist sentiment.

THE ORIGINS OF CAPITAL PUNISHMENT IN AFRICA

In Shakespeare's *The Merchant of Venice*, Shylock says, "The villainy you teach me, I will execute, and it shall go hard but I will better the instruction." Capital punishment as it is currently practiced in Africa is very much a part of the legacy of colonialism. As Amnesty International has pointed out, "Capital punishment as it is now practised in Africa was introduced by the colonial powers."[8] The colonialist origin of capital punishment, along with its incompatibility with indigenous culture, was demonstrated in the individual reasons of Justice Albie Sachs of the South African Constitutional Court, in the judgment in *Makwanyane and Mchunu v. The State*. Justice Sachs was responding to arguments submitted by an intervener in the case, the Black Advocates Forum, which had implied that abolitionists were attempting to foist a Eurocentric ideology on African justice. However, counsel for the Black Advocates Forum had not researched the question, and so Justice Sachs undertook the task himself.

Justice Sachs began by noting that systems of law enforcement based on rational procedures were well entrenched in traditional African society.[9] Referring to academic authorities, he presented a number of examples of sophisticated judicial mechanisms in place in Africa prior to the arrival of European colonizers. According to Justice Sachs's research, the death penalty was almost nonexistent in southern Africa at the time, being confined essentially to cases of suspected witchcraft. Quoting the *Cape Law Journal* from the end of the nineteenth century, Justice Sachs noted that the death sentence "seldom followed even murder, when committed without the aid of supernatural powers; and as banishment, imprisonment and corporal punishment are all unknown in (African) jurisprudence, the property of the people constitutes the great fund out of which debts of justice are paid."[10] Other African communities provided comparable patterns of criminal justice, noted Justice Sachs.[11] According to Justice Sachs,

> if these sources are reliable, it would appear that the relatively well-developed judicial processes of indigenous societies did not in general encompass capital punishment for murder. Such executions as took place were the frenzied, extra-judicial killings of supposed witches, a spontaneous and irrational form of crowd behavior that has unfortunately continued to this day in the form of necklacing and witch-burning. In addition, punishments by military leaders in terms of military discipline were frequently of the harshest kind and accounted for the lives of many persons. Yet, the sources referred to above indicate that, where judicial procedures were followed, capital punishment was in general not applied as a punishment for murder.[12]

Justice Sachs cautioned against invoking "every aspect of traditional law" as a source of values.[13] "I am sure that there are many aspects and values of traditional African law which will also have to be discarded or developed in order to ensure compatibility with the principles of the new constitutional order," he added. Justice Sachs found it helpful to examine the behavior of the colonists in Africa. He noted that torture was used by the Dutch settlers until the end of the eighteenth century as an integral part of the judicial process. When the British took over, at the time of the Napoleonic wars, some reforms were enacted, and the most brutal aspects of European-style capital punishment were suppressed. This brought a reaction from the settler communities. "The incumbent judges protested that whatever might have been appropriate in Britain, in the conditions of the Cape to rely merely on hangings, corporal punishment and prison was to invite slave uprisings and mayhem," wrote Justice Sachs. "The public executioner was so distressed that he hanged himself. All this is a matter of record."[14]

SOUTHERN AFRICA

With the decision of the South African Constitutional Court, in June 1995, southern Africa becomes a virtual bastion of abolitionism within the continent. South Africa joins, within the region, Mozambique, Namibia, and Angola, all of which abolished the death penalty in the early 1990s. Four other southern African states are de facto abolitionist or about to become so: Swaziland, where the last execution dates to 1983; Lesotho, where the last was in 1984; Madagascar, whose last known execution was in 1956[15]; and Comoros, which has not had any executions since obtaining independence in the 1970s. Botswana was on the verge of becoming a de facto abolitionist state when it proceeded to hang five people on August 26, 1995, at Gaborone Maximum Security Prison.[16] It had been nine years without an execution.

The positions of Mozambique, Namibia, and Angola have been interpreted as a response to the repression that these states endured under decades of oppressive white rule.[17] Abolition was effected in Mozambique and Namibia in 1990, by means of express constitutional provisions outlawing the death penalty.[18] Both states subsequently ratified the Second Optional Protocol.[19] As Namibia's representative, Ms. de Wet, stated during the 1994 debate on capital punishment in the United Nations General Assembly, "The historical perspective and the social cultural and political reality of Namibia prior to independence had played a major role in shaping its Constitution. Capital punishment was therefore clearly and expressly banned. . . ."[20] According to Justice Albie Sachs,

> The positions adopted by the framers of the Mozambican and Namibian constitutions were not apparently based on bending the knee to foreign ideas, as was implicit in Ms. David's contention, but rather on memories of massacres and martyrdom in their own countries. As Churchill is reputed to have said, the grass never grows green under the gallows. Germany after Nazism, Italy after fascism, and Portugal, Peru, Nicaragua, Brazil, Argentina, the Philippines and Spain all abolished capital punishment for peacetime offences after emerging from periods of severe repression. They did so mostly through constitutional provisions.[21]

In 1990, while Mozambique and Namibia were abolishing the death penalty by constitutional amendment, the Supreme Court of Zimbabwe began its attack on the country's capital punishment practice.[22] The Court asked for full argument on whether execution by hanging was consistent with section 15(1) of the Constitution. Specifically, the Court requested that counsel present evidence on procedures involved in hanging, and on any physical pain and mental anguish that might be attendant.[23] But prior to the hearing, a constitutional amendment bill was published that upheld the constitutionality of executions by hanging, in effect "preempting" the Court.[24] It later became section 15(4) of the Constitution of Zimbabwe.[25] Defending the amendment in Parliament, Zimbabwe's minister of Justice, Legal and Parliamentary Affairs said any conclusion to the contrary by the Court "would be untenable to a government which holds the correct and firm view . . . that Parliament makes the laws and the courts interpret them." According to the minister, abolition was not a matter for the courts: "[G]overnment will not and cannot countenance a situation where the death penalty is *de facto* abolished through the back door."[26] But a Tanzanian High Court judge, commenting on the case in 1994, charged that the Zimbabwe government "impliedly concedes that hanging is ugly and cruel and that is why they do it in secret so that the people should not witness such a cruel spectacle."[27] The following year, Zimbabwe's Supreme

Court considered the appalling conditions on death row and ordered significant changes in the custodial regime.[28]

The Zimbabwe Supreme Court returned to the issue of the death penalty in March 1993, when the minister of Justice, Legal and Parliamentary Affairs announced that four individuals, Timothy Mhlanga, Martin Bechani Bakaka, Luke Kingsize Chiliko, and John Chakara Zacharia Marichi, who had been on death row for periods of approximately five years, were soon to be executed. Within days, a petition lodged on behalf of the condemned men by a local non-governmental organization, the Catholic Commission for Justice and Peace in Zimbabwe, was filed in court. The petitioners claimed that execution following such prolonged detention on death row would constitute cruel, inhuman, and degrading treatment or punishment, contrary to section 15(1) of the Constitution. In an eloquent judgment,[29] Chief Justice Gubbay granted the application, relying heavily on the ruling of the European Court of Human Rights in *Soering v. United Kingdom*[30] and on the dissenting views of Christine Chanet, in the Human Rights Committee case of *Barrett and Sutcliffe v. Jamaica*,[31] and rejecting judgments of the courts of the United States[32] and Canada.[33] He also reversed an earlier Rhodesian precedent holding that the only remedy for protracted detention prior to execution was an order to the executioner to speed things up![34] Chief Justice Gubbay spoke of the "impressive judicial and academic consensus concerning the death row phenomenon,"[35] referring at a number of points in his judgment to the "demeaning" or "harsh" conditions of detention.[36]

> From the moment he enters the condemned cell, the prisoner is enmeshed in a dehumanizing environment of near hopelessness. He is in a place where the sole object is to preserve his life so that he may be executed. The condemned prisoner is "the living dead."[37]

Chief Justice Gubbay said it was not a question of condoning the evils committed by the offenders, but rather "whether the acute mental suffering and brooding horror of being hanged which has haunted them in their condemned cells over the long lapse of time since the passing of sentence of death is consistent with the guarantee against inhuman or degrading punishment or treatment."[38]

Once again, the judgment provoked a vigorous riposte from Zimbabwe's legislature, and a constitutional amendment to neutralize its effects was adopted in the months that followed. The amendment stated, "Delay in execution of a sentence of death, imposed upon a person in respect of a criminal offence of which he has not been convicted, shall not be held to be a contravention" of the provision prohibiting cruel, inhuman, and degrading treatment or punishment.[39] However, Zimbabwe's Supreme Court has not let the matter lie, and, in a judgment subsequent to the constitutional amendment, Chief Justice Gubbay held the latter to be inapplicable, at least with respect to persons sentenced to death prior to the amendment's coming into force.[40]

Thus, judicial abolition has been blocked in Zimbabwe by aggressive legislators; but the behavior of the Supreme Court shows that abolitionist sentiment is hardly marginalized within the country. Indeed, there have been no reported executions in Zimbabwe since 1990, and the minister of Home Affairs regularly commutes death sentences of individuals who have spent lengthy periods of time on death row.[41] Two other southern African states, Zambia and Malawi, also retain the death penalty. Zambia, though, last conducted executions in 1989, when eighteen offenders were put to death at Mukobeko Maximum Security Prison in Kabwe, the first known executions since 1985.[42] In 1992, the Zambian government said that it was undertaking a research project on public opinion, in order to determine whether to abolish the death penalty.[43] Meanwhile, Zambia's death row population continues to grow.[44] Malawi last conducted executions in 1992, and it also has a burgeoning death row population.[45] Thus, in recent years the three retentionist states in southern Africa are applying a form of de facto moratorium on executions, as can be seen from the large numbers on their respective death rows. Is it unreasonable to surmise that they are being influenced by their abolitionist neighbors? And if this is the case, recent developments in South Africa can only enhance the evolution of abolitionism within the entire region.

The Republic of South Africa has a long and unhappy history of capital punishment. During the 1980s South Africa became one of the world leaders in capital punishment.[46] On a number of occasions,

United Nations General Assembly and Security Council resolutions protested South Africa's use of the noose as a means of political repression directed against the antiapartheid movement.[47] When the white supremacist regime finally began to unravel, in early 1990, President F. W. de Klerk suspended executions. The last judicial execution in South Africa proper had taken place the previous November, although there was one execution in Bophuthatswana during 1990. In Ciskei, another of the so-called homelands within South Africa, the death penalty was officially abolished in June 1990.[48] A formal moratorium on executions throughout the country was proclaimed by the minister of Justice on March 27, 1992.

South African legislators did not abolish capital punishment, however, and the courts continued to impose sentences of death, while politicians, legislators, and constitutional lawyers continued to debate the matter. Following President de Klerk's suspension of executions, Parliament amended the law so as to broaden judicial discretion in imposition of the death penalty and provide for an automatic right of appeal.[49] In August 1991, the South African Law Commission rejected suggestions made in a working paper that the future bill of rights recognize a right to life subject to use of the death penalty for serious crimes, and instead it proposed what it called a "Solomonic solution." The matter was intentionally left to the yet-to-be-created constitutional court to determine whether the death penalty could be "saved," as a permissible limit to the right to life or to the prohibition of cruel, inhuman, and degrading treatment or punishment, pursuant to the interim constitution's general limitations clause.[50]

When the new South African Constitutional Court began sitting in February 1995, its president, Arthur Chaskalson, decided that the very first case to be heard would be a challenge to the constitutionality of the death penalty. The day prior to the hearing, President Nelson Mandela had administered the oath of office to his former attorney, Arthur Chaskalson, and to the other ten justices, reminding South Africans that the last time he had appeared before a court it was to learn whether he was to be sentenced to death.[51] The case before the Constitutional Court involved appellants Themba Makwanyane and Mavusa Mchunu, two among the hundreds of individuals who had been sentenced to death during the moratorium, pursuant to section 277 of the Criminal Procedure Act, 1977.[52] The accused challenged section 277 as being incompatible with sections 9 (right to life), 10 (right to respect for and protection of the dignity of human beings), and 11(2) (prohibition of physical, mental, and emotional torture and of cruel, inhuman, and degrading treatment and punishment) of the Bill of Rights, which is contained in Chapter III of the Constitution of the Republic of South Africa, 1993 (the "interim constitution").[53] The minister of Justice, representing the government and acting pursuant to a cabinet decision, intervened to support the appellants.[54]

All eleven judges of the South African Constitutional Court agreed that the death penalty was incompatible with South Africa's interim constitution, although in eleven individual decisions they advanced a variety of different reasons for their conclusions. All but one, Justice Johann Kriegler, rallied to the conclusions of President Chaskalson to the effect that the death penalty breached the norm prohibiting cruel, inhuman, or degrading treatment or punishment set out in section 11(2) of the interim constitution. Justice Kriegler preferred to base his reasoning solely on the protection of the right to life, although he made a point of adding that he did "not want to be understood as disagreeing with the views expressed by any of my colleagues" on the subject of section 11(2).[55] Some of the judges were less comfortable with arguments based on the right to life, apparently nervous about consequences that its interpretation may have for the abortion debate, which is sure to confront the court in the future.[56]

The lead judgment, signed by President Chaskalson, makes abundant use of international and comparative law sources. President Chaskalson distinguished the South African interim constitution from other instruments, such as the United States Bill of Rights and European Convention of Human Rights,[57] both of which allow for the death penalty in more or less express terms. "When challenges to the death sentence in international or foreign courts and tribunals have failed, the constitution or the international instrument concerned has either directly sanctioned capital punishment or has specifically provided that the right to life is subject to exceptions sanctioned by law," he wrote.[58] President Chaskalson referred to several courts that have concluded capital punishment to constitute cruel, inhuman, and degrading treatment: the Supreme Court of California,[59] the Supreme Judicial Court of Massachusetts,[60] the Constitutional Court of Hungary,[61] and by what is probably a majority of the Supreme Court of Canada.[62] He also relied heavily on the plurality opinions of the United States Supreme Court in *Furman v. Georgia*[63] and the views of the minority in *Gregg v. Georgia*.[64] In what is a clear departure from the majority trend in United States jurisprudence, President Chaskalson argued that imposition of the death penalty is inherently arbitrary because "race and poverty"[65] mean that some offenders are more likely than others to be condemned to die. "Accused persons who have the money to do so," he explained, "are able to retain experienced attorneys and counsel, who are paid to undertake the necessary investigations and research, and as a result they are less likely to be sentenced to death than persons similarly placed who are unable to pay for such services."[66] Although such arbitrariness is inherent in all criminal proceedings, the fatal consequences of death penalty cases give this problem paramount importance; any injustice becomes irrevocable, because "death is different."[67]

It is clear that in determining the scope of the terms "cruel, inhuman, or degrading" judges are required to make a value judgment. In this context, President Chaskalson rejected invitations to canvass public opinion, conceding, at least for the sake of argument, "that the majority of South Africans agree that the death sentence should be imposed in extreme cases of murder."[68] Nevertheless, he stated, "The question before us, however, is not what the majority of South Africans believe a proper sentence for murder should be. It is whether the Constitution allows the sentence."[69] Here he cited the reasons of Justice Powell in *Furman v. Georgia*:

> ... the weight of the evidence indicates that the public generally has not accepted either the morality or the social merit of the views so passionately advocated by the articulate spokesmen for abolition. But however one may assess the amorphous ebb and flow of public opinion generally on this volatile issue, this type of inquiry lies at the

periphery—not the core—of the judicial process in constitutional cases. The assessment of popular opinion is essentially a legislative, and not a judicial, function.[70]

On this subject, Justice Yvonne Mokgoro, in her individual reasons, referred to section 35(1) of the interim constitution, which appeals to the courts to "promote the values which underlie an open and democratic society based on freedom and equality."[71] Justice Mokgoro argued that "an all-inclusive value system, or common values in South Africa, can form a basis upon which to develop a South African human rights jurisprudence."[72] Here she proposed an activist role for the court, recognizing that South Africa's history makes it difficult to establish an underpinning of existing values because these have been so corrupted by the country's wretched past. The court and its case law have a role to play in building the human rights culture of the new South Africa, she suggested. Similar comments appear in the judgment of Justice Katherine O'Regan, who noted that "[t]he values urged upon the court are not those that have informed our past."[73] The court is directed to the future, said Justice O'Regan, "to look forward not backward, to recognize the evils and injustices of the past and to avoid their repetition."[74]

In his submissions in defense of the death penalty, South Africa's attorney general had argued that the moratorium on the death penalty that began in February 1990 and the dramatic increase in violent crime including murder since that time were related. Because capital punishment was not being used, he speculated, criminals were not being deterred.[75] However, President Chaskalson noted that the crime wave had begun before the moratorium was announced. Furthermore, the moratorium could have ended at any time, and murderers had therefore no assurance whatsoever that they would not be subject to the death penalty.[76] Justice Didcott was even more affirmative on this point, arguing that the statistics tendered in evidence actually demonstrated that the moratorium had no effect whatsoever on the murder rate.[77] And acting Justice Kentridge went still further, opining that the proclamation of the moratorium might actually be used to support contentions that South African public opinion is in fact ambivalent on the subject of capital punishment.[78]

The crime wave in modern-day South Africa is explained by a

number of factors, noted President Chaskalson, including political violence, homelessness, unemployment, poverty, and the frustration consequent upon such conditions.[79] Citing evidence before the court showing that the bulk of violent crime is never solved, President Chaskalson stated that the most effective deterrent is the knowledge that the offender will probably be caught, convicted, and punished.[80] In the final analysis, as Justice Kriegler observed, "No empirical study, no statistical exercise and no theoretical analysis has been able to demonstrate that capital punishment has any deterrent force greater than that of a really heavy sentence of imprisonment."[81] Therefore, "It simply cannot be reasonable to sanction judicial killing without knowing whether it has any marginal deterrent value."[82]

Eight of the eleven members of the court concluded that the right to life, proclaimed in section 9 of the interim constitution, had also been breached.[83] Justice Sachs insisted that the right to life, and not the guarantee against cruel, inhuman, and degrading punishment, should be "the starting-off point for an analysis of capital punishment."[84] Justice Ismael Mahomed examined the other issues encompassed by the right to life, including abortion and euthanasia.[85] He said it is unnecessary to resolve these matters, and that for the purposes of the case before the court, the issue should be to determine whether the right to life includes a right "not to be deliberately killed by the State, through a systematically planned act of execution sanctioned by the State as a mode of punishment and performed by an executioner remunerated for this purpose from public funds?"[86] This readily distinguishes the question of capital punishment from other forms of state-sanctioned homicide, "for example the right of a person in life-threatening circumstances to take the life of the aggressor in self-defence or even the acts of the State, in confronting an insurrection or in the course of War."[87]

South Africa is currently determining the content of its permanent constitution. A working draft, published on November 22, 1995, envisages three different hypotheses. First, the right-to-life provision could explicitly exclude the death penalty. Second, it could explicitly allow it. Third, the constitution could simply enshrine the right to life without any comment on the death penalty, in which case the case law of the Constitutional Court would simply continue to apply. Although retentionists have not given up the fight, it will be very hard for them to overcome the momentum created by a unanimous judgment of the court. But the court's judgment is sure to have enormous influence beyond South Africa's borders, and particularly elsewhere on the continent. Moreover, it is bound to be a precious aid in interpreting the African Charter of Human and People's Rights,[88] which resembles the South African interim constitution to the extent that it, too, takes no clear position on the death penalty and leaves the matter to subsequent judicial interpretation.

EAST AFRICA AND THE HORN

None of the states in the East Africa/Horn region, with the exception of Djibouti, can be classified as abolitionist, either de facto or de jure. However, in recent years there have been no executions in three states, Eritrea (since independence in 1993),[89] Ethiopia (since the fall of the Mengistu regime in 1991),[90] and Kenya (since at least 1990).[91] A symptom of an increase in abolitionist sentiment, Kenya's death row population has continued to grow throughout the 1990s, indicating a form of de facto moratorium on executions. By the end of 1994, there were nearly six hundred offenders awaiting execution in Kenya, of whom several hundred had been waiting for more than five years.[92] However, a parliamentary motion calling for abolition of the death penalty was defeated in December 1994.[93]

Somalia, Uganda, and Tanzania all continue to practice capital punishment. In Somalia in 1994, a man was condemned to death by stoning for rape, and the sentence was immediately carried out. Two others were also executed in Somalia in 1994.[94] In Uganda, executions have been conducted regularly since 1990. There were nine reported executions in 1993,[95] and one reported execution in 1994, by firing squad, of a soldier found guilty of murder. The death row at Uganda's Luzira Maximum Security Prison is said to house at least two hundred prisoners.[96] Under the Ugandan Penal Code, the death penalty is mandatory for a wide range of offenses, including murder, kidnapping with intent to murder, armed robbery, and armed smuggling. In 1990, amendments added rape, defilement of girls under eighteen, and sexual intercourse with a prisoner to the list of capital offenses, apparently in an attempt to prevent the spread of AIDS.[97] Moreover, the Ugandan Constitution, adopted in early 1995, expressly reserves capital punishment as an exception to the right to life, although there were proposals during its preparation that the instrument expressly abolish the death penalty.

Tanzanian law provides a mandatory death penalty for murder. Its 1984 Bill of Rights allows for capital punishment as an exception to the right to life, by specifying, in a provision that effectively deprives the provision of any constitutional significance, that life may be limited "subject to law."[98] Between 1985 and 1990, there were approximately twenty-five executions, and a total of two-hundred offenders were confined to death row during the period. In the early 1990s, Tanzania appeared to lose enthusiasm for capital punishment. In 1991, there were eight death sentences and three executions, in 1992, one sentence and no executions,[99] and in 1993, three sentences and no executions.[100] Also, a law reform commission headed by Justice Nyalali recommended abolition of the death penalty, declaring it to be an inhuman and cruel punishment. There were, however, rumors that executions continued in secret during this period of apparent moratorium.[101] In 1994, Tanzania resumed executions, when at least three people were sentenced to death and eight were executed.[102]

That same year, a courageous High Court judge in Tanzania found the death penalty to be contrary to the cruel, inhuman, and degrading treatment or punishment provision of the country's Constitution. Justice Mwalusanya reviewed the entire range of abolitionist arguments, including the unacceptability of prolonged confinement on death row, the inherent cruelty of hanging as a method of execution, and the danger of "botched" executions. Dealing with the issue of public opinion and its presumed support for capital punishment, Justice Mwalusanya stated,

> The government must assume responsibility for ensuring that their citizens are placed in a position whereunder they are able to base their views about the death penalty *on a rational and properly informed assessment.* It is clear that many people base their support for the penalty on an erroneous belief that capital punishment is the most effective deterrent punishment, and so the government has a duty to

put the true facts before them instead of holding out to the public that the death penalty is an instant solution to violent crime.[103]

Justice Mwalusanya even held that the death penalty also violated the right to life, despite the fact that the Tanzanian constitution only protected the right to life "subject to law." He held that Tanzania's death penalty legislation was not "lawful law" and that consequently the limiting phrase within the right to life provision was ineffective.

However, Justice Mwalusanya's judgment was overturned by the Tanzanian Court of Appeal in January 1995. The court relied on a constitutional provision authorizing limitations on fundamental rights. The judges rejected arguments contending that Tanzania's mandatory death penalty for murder was arbitrary because decisions as to guilt or innocence are taken not by juries but by judges. Essentially, the appellate court held that capital punishment was a matter for society, and not the courts, to determine, and that society generally favored the death penalty.[104] Therefore, it was a "reasonable and necessary" limitation on constitutional guarantees. Criticizing the decision, President Arthur Chaskalson of the South African Constitutional Court wrote that constitutional interpretation was a role for the courts, and not society or Parliament, although societal attitudes were not totally irrelevant. Nevertheless, "ultimately the decision must be ours. If the decision of the Tanzanian Court of Appeal is inconsistent with this conclusion, I must express my disagreement with it."[105]

GREAT LAKES REGION

The Great Lakes region, which has suffered from some of the most horrible ethnic violence and genocide in history, as well as a wide range of human rights abuses perpetrated by corrupt regimes, nevertheless presents a rather positive profile on the subject of capital punishment. Neither Burundi nor Rwanda has conducted judicial executions since 1982, and both are therefore classified as de facto abolitionist states. Zaire will soon join this category, not having conducted executions since before 1990.[106]

The issue of capital punishment resurfaced dramatically in 1994, following the genocide of more than half a million Tutsis in Rwanda. In November 1994 the United Nations Security Council decided to set up an ad hoc tribunal to try genocide, crimes against humanity, and war crimes committed in Rwanda that year. As it had done with the ad hoc tribunal for the former Yugoslavia that had been created the previous year,[107] the Security Council decided to exclude capital punishment and provide a maximum sentence of life imprisonment. Rwanda, which by pure chance was one of the elected members of the council at the time, opposed the prohibition on capital punishment, which it still retains in its own domestic legislation for murder.[108] It claimed there would be a fundamental injustice in exposing criminals tried by its domestic courts to execution if those tried by the international tribunal—presumably the masterminds of the genocide—would be subject only to life imprisonment.[109] "Since it is foreseeable that the Tribunal will be dealing with suspects who devised, planned and organized the genocide, these may escape capital punishment whereas those who simply carried out their plans would be subjected to the harshness of this sentence," said Rwanda's representative to the Council. "That situation is not conducive to national reconciliation in Rwanda."[110] To counter this argument, however, the representative of New Zealand stated, "For over three decades the United Nations has been trying progressively to eliminate the death penalty. It would be entirely unacceptable—and a dreadful step backwards—to introduce it here."[111]

Rwanda's own position on the death penalty is far from unequivocal. The death penalty has not been imposed in Rwanda since the early 1980s, and the program of the Rwandan Patriotic Front, which won military victory in July 1994, calls for its abolition. Furthermore, in the 1993 Arusha peace accords, which have constitutional force in Rwanda, the government undertook to ratify the Second Optional Protocol,[112] although it has not yet formally taken this step.[113] Rwanda is faced with a dilemma. It seems unthinkable that the masterminds of the genocide, who will, it is hoped, be judged by the international tribunal in Arusha, receive sentences of detention, while their subordinates find themselves condemned to death. Nevertheless, draft legislation currently being examined by the National Assembly provides for the death penalty in the case of genocide and crimes against humanity. The Rwandan government could, of course, recognize the unfairness of the situation and carry through with its obligations, under the Rwandan Patriotic Front program and the Arusha agreements, to abolish capital punishment.[114] Failing such an initiative, it will be left to Rwanda's judges to see that death sentences are not imposed.[115] They should be encouraged to take such a course, if for no other reason than that modern sentencing theory and the imperatives of reconciliation require it. The death penalty is the only sanction that can be justified solely from the standpoint of retribution. As for deterrence, the other basic argument in favor of severe sanctions, modern criminology and jurisprudence indicate that capital punishment has no demonstrably greater deterrent effect than lengthy imprisonment. But should a country anxious to rebuild and to reconcile its citizens base its criminal law policy on retribution, or, to be more accurate, on vengeance? Such a course can only doom Rwanda to new cycles of violence and brutality. As Chief Justice Gubbay of the Zimbabwe Supreme Court stated, "retribution has no place in the scheme of civilized jurisprudence."[116]

WEST AFRICA AND THE SAHEL

A majority of states in West Africa have abolished the death penalty, either de facto or de jure. However, the region also harbors one of the world's most egregious users of the noose and the firing squad, Nigeria. Three states—Cape Verde, São Tomé and Principe, and Guinea-Bissau—can be considered as abolitionist de jure, and several states in the region are now abolitionist de facto: Central African Republic, Congo, Gambia, Guinea, Ivory Coast, Mali, Niger, Senegal, and Togo. Others are well on their way to joining this category; four states have no reported executions since before 1990: Burkina Faso[117]; Gabon[118]; Benin[119]; Cameroon.[120]

Three of the de facto abolitionist states have been the source of rumblings in recent years that show there is pressure to reintroduce capital punishment. In December 1994, the government of Guinea announced that capital punishment would be imposed by the courts and carried out. There have been no reported executions in Guinea since 1984, when president Lansana Conté took power.[121] Although Ivory Coast has not executed anyone since independence in 1960, in 1995 its National Assembly adopted a law extending capital punishment to cover cases of armed robbery and providing that executions be performed publicly by firing squad.[122] Finally, in August 1995, Gambia's Armed Forces Provisional Ruling Council reinstated the death penalty, which Gambia had abolished de jure in April 1993. At the June 1993 World Conference on Human Rights, Gambia's president, Sir Dawda Jwara, had stated that "the death penalty is increasingly difficult to reconcile with evolving human rights standards . . . it has no value, no useful purpose in relation to crime prevention and control." He also declared Gambia's intention to ratify the Second Optional Protocol.[123] The current authorities came to power in a military coup in July 1994.

Several other countries in the region continue to make regular use of the death penalty. Twelve soldiers were executed in Sierra Leone in 1994,[124] and at least twenty-six people were executed in 1992 for coup attempts.[125] The most recent judicial executions in Chad date to 1991, of three soldiers and a civilian who were convicted by a special military court that allowed no right of appeal.[126] From Equatorial Guinea, there are reports of a conviction and an execution the same day in 1994, after a trial for which there was no right of appeal.[127] Ghana reports executions of twelve persons by firing squad in 1993, the first executions since the beginning of 1990.[128] There were no reported death sentences or executions there in 1994, and prisoners who had been on Ghana's death row for more than ten years had their sentences commuted.[129] In Liberia, there have been executions as recently as November 1995.[130]

These retentionist states all pale in comparison with their neighbor, Nigeria, which is among the world leaders in number of executions. There was widespread use of the death penalty in Nigeria in the 1980s,[131] but it appeared to fall off early in the 1990s.[132] In the two years prior to the 1993 presidential elections, there were no executions whatsoever.[133] However, capital punishment resumed in 1994, when at least one hundred persons were executed, usually in public by firing squads.[134] Amnesty International has estimated that in 1995 at least eighty-six persons were executed in public after conviction by the Robbery and Firearms Tribunal.[135] Most executions in Nigeria are for armed robbery, where suspects are tried by the Robbery and Firearms Tribunal, and from which there is no right of appeal. The death sentence for armed robbery, introduced in 1970, is mandatory.[136] Coup suspects are tried by a military tribunal that sits in camera and from which there is also no right of appeal.[137]

Nigeria has been condemned at least twice by the African Commission on Human and People's Rights for violations of the African

Charter on Human and People's Rights, in cases initiated by the Constitutional Rights Project on behalf of death row inmates.[138] The first petition challenged imposition of the death sentence by the Robbery and Firearms Tribunal. In both decisions, the commission concluded that there had been a violation of various provisions of article 7, specifically the right to appeal a conviction (7.1a), the right to defense, including the right to be defended by counsel of choice (7.1c), and the right to be tried by an impartial tribunal (7.1d). The commission considered that the composition of the special tribunal suggested impartiality. Also, the commission concluded that the condemned petitioners were entitled to be released.[139] In the second application, the commission made similar findings with respect to death sentences imposed by the special Civil Disturbances Tribunal.[140]

Nigeria's frequent use of capital punishment following trials that fail to respect international guidelines came to the attention of the world in November 1995 with the hanging of Ken Saro-Wiwa, Barinem Kiobel, and several others. They were tried by a Civil Disturbances Special Tribunal, set up especially for the cases by General Sani Abacha, the head of state.[141] Although the sentences were subject to confirmation by the Nigerian Provisional Ruling Council, there was no right of appeal before an independent tribunal. Amnesty International described the trials as "blatantly unfair."[142] Following the executions, Nigeria's membership in the Commonwealth was suspended. Nigeria was condemned in the United Nations General Assembly, by a resolution adopted on December 22, 1995, with 101 votes in favor, 14 against, and 47 abstentions.[143] The General Assembly condemned the arbitrary execution, after a flawed judicial process, of Ken Saro-Wiwa and his eight codefendants, and it emphasized that everyone charged with a penal offense has the right to be presumed innocent until proved guilty according to law in a public trial with all the guarantees necessary for defense.

NORTHERN AFRICA

Although the Arab states of northern Africa are all retentionist, it would be incorrect to paint them as a monolith. Some, like Tunisia, have used the death penalty only occasionally in recent years.[144] During the 1994 United Nations General Assembly vote on an Italian-sponsored resolution calling for a moratorium on the death penalty,[145] the Tunisian government instructed its permanent representative to support the initiative. However, the permanent representative eventually succumbed to pressure from other members of the Arab caucus. Since 1982, Morocco has actually conducted only one execution, in 1993.[146] In 1994, no new death sentences were imposed in Morocco, and 196 sentences were commuted to terms of detention.[147] Morocco's third periodic report to the Human Rights Committee describes the death penalty as being only "theoretically" applicable, and adds that in practice, death sentences are generally commuted to life imprisonment.[148] Mauritania has reported no death sentences or executions since before 1990.[149]

Egypt, Algeria, Libya, and Sudan are all rather more enthusiastic partisans of the death penalty, often taking the stage in international meetings to defend its use.[150] Both Egypt and Algeria show an upsurge in their use of the death penalty. In Algeria in 1994, six hundred people were sentenced to death, and there were reports of several executions being carried out.[151] Twenty-six people were executed by firing squad in 1993, the first reported executions since 1989.[152] In Egypt in 1994, thirty-nine were sentenced to death, and thirty-one were executed in what Amnesty International characterized as a "dramatic increase" in the use of capital punishment.[153] Libya executed seventeen people in 1994, some of them publicly on television.[154] Curiously, Libya declares from time to time its intention to abolish the death penalty. This was its claim to the United Nations Human Rights Committee when it presented its second periodic report.[155] On the other hand, Libya continues to maintain capital punishment for such crimes as damage to or destruction of food warehouses.[156]

In recent years, Sudan has sentenced offenders to execution by crucifixion, although it is not known whether any of the sentences was actually carried out.[157] When the Commission on Human Rights rapporteur Gaspar Biro suggested in February 1994 that the death penalty as imposed in the Sudan was contrary to articles 6 and 7 of the Covenant, his "blasphemy" in attacking "Islamic punishments" was condemned. Biro's report focused on a provision of Sudanese criminal law providing that "in case of murder, retribution shall be death by hanging and, if the court sees fit, it shall be in the same manner in which the offender has caused death." Biro described the practice as being "inconsistent with relevant international norms," adding that "[s]ince the Sudan has ratified the *International Covenant on Civil and Political Rights* and the *Convention on the Rights of the Child*, the cultural argument that this practice is deeply rooted in the tradition of the country and is accepted by the people is irrelevant."[158] The Sudanese representative, Abdelaziz Shiddo, accused Biro of insulting religious values in a "Satanic paragraph" of his report, adding that "he must assume the responsibility" for his comments. The report, continued Ambassador Shiddo, was "flagrant blasphemy and a deliberate insult to the Islamic religion."[159] Later that year, during debate at the autumn session of the General Assembly, the Sudanese delegate affirmed that " . . . capital punishment was a divine right according to some religions, in particular Islam. . . . [C]apital punishment was enshrined in the Koran and millions of inhabitants of the Muslim world believed that it was a teaching of God."[160]

Clearly, little progress will be made in promoting abolition of the death penalty in northern Africa until the religious issues are tackled. That Islamic culture will dictate interpretations of the terms "cruel, inhuman, and degrading" that are "significantly, if not radically, different from perceptions of the meaning of this clause in other parts of the world" is evoked in the writings of Professor Abdullahi Ahmed An-Na'im.[161] The recent Arab Charter of Human Rights, adopted September 15, 1994, but not yet ratified by any members of the League of Arab States, proclaims the right to life like the other international instruments. However, three distinct provisions, articles 10, 11, and 12, recognize the legitimacy of the death penalty in the case of "serious violations of general law," prohibit the death penalty for political crimes, and exclude capital punishment for crimes committed under the age of eighteen and for both pregnant women and nursing mothers, for a period of up to two years following childbirth.[162]

In October 1995 at Tunis, the Arab Institute for Human Rights and the Citizens' and Parliamentarians' League for the Abolition of the Death Penalty Worldwide by the Year 2000 ("Hands Off Cain") held an international conference on the death penalty in the legislation of Arab states. The bold initiative brought together human rights activists from throughout the Arab world, including many who were far from convinced at the start of the conference that abolition of the death penalty belonged in their program. In a report to the meeting, Egyptian jurist Aly Fahmi analyzed the legislation in force in various Arab criminal jurisdictions, concluding "that Arab countries should agree on the abolition of the death penalty from the Arab penal legislation as a strategic goal, by starting limiting its application to some odd cases and gradually working for a socio-cultural climate to settle a full abolition as the next step."[163] Fahmi's recommendation was adopted by the conference in its final statement. The Tunis conference showed both that there is a solid and significant body of thought within Arab countries favorable to abolition of the death penalty and that Islamic religion can be reconciled with elimination of capital punishment as a judicial sanction.

The African Charter of Human and People's Rights

The African Charter of Human and People's Rights,[164] adopted in 1981 by the Organization of African Unity, makes no mention of the death penalty, in contrast to the regional conventions of the European and American systems.[165] It does, of course, provide for a right to life, for a protection against inhuman treatment, and for procedural safeguards in criminal proceedings. According to article 4 of the African Charter, no individual may be deprived "arbitrarily" of his life, a term that echoes article 6§1 of the International Covenant on Civil and Political Rights[166] and that most certainly includes the arbitrary use of capital punishment.[167] Furthermore, the African Charter envisages reference to such instruments as the Universal Declaration of Human Rights[168] for purposes of interpretation.[169] To this extent, an analysis of the death penalty in light of article 3 of the Universal Declaration may be useful.[170] Whether the drafters of the African Charter intentionally omitted mention of the death penalty and what conclusions are to be drawn from such an omission are questions to which we cannot provide a thorough answer, because of the paucity of available materials. One scholar, Etienne-Richard Mbaya, writes that article 4 of the African Charter permits the death penalty, which is widespread in Africa, providing it is imposed in accordance with the law.[171] Professor Benoît S. Ngom decries what he calls the indifference of African human rights law to the debate surrounding abolition of the death penalty.[172] A brochure prepared by Amnesty International on the subject of the African Charter provides a comment on article 4:

> [The right to life] also means that in states which have not yet abolished the death penalty prisoners may never be executed without a fair trial. A fair trial includes the right to appeal and the right to apply for a reduction in sentence or a pardon. . . .
> Some people, including all members of Amnesty International, interpret the right to life to mean that nobody should ever be sentenced to death or executed—even prisoners who have been found guilty in fair trials of committing serious crimes.[173]

The African Commission on Human Rights, in its examination of periodic reports pursuant to the African Charter, appears to avoid the question of article 4 and and its application to the death penalty.[174] Nigeria, in its periodic report dated 1993, referred to abolition of the death penalty for drug trafficking, unlawful dealing in petroleum products, and counterfeiting of currency, and its replacement with life imprisonment.[175] In two individual communications to the commission, first published in 1996, the commission concluded that judicial guarantees had not been respected during death penalty trials in Nigeria and held that there had been a breach of article 7 of the Charter.[176] Litigants before domestic courts have now begun to argue that the "death row phenomenon" is incompatible with the current state of African human rights law and more specifically with the African Charter of Human and People's Rights,[177] and this position is undoubtedly strengthened by developments such as the judicial abolition of the death penalty in the Republic of South Africa.[178]

A much more recent instrument, the African Charter of the Rights and Welfare of the Child, provides that the death penalty shall not be pronounced for crimes committed by children below the age of eighteen, and that a death sentence shall not be imposed on expectant mothers and mothers of young children.[179] Its universal counterpart, the Convention on the Rights of the Child, prohibits execution of children and adolescents.[180] Like the African Charter of Human and People's Rights, the Charter of Rights of the Child is to be construed with reference to international human rights law, and specifically the Convention on the Rights of the Child and the Universal Declaration of Human Rights.[181]

Conclusion

Africa is a continent plagued with human rights violations. Yet it is also a continent where some of the most remarkable progress in the protection of human rights is being achieved, as the debate on capital punishment makes clear. From a situation at the beginning of the decade where only a handful of states could be qualified as abolitionist, the retentionists have steadily and inexorably lost ground. Not quite half of the African states no longer use the death penalty, and several others have mushrooming death row populations, proof that there is significant hesitation about its continued employment. The June 1995 judgment of the South African Constitutional Court stands as a major milestone in this movement, although it is not alone, and there are important developments in many other states.

Conditions on death row continue to pose a major problem. Reports in the cases of conditions on African death rows are appalling.[182] While it is true, as Lord Diplock once said, "where there's life, there's hope,"[183] prolonged detention on death row is increasingly viewed as a violation of the guarantee against cruel, inhuman, and degrading treatment or punishment.[184] Ironically, it is the unwanted byproduct of moratoria on capital punishment.

Africa, then, provides convincing evidence of the international trend towards abolition of the death penalty. Interestingly, the pace of developments is much more rapid than in other continents, including Europe. If it continues at the same rate, it is not unrealistic to envisage a continent that will have virtually freed itself of capital punishment by the end of the decade. The indigenous humanity of Africa's human rights culture may, as Justice Albie Sachs implied, have lessons to teach the rest of the world.

Notes

William A. Schabas is Professor and Chair, Département des sciences juridiques, Université du Québec à Montréal and senior policy advisor, International Center for Human Rights and Democratic Development, Montréal. B.A. 1972, M.A. 1974, University of Toronto; LL.B. 1983, LL.M. 1990, LL.D. 1992, Université de Montréal.

1. *Makwanyane and Mchunu* v. *The State*, (1995) 16 *Human Rights L.J.* 154 (Constitutional Court of South Africa). See: William A. SCHABAS, "South Africa's Constitutional Court Outlaws the Death Penalty" (1995), 16 *Human Rights L.J.* 133.

2. "Nigeria: Amnesty International Condemns Execution of Ken Saro-Wiwa and Eight Others," AI Index: AFR 44/31/95.

3. Second Optional Protocol to the International Covenant on Civil and Political Rights Aimed at Abolition of the Death Penalty, G.A. Res. 44/128 (1990), 29 *I.L.M.* 1464.

4. U.N. Doc. A/44/PV.82, at p. 11.

5. Cameroon, Djibouti, Egypt, Morocco, Nigeria, Sierra Leone, Somalia, United Republic of Tanzania, Sudan.

6. Algeria, Botswana, Burkina Faso, Burundi, Congo, Ivory Coast, Ethiopia, Gambia, Ghana, Guinea, Kenya, Lesotho, Liberia, Libyan Arab Jamahiriya, Madagascar, Malawi, Mali, Mauritius, Mozambique, Rwanda, Senegal, Uganda, Zambia, Zimbabwe.

7. "Capital punishment and implementation of the safeguards guaranteeing the protection of the rights of those facing the death penalty, Report of the Secretary-General," U.N. Doc. E/1995/78, §36.

8. Amnesty International, "Africa: Towards abolition of the death penalty," AI Index: AFR 01/01/91.

9. *Makwanyane and Mchunu* v. *The State, supra* note 1, §376.

10. *Ibid.*, §377.

11. *Ibid.*, §378.

12. *Ibid.*, §381.

13. *Ibid.*, §382.

14. *Ibid.*, §385.

15. U.N. Doc. A/46/40, §541.

16. "Death Penalty News," AI Index: ACT 53/03/95, September 1995, at p. 6. Until that point, there had been no executions in Botswana since 1986. On the death penalty in Botswana, see: D. D. NSEREKO, J.A. GLICKMAN, "Capital Punishment in Botswana" (1986), pp. 12–13, *Crime Prevention and Criminal Justice Newsletter* 51; D. D. NSEREKO, "Extenuating Circumstances in Capital Offenses in Botswana" (1991), 2 *Criminal Law Forum* 235.

17. *Makwanyane and Mchunu* v. *The State, supra* note 1, §386. Note that Portugal has been one of the world's most resolutely abolitionist states and that its

former colonies did not have the death penalty, at least for common crimes, while under colonial rule.

18. Article 70§2 of Mozambique's Constitution states: "In Mozambique there will be no death penalty." Article 6 of Namibia's Constitution declares: "The right to life shall be respected and protected. No law may prescribe death as a competent sentence. No Court or Tribunal shall have the power to impose a sentence of death upon any person. No execution shall take place in Namibia."

19. Second Optional Protocol to the International Covenant on Civil and Political Rights Aimed at Abolition of the Death Penalty, *supra* note 3.

20. U.N. Doc. A/C.3/49/SR.43, §68.

21. *Makwanyane and Mchunu* v. *The State, supra* note 1, §387 (references omitted).

22. For background on the question of capital punishment in Zimbabwe, see: A. DUMBUTSHENA, "The Death Penalty in Zimbabwe" (1987), 58 *Revue internationale de droit pénal* 521.

23. *Chileya* v. *S.*, S.C. 64/90 (unreported).

24. *Republic* v. *Mbushuu et al.* [1994], 2 L.R.C. 335 (High Court of Tanzania), at p. 345.

25. Gino J. NALDI, "Constitutional Developments in Zimbabwe and Their Compatibility with International Human Rights" (1991), 3 *African J. Int'l Comp. L.* 372, at pp. 376–380; John HATCHARD, "Capital Punishment in Southern Africa: Some Recent Developments" (1994), 43 *I.C.L.Q.* 923, at pp. 924–925.

26. ZIMBABWE, *Parliamentary Debates*, December 6, 1990.

27. *Republic* v. *Mbushuu et al., supra* note 24, at p. 351.

28. *Conjwayo* v. *Minister of Justice*, [1992] 2 S.A. 56 (Z.S.C.), [1991] 1 Z.L.R. 105, [1992] 2 S.A. 56 (Z.S.C.).

29. *Catholic Commission for Justice and Peace in Zimbabwe* v. *Attorney-General, Zimbabwe* et al., [1993] 4 S.A. 239 (Z.S.C.), [1993] 1 Z.L.R. 242 (S), 14 *Human Rights L.J.* 323, at pp. 245–246 (S.A.) (*per* Gubbay, C.J.). See: Laurel ANGUS, "Delay Before Execution: Is It Inhuman and Degrading Treatment?" (1993), 9 *South African J. Human Rights* 432.

30. *Soering* v. *United Kingdom and Germany*, July 7, 1989, Series A, Vol. 161, 11 E.H.R.R. 439.

31. *Barrett and Sutcliffe* v. *Jamaica* (Nos. 270/1988 and 271/1988), U.N. Doc. CCPR/C/44/D/1988 and 271/1988, U.N. Doc. A/47/40, at p. 246.

32. *Richmond* v. *Lewis*, 948 F. 2d. 1473 (9th Cir. 1990), *rev'd on other grounds*, 113 S.Ct. 528, 121 L.Ed.2d 411 (1992), *vacated*, 986 F.2d 1583 (9th Cir. 1993).

33. *Kindler* v. *Canada*, [1991] 2 S.C.R. 779, 67 C.C.C. (3d) 1, 84 D.L.R. (4th) 438, 6 C.R.R. (2d) 193.

34. *Dhlamini et al.* v. *Carter N.O. et al*, [1968] 1 R.L.R. 136 (A.), [1968] 2 S.A. 445.

35. *Catholic Commission for Justice and Peace in Zimbabwe* v. *Attorney-General, Zimbabwe* et al., *supra* note 29, at pp. 239, 270 (S.A.).

36. *Ibid.*, at pp. 244, 245, 249, 250, 264, 270 (S.A.).

37. *Ibid.*, at p. 268 (S.A.).

38. *Ibid.*, at p. 270 (S.A.).

39. Constitution of Zimbabwe Amendment (No. 13) Act 1993.

40. *Nkomo et al.* v. *Attorney-General, Zimbabwe* et al., [1994] 3 S.A. 34 (Z.S.C.) (*per* Gubbay, C.J.).

41. *Amnesty International Report 1995*, at p. 322.

42. *Amnesty International Report 1990*, at p. 269.

43. *Amnesty International Report 1993*, at p. 319.

44. *Amnesty International Report 1991*, at p. 257; *Amnesty International Report 1992*, at p. 284; *Amnesty International Report 1993*, at p. 319; *Amnesty International Report 1994*, at p. 325; *Amnesty International Report 1995*, at p. 321.

45. *Amnesty International Report 1993*, at p. 179; *Amnesty International Report 1994*, at p. 203; *Amnesty International Report 1995*, at p. 203.

46. Nathan V. HOLT, Jr., "Human Rights and Capital Punishment: The Case of South Africa" (1989), 30 *Virginia J. Int'l L.* 273; Christina MURRAY, Julia SLOTH-NIELSEN, "Hangings in South Africa: The Last Ten Years" (1989), 5 *South African J. Human Rights* 490; Christina MURRAY, Julia SLOTH-NIELSEN, Colin TREDOUX, "The Death Penalty in the Cape Provincial Division: 1986–1988" (1989), 5 *South African J. Human Rights* 154; Laurel ANGUS, Evadné GRANT, "Sentencing in Capital Cases in the TPC and WLD: 1987–1989" (1991), 7 *South African J. Human Rights* 50; T. P. MCNALLY, "Capital Punishment: An Orange Free State Perspective" (1989), 2 *South African J. Criminal Justice* 239; R. N. LEON, "The Abolition of the Death Penalty in South Africa" (1989), 106 *South African L. Journal* 42; E. KAHN, "Death Penalty in South Africa" (1970), 33 *J. Contemporary Roman-Dutch L.* 108.

47. U.N. Doc. S/RES/191 (1964), §4(a); U.N. Doc. A/RES/37/69 A (1982), §1; U.N. Doc. A/RES/42/23 A (1987), §3(a); U.N. Doc. A/RES/44/27 A (1989), §3.

48. Criminal Procedure Second Amendment Decree, 1990, Decree No. 16 of 1990 of the Council of State of the Republic of Ciskei, June 8, 1990, as amended. See: *S.v. Qeqe and Another* [1990], 2 S.A.C.R. 654 (Ck.A.D.).

49. Criminal Law Amendment Act No. 107 of 1990, assented to June 28, 1990, *Government Gazette*, Vol. 301, No. 12644. See: Jan H. VAN ROOYEN, "South Africa's New Death Sentence: Is the Bell Tolling for the Hangman?" (1991), 4 *South African J. Criminal Justice* 79; A. GOLDFARB, "The Dilemma of Discretion: A U.S. Perspective on the Proposal for Reform of the South African Death Penalty for Murder" (1990), 6 *South African J. Human Rights* 266; John HATCHARD, *supra* note 25.

50. SOUTH AFRICAN LAW COMMISSION, *Interim Report on Group and Human Rights, Project 58*, August 1991, §§7.33, 7.36, cited in *Makwanyane and Mchunu* v. *The State*, *supra* note 1, §22 (*per* Chaskalson P.).

51. See: Nelson MANDELA, *A Long Walk to Freedom*, Boston: Little, Brown and Company, 1994, at pp. 327–328.

52. As amended by Criminal Law Amendment Act No. 107 of 1990, *supra* note 49, s. 4.

53. Constitution of the Republic of South Africa, Act 200 of 1993, assented to January 25, 1994, date of commencement April 27, 1994, *Government Gazette*, Vol. 343, No. 15466.

54. During the hearing, Advocate George Bizos, SC, acted for the minister. Mr. Bizos has been the Mandela family lawyer since the 1960s.

55. *Makwanyane and Mchunu* v. *The State, supra* note 1, §214.

56. See, for example, the reasons of acting Justice Sydney Kentridge, *ibid.*, §196.

57. Convention for the Protection of Human Rights and Fundamental Freedoms (1955), 213 U.N.T.S. 221, E.T.S. 5, art. 2.

58. *Makwanyane and Mchunu* v. *The State, supra* note 1, §38.

59. *People* v. *Anderson*, 6 Cal.3d 628, 100 Cal.Rptr. 152, 493 P.2d 880 (1972), *cert. denied*, 406 U.S. 958, 92 S.Ct. 2060, 32 L.Ed.2d 344 (1972).

60. *District Atty. for Suffolk Dist.* v. *Watson*, 381 Mass.648, 411 N.E.2d 1274 (1980).

61. Decision no 23/1990 (X.31.) AB. See: Tibor HORVATH, "L'abolition de la peine de mort en Hongrie" [1992], 2 *Revue internationale de criminologie et de police technique* 167.

62. *Kindler* v. *Canada* [1991], 2 S.C.R. 779, 67 C.C.C. (3d) 1, 84 D.L.R. (4th) 438, 6 C.R.R. (2d) 193; cited in *Makwanyane and Mchunu* v. *The State, supra* note 1, §§60–61. See: William A. SCHABAS, "*Kindler* v. *Canada*" (1993), 87 *A.J.I.L.* 128; William A. SCHABAS, "Kindler and Ng: Our Supreme Magistrates Take a Frightening Step into the Court of Public Opinion" (1991), 51 *Revue du Barreau* 673; John PAK, "Canadian Extradition and the Death Penalty: Seeking a Constitutional Assurance of Life" (1993), 26 *Cornell Int'l L. J.* 239.

63. *Furman* v. *Georgia*, 408 U.S. 238, 92 S.Ct. 2726, 33 L.Ed.2d 346 (1972).

64. *Gregg* v. *Georgia*, 428 U.S. 153, 96 S.Ct. 2909, 49 L.Ed.2d 859 (1976).

65. *Makwanyane and Mchunu* v. *The State, supra* note 1, §51.

66. *Ibid.*, §49.

67. See also the reasons of Ackermann, J., *ibid.*, §164; Kentridge, A.J., *ibid.*, §196.

68. *Ibid.*, §87. On this subject, see: J. MIDGLEY, "Public Opinion and the Death Penalty in South Africa" (1974), 14 *British J. Criminology* 347; J. J. RAY, "Attitude to the Death Penalty in South Africa with Some International Comparisons" (1982), 116 *J. Social Psychology* 287; Keith I. SMITH, "The Penalty of Death: Public Attitudes in South Africa" (1989), 2 *South African J. Criminal Justice* 256.

69. *Makwanyane and Mchunu* v. *The State, supra* note 1, §87.

70. *Supra* note 63, at p. 443 (U.S.); cited in *ibid.*, §89.

71. *Makwanyane and Mchunu* v. *The State, supra* note 1, §305. See also: Sachs, J., *ibid.*, §373.

72. *Ibid.*, §307.

73. *Ibid.*, §322.

74. *Ibid.*, §323.

75. *Ibid.*, §118.

76. *Ibid.*, §§119, 120. See also: Langa, J., *ibid.*, §219.

77. *Ibid.*, §182. See also: Mahomed, J., *ibid.*, §292.

78. *Ibid.*, §201.

79. *Ibid.*, §§119–120.

80. *Ibid.*, §122. See also: Mahomed, J., *ibid.*, §287.

81. *Ibid.*, §212.

82. *Ibid.*, §213.

83. Ackermann, J., *ibid.*, §166; Didcott, J., *ibid.*, §174; Kriegler, J., *ibid.*, §214; Langa, J., *ibid.*, §216; Mahomed, J., *ibid.*, §269; Mokgoro, J., *ibid.*, §317; O'Regan, J., *ibid.*, §318; Sachs, J., *ibid.*, §350.

84. *Ibid.*, §346.

85. *Ibid.*, §268.

86. *Ibid.*, §269.

87. *Ibid.*, §269.

88. African Charter on Human and People's Rights, O.A.U. Doc. CAB/LEG/67/3 rev. 5, 4 E.H.R.R. 417, 21 *I.L.M.* 58.

89. *Amnesty International Report 1994*, at p. 128; *Amnesty International Report 1995*, at pp. 127–128.

90. *Amnesty International Report 1992*, at p. 116; *Amnesty International Report 1993*, at p. 130; *Amnesty International Report 1994*, at pp. 129–132; *Amnesty International Report 1995*, at p. 131.

91. *Amnesty International Report 1991*, at p. 136; *Amnesty International Report 1992*, at p. 16; *Amnesty International Report 1993*, at p. 180; *Amnesty International Report 1994*, at p. 183; *Amnesty International Report 1995*, at p. 296.

92. *Amnesty International Report 1991*, at p. 136; *Amnesty International Report 1992*, at p. 16; *Amnesty International Report 1993*, at p. 180; *Amnesty International Report 1994*, at p. 183; *Amnesty International Report 1995*, at p. 296.

93. *Amnesty International Report 1995*, at p. 183.

94. *Amnesty International Report 1995*, at p. 262.

95. *Amnesty International Report 1994*, at p. 301. Also: AI Index: AFR 59/06/93; AI Index: AFR 59/02/93.

96. *Amnesty International Report 1995*, at p. 296.

97. AMNESTY INTERNATIONAL, *Uganda, The failure to safeguard human rights*, London, 1992, at pp. 57–62; also: "Uganda: The Death Penalty: A Barrier to Improving Human Rights," AI Index: AFR 59/03/93.

98. F.D.A.M. LUOGA, "The Tanzanian Bill of Rights," unpublished paper, April 1995, at p. 10.

99. Alan SMITH, "Tanzania," in Peter BAEHR, Hilde HEY, Jacqueline SMITH, Theresa SWINEHART, eds., *Human Rights in Developing Countries Yearbook 1994*, Deventer: Kluwer, 1994, at pp. 397, 412.

100. *Amnesty International Report 1994*, at p. 286.

101. AI Index: AFR 56/02/94.

102. *Amnesty International Report 1995*, at p. 282.

103. *Republic* v. *Mbushuu et al., supra* note 24, at p. 351.

104. *Mbushuu and Another* v. *Republic*, unreported judgment of the Court of Appeal of Tanzania, Criminal Appeal No. 142 of 1994, January 30, 1995.

105. *Makwanyane and Mchunu* v. *The State, supra* note 1, §115.

106. *Amnesty International Report 1991*, at p. 256; *Amnesty International Report 1992*, at p. 283; *Amnesty International Report 1993*, at p. 318; *Amnesty International Report 1994*, at p. 324; *Amnesty International Report 1995*, at p. 320.

107. "Statute of the International Tribunal for the Former Yugoslavia," S/RES/827 (1993), annex, art. 24(1).

108. Despite Rwanda's opposition, the Statute of the Tribunal, like its counterpart for the former Yugoslavia, excludes capital punishment: "Statute of the International Tribunal for Rwanda," S/RES/955 (1994), annex, art. 23(1).

109. U.N. Doc. S/PV.3453, at p. 16.

110. *Ibid.*

111. *Ibid.*, at p. 5.

112. Second Optional Protocol to the International Covenant on Civil and Political Rights Aimed at Abolition of the Death Penalty, *supra* note 3.

113. "Protocole d'Accord entre le Gouvernement de la République Rwandaise et le Front Patriotique Rwandais portant sur les questions diverses et dispositions finales signé à Arusha," August 3, 1993, *Journal officiel,* Year 32, no. 16, August 15, 1993, p. 1430, art. 15.

114. See: "Justice for Some," *The Economist*, January 6, 1996, pp. 32–33.

115. For an attempt by a European scholar to justify use of the death penalty in post-genocide Rwanda, see: Gérald PRUNIER, *The Rwanda Crisis, History of a Genocide, 1959–1994,* Kampala: Fountain Publishers, 1995, at p. 355. In an emotional conclusion to his overview of the Rwandan genocide, Prunier says that perhaps a hundred individuals "have to die. This is the only ritual through which the killers can be cleansed of their guilt and the surviors brought back to the community of the living."

116. *Catholic Commission for Justice and Peace in Zimbabwe* v. *Attorney-General, Zimbabwe et al., supra* note 29, at p. 270 (S.A.).

117. *Amnesty International Report 1991*, at pp. 51–52; *Amnesty International Report 1992*, at pp. 75–76; *Amnesty International Report 1993*, at p. 78.

118. *Amnesty International Report 1991*, at p. 95; *Amnesty International Report 1995*, at pp. 134–135.

119. *Amnesty International Report 1991*, at pp. 42–43; *Amnesty International Report 1992*, at pp. 66–67; *Amnesty International Report 1993*, at pp. 65–66; *Amnesty International Report 1994*, at pp. 72–73; *Amnesty International Report 1995*, at pp. 71–72.

120. "Second periodic report of Cameroon," U.N. Doc. CCPR/C/63/Add.1, §50.

121. *Amnesty International Report 1995*, at p. 146.

122. See: "Open letter to His Excellency Mr. Henri Konan Bédie, president of Côte d'Ivoire on the proposed extension of the scope of the death penalty," AI Index: AFR 31/04/95 EXT: Open letter.

123. Second Optional Protocol to the International Covenant on Civil and Political Rights Aimed at Abolition of the Death Penalty, *supra* note 3. See: *Amnesty International Report 1994*, at p. 134.

124. *Amnesty International Report 1995*, at p. 259.

125. *Amnesty International Report 1993*, at p. 256.

126. AI Index: AFR 20/01/95; AI Index: AFR 20/03/95.

127. *Amnesty International Report 1995*, at p. 126.

128. *Amnesty International Report 1994*, at p. 140.

129. *Amnesty International Report 1995*, at p. 140.

130. AI Index: AFR 34/04/95

131. U.N. Doc. E/CN.4/1989/25, §§195–198; AMNESTY INTERNATIONAL, *When the State Kills . . .*, New York, 1989, at pp. 185–187; A. ADEYEMI, "Death Penalty: Criminological Perspectives. The Nigerian Situation" (1987), 58 *Revue internationale de droit pénal* 485.

132. Mike IKHARIALE, "Death Penalty in Nigeria: A Constitutional Aberration" (1992), 2 *J. Human Rights Law and Practice* 40.

133. *Amnesty International Report 1995*, at p. 229.

134. COMMITTEE FOR THE DEFENCE OF HUMAN RIGHTS, *1990 Annual Report on Human Rights Situation in Nigeria*, at pp. 1–3; *Amnesty International Report 1995*, at pp. 229–230; "Nigeria: A Travesty of Justice—Secret Treason Trials and Other Concerns," AI Index: AFR 44/23/95, at pp. 20–21.

135. AI Index: AFR 44/17/95.

136. "Nigeria: Public Executions and Death Sentence for Armed Robbery," AI Index: AFR 44/07/91; "Nigeria: Death Sentences and Executions for Armed Robbery," AI Index: AFR 44/11/92.

137. COMMITTEE FOR THE DEFENCE OF HUMAN RIGHTS, *1990 Annual Report on Human Rights Situation in Nigeria, supra* note 134.

138. African Charter on Human and People's Rights, *supra* note 88.

139. *Constitutional Rights Project (in respect of Nahab Akama, G. Adega et al.)* (Comm. no. 60/91) (1996), 3 I.H.R.R. 132.

140. *Constitutional Rights Project (in respect of Zamani Lakwot et al.)* (Comm. no. 87/93) (1996), 3 I.H.R.R. 137.

141. "Nigeria, The Ogoni Trials and Detentions," AI Index AFR 44/20/95.

142. "Nigeria: Amnesty International Condemns Death Sentences Imposed on Ken Saro-Wiwa and Other Ogoni Detainees after Blatantly Unfair Trials," AI Index: AFR 44/26/95.

143. U.N. Doc. GA/9046. In the Third Committee: U.N. Doc. GA/SHC/3351. For the statement of representative Ibrahim Gambari, defending the legality of the executions: U.N. Doc. GA/SHC/3348.

144. "Fourth periodic report of Tunisia," U.N. Doc. CCPR/C/84/Add.1, §84; *Amnesty International Report 1992*, at p. 256.

145. U.N. Doc. A/49/234 and Add.1 and Add.2, later revised by U.N. Doc. A/C.3/49/L.32/Rev.1.

146. *Amnesty International Report 1993*, at p. 214; *Amnesty International Report 1994*, at p. 216.

147. *Amnesty International Report 1994*, at p. 216.

148. "Third periodic report of Morocco," U.N. Doc. CCPR/C/76/Add.3, §31.

149. *Amnesty International Report 1991*, at pp. 153–155; *Amnesty International Report 1992*, at pp. 183–185; *Amnesty International Report 1993*, at pp. 204–206; *Amnesty International Report 1994*, at pp. 208–209; *Amnesty International Report 1995*, at pp. 208–209.

150. Sudan: U.N. Doc. A/C.3/49/SR.36, §§57–59; Libya: U.N. Doc. A/C.3/49/SR.43, §53; Egypt: U.N. Doc. A/C.3/49/SR.43, §§57–60; U.N. Doc. A/CONF.87/14/Rev.1, at p. 60.

151. U.N. Doc. E/CN.4/1995/61, §45; *Amnesty International Report 1995*, at p. 54.

152. *Amnesty International Report 1994*, at p. 56. Also: U.N. Doc. E/CN.4/1994/7, §109, 114. For Algeria's defense of use of the death penalty, see also: U.N. Doc. E/CN.4/1992/30, §§42–47. For criticism by the Human Rights Committee of a provision of Algerian law allowing the death penalty for economic crimes, see: U.N. Doc. CCPR/C/79/Add.1, §5.

153. *Amnesty International Report 1995*, at p. 121. Also U.N. Doc. E/CN.4/1995/61, §119.

154. *Amnesty International Report 1995*, at p. 199.

155. "Second Periodic Report of Libyan Arab Jamahiriya," U.N. Doc. CCPR/C/28/Add.16, §19.

156. U.N. Doc. CAT/C/SR.202, §13.

157. *Amnesty International Report 1993*, at p. 256.

158. U.N. Doc. E/CN.4/1994/48, §§60–61.

159. "Statement by H.E. Mr. Abdelaziz Shiddo, Minister of Justice and Attorney-General of the Republic of the Sudan and Leader of Sudan Delegation to the 50th Session of the Commission on Human Rights, Commenting on the report of Dr. Gaspar Biro, Special Rapporteur on Human Rights situation in the Sudan under agenda item (12)," Geneva, February 25, 1994. See also: U.N. Doc. E/CN.4/1994/122, §58–64.

160. U.N. Doc. A/BUR/49/SR.5, §13.

161. Abdullahi Ahmed AN-NA'IM, "The Meaning of Cruel, Inhuman or Degrading Treatment or Punishment," in Abdullahi Ahmed AN-NA'IM, ed., *Human Rights in Cross-Cultural Perspectives, A Quest for Consensus*, Philadelphia: University of Pennsylvania Press, 1992, pp. 19–43, at p. 33. On capital punishment in Islamic law, see: Frédéric SUDRE, *Droit international et européen des droits de*

l'homme, Paris: Presses universitaires de France, 1989, at pp. 85–87; A. WAZIR, "Quelques aspects de la peine de mort en droit pénal islamique" (1987), 58 *Revue internationale de droit pénal* 421; CENTRE DES ÉTUDES DE SÉCURITÉ (ARABIE SAOUDITE), "L'égalité et commodité de la peine de mort en droit musulman" (1987), 58 *Revue internationale de droit pénal* 431; N. HOSNI, "La peine de mort en droit égyptien et en droit islamique" (1987), 58 *Revue internationale de droit pénal* 407. In an interesting twist on this debate, an individual challenged Malaysia's mandatory death penalty for drug trafficking as being unconstitutional because it was contrary to Islamic law and, consequently, in breach of the Constitution of Malaysia, art. 3: *Che Omar bin Che Soh* v. *Public Prosecutor* [1988], L.R.C. (Const.) 95 (Malaysia Supreme Court).

162. Charte arabe des droits de l'homme (1995), 7 *Revue universelle des droits de l'homme* 212.

163. ARAB INSTITUTE FOR HUMAN RIGHTS, HANDS OFF CAIN, *The Death Penalty in International Law and in the Legislations of the Arab Countries*, 1995, at p. 62.

164. *Supra* note 88.

165. For further reading on the subject of human rights and the African regional system, see: B. Obinna OKERE, "The Protection of Human Rights in Africa and the African Charter on Human and Peoples' Rights: A Comparative Analysis with the European and American Systems" (1984), 6 *Human Rights Quarterly* 143; Richard GITTLEMAN, "The African Charter on Human and Peoples' Rights: A Legal Analysis" (1982), 22 *Virginia J. Int'l L.* 667; Manfred NOWAK, "The African Charter on Human and Peoples' Rights" (1986), 7 *Human Rights L.J.* 399; A. OJO, A. SESAY, "The O.A.U. and Human Rights: Prospects for the 1980s and Beyond" (1986), 8 *Human Rights Quarterly* 89; E. G. BELLO, "The African Charter on Human and People's Rights. A Legal Analysis" (1985), 194 *R.C.A.D.I.* 91; O. U. UMOZURIKE, "The African Charter of Human Rights" (1983), 77 *A.J.I.L.* 511; Ibrahim BADAWI EL-SHEIKH, "The African Commission on Human and Peoples' Rights: Prospect and Problems" (1989), 3 *N.Q.H.R.* 281.

166. (1976) 999 U.N.T.S. 171.

167. For comments on the right to life provision in the African Charter, see Johannes G. C. VAN AGGELEN, *Le rôle des organisations internationales dans la protection du droit à la vie*, Brussels: E. Story-Scientia, 1986, at p. 41; Tunguru HUARAKA, "The African Charter on Human and Peoples' Rights: A Significant Contribution to the Development of International Human Rights Law," in Daniel PRÉMONT, ed., *Essais sur le concept de "droit de vivre" en mémoire de Yougindra Khushalani*, Brussels: Bruylant, 1988, pp. 193–211, at p. 203.

168. G.A. Res. 217 A (III), U.N. Doc. A/810.

169. *Supra* note 88, art. 60.

170. Amos WAKO, "Comparison of the *African Charter of Human and Peoples' Rights* and the *Optional Protocol* to the *International Covenant on Civil and Political Rights*," [1991–92] *Canadian Human Rights Yearbook* 145. On the Universal

Declaration and the death penalty, see: Lilly E. LANDERER, "Capital Punishment as a Human Rights Issue Before the United Nations" (1971), 4 *Human Rights J.* 511; Alfred VERDOODT, *Naissance et signification de la Déclaration universelle des droits de l'homme*, Louvain, Paris: Nauwelaerts, 1963, at pp. 99–100; William A. SCHABAS, *The Abolition of the Death Penalty in International Law*, Cambridge: Cambridge University Press (Grotius Publications), 1993, at pp. 30–45.

171. Etienne-Richard MBAYA, "À la recherche du noyau intangible dans la Charte africaine," in *Le noyau intangible des droits de l'homme*, Fribourg: Éditions universitaires Fribourg Suisse, 1991, at pp. 207–226, at p. 221. See also: Keba MBAYA, *Les droits de l'homme en Afrique*, Paris: Pedone, 1992, at p. 197.

172. Benoît S. NGOM, *Les droits de l'homme et l'Afrique*, Paris: Silex, 1984, at p. 51.

173. AMNESTY INTERNATIONAL, *A Guide to the African Charter on Human and People's Rights*, London, 1991, at pp. 18–19.

174. Astrid DANIELSEN, *The State Reporting Procedure under the African Charter*, Copenhagen: Danish Centre for Human Rights, 1994; Felice D. GAER, "First Fruits: Reporting by State under the African Charter on Human and Peoples' Rights" (1992), 10 *N.Q.H.R.* 29.

175. O.A.U. Doc. ACHPR/MOC/XIII/006. But other states make no reference whatsoever to the death penalty in their reports; *e.g.*, "Periodic Report of Cape Verde," O.A.U. Doc. ACHPR/MOC/XIII/009; "Periodic Report of Ghana," O.A.U. Doc. ACHPR/MOC/XIII/008; "Periodic Report of Togo," O.A.U. Doc. ACHPR/MOC/XIII/010.

176. *Constitutional Rights Project (in respect of Nahab Akama, G. Adega et al.)*, *supra* note 139; *Constitutional Rights Project (in respect of Zamani Lakwot et al.)*, *supra* note 140.

177. *Nemi v. The State*, [1994] 1 L.R.C. 376 (Supreme Court of Nigeria), at p. 386 (Bello, C.J.N.); also at p. 400 (Uwais, J.S.C.).

178. *Makwanyane and Mchunu v. The State*, *supra* note 1.

179. O.A.U. Doc. CAB/LEG/24.9/49 (1990), arts. 5§3, 30(e).

180. Convention on the Rights of the Child, G.A. Res. 44/25, 28 I.L.M. 1448, art. 37(*a*).

181. *Supra* note 88, art. 46.

182. *Conjwayo v. Minister of Justice*, *supra* note 28; *Catholic Commission for Justice and Peace in Zimbabwe v. Attorney-General, Zimbabwe* et al., *supra* note 29; *Republic v. Mbushuu et al.*, *supra* note 24. See also: Lloyd VOGELMAN, "The Living Dead: Living on Death Row" (1989), 5 *South African J. Human Rights* 183.

183. *Abbott v. A.-G. of Trinidad and Tobago*, [1979] 1 W.L.R. 1342, 32 W.I.R. 347 (J.C.P.C.), at p. 1345 (W.L.R.) (*per* Lord Diplock).

184. *Pratt et al. v. Attorney General for Jamaica et al.*, [1993] 4 All.E.R. 769, [1993] 2 L.R.C. 349, [1994] 2 A.C. 1, [1993] 3 W.L.R. 995, 43 W.I.R. 340, 14 *H.R.L.J.* 338, 33 I.L.M. 364 (J.C.P.C.). See also: *Guerra v. Baptiste*, [1995] J.C.J. No. 43.

ERIC PROKOSCH

Death Penalty Developments

Abolition of the Death Penalty

In Italy, a bill eliminating the death penalty from the Military Penal Code in Time of War received its final approval from the parliament on October 5, 1994, and was promulgated on October 25. As a result, Italy has now abolished the death penalty for all crimes.

The effort to abolish the death penalty in Italy has a long history. In 1786, Grand Duke Leopold of Tuscany promulgated a penal code that completely eliminated the death penalty. This action was one of a number of early abolitionist efforts inspired by the publication in 1764 of Cesare Beccaria's *On Crimes and Punishments*, a book that contained the first sustained, systematic critique of the death penalty. The death penalty was reintroduced some years later, but the experience of Tuscany was cited as a successful experiment by people arguing for abolition elsewhere.

In 1889, Italy abolished the death penalty for all crimes under a new penal code, but the penalty was reintroduced for certain crimes against the state in 1926 under the government of Benito Mussolini, and its scope was broadened in 1931. It was finally abolished for common criminal offenses and military offenses committed in peacetime under the new Constitution of the Republic of Italy of December 27, 1947.[1]

In recent years the subject of the death penalty as an international issue has attracted considerable public interest in Italy in the form of scholarly discussions, popular books, and articles. One recent book follows the cases of prisoners facing imminent execution in four countries—Sudan, Taiwan, the Soviet Union, and the United States of America (Sandro Veronesi, *Occhio per occhio: La pena di morte in quattro storie*, Milan: Mondadori, 1992)—and public campaigns against the use of the penalty abroad. An international colloquium was held in Bologna in 1982. The report of the colloquium, *La pena di morte nel mondo: Convegno internazionale di Bologna (28–30 ottobre 1982)* (Casale Monferrato, Marietti, 1983), includes the results of an opinion poll conducted by two researchers at the Carlo Cattaneo Institute in Bologna. In 1987, an international conference on the death penalty was held in Siracusa under the auspices of the International Institute of Higher Studies in International Criminal Sciences.[2]

In November 1995, Spain also took the step of abolishing the death penalty for all crimes. A bill signed by the king removed the death penalty from the Military Penal Code. In 1932 the death penalty was originally abolished in Spain for common criminal offenses, but was reintroduced by the Franco regime in 1938. Spain's last executions date to September 17, 1975, when five men were executed by firing squad. The post-Franco constitution, which was endorsed by referendum in 1978, abolished the death penalty for offenses committed in peacetime but retained it for military offenses committed in time of war. In 1994, the senate unanimously adopted a bill requesting that the government abolish the death penalty. The relevant legislation was then adopted by the Congress of Deputies, approved by the senate, and signed by the king.

Spain and Italy are the latest in a series of countries that, having abolished the death penalty for common crimes, have gone on to abolish it for military and other exceptional crimes. Countries that have taken this path since the Second World War are Austria in 1968, Finland and Sweden in 1972, Portugal in 1976, Denmark in 1978, Norway in 1979, the Netherlands in 1982, New Zealand in 1989, Switzerland in 1992, and Greece in 1993.[3]

The standard arguments against the death penalty for common crimes—that it violates human rights, that there is an inherent risk of executing the innocent, that it negates the possibility of rehabilitating the offender—apply to the death penalty for wartime and other exceptional crimes, but there are also special arguments relating to the latter. These arguments were brought together in a paper issued by Amnesty International in 1994.[4] The paper was based on research conducted by the death penalty theme group of Amnesty International's Dutch Section. The arguments are often cited in debates over the issue.

By the end of 1995, sixty countries and territories had abolished the death penalty for all offenses. The figure of sixty included the Republic of Palau, which became independent in October 1994, and South Africa, which brought an end to the death penalty by judgment of the Constitutional Court in June 1995. Fourteen countries had abolished the penalty for all but exceptional crimes, while at least thirty-five countries and territories that retained the death penalty in law could be classified as abolitionist de facto, in that they had not carried out any executions for the last ten years or more. Eighty-two countries retained the death penalty. The year 1995 marked a turning point, in that for the first time in history it could be stated that a majority of states in the world had abolished the death penalty, either de facto or de jure.

Figures compiled by Amnesty International in 1994 showed the enormous advances made in the abolition of the death penalty in recent years. At year end, the number of countries that had abolished the death penalty for all crimes had more than doubled since 1980, and the number of countries abolitionist in law or practice had risen from sixty-two to ninety-seven over the same period. The first country permanently to abolish the death penalty for all crimes, Venezuela, did so in 1963; by 1975 the number had risen to twenty, an average increase of one country every seven months. In 1980 the number had risen to twenty-five, and at the end of 1994 it stood at fifty-five. Since 1976, an average of nearly two countries per year have become totally abolitionist, and the rise in the number of totally abolitionist countries has accelerated since 1988. The death penalty is being abolished today faster than ever before in history.

Regional Developments

Eastern Europe was the focus of dramatic developments in terms of abolition of the death penalty, a consequence of the insistence of the Council of Europe that new members impose a moratorium on the death penalty and undertake to ratify the Protocol No. 6 to the Convention for the Protection of Human Rights and Fundamental Freedoms Concerning the Abolition of the Death Penalty. In 1995 alone, Moldava, Ukraine, Albania, and Bosnia-Herzegovina made such commitments.

The year 1996 began with the commitment by the Russian Federation to abolish the death penalty within one year, to ratify the Protocol and to impose an immediate moratorium on all sentences of death. In 1990, Russia executed seventy-six persons, but the number has declined steadily, to three in 1993 and four in 1994. This decrease is attributed principally to the use of executive clemency by President Yeltsin. Russia has also reduced the number of offenses punishable by death and has exempted men over sixty-five and all women from its scope.

By virtue of the Dayton Peace Agreement, signed at Paris on December 14, 1995, the new state of Bosnia and Herzegovina is held to the highest standard of compliance with contemporary human rights norms. This includes ratification of Protocol No. 6 of the European Convention on Human Rights and the incorporation of its terms as the fundamental law of the new republic.[5] Bosnia and Herzegovina has not performed executions since achieving independence in 1992. Ironically, the Dayton agreement was negotiated in a state that still retains the death penalty, Ohio.

Africa was also the scene of very significant progress in terms of abolition of the death penalty. The highlight was the June 1995 judgment of the Constitutional Court of South Africa, declaring the death penalty to be contrary to the country's new constitution. On recent developments favoring abolition of the death penalty in Africa, see the article by William A. Schabas earlier in this volume.

Defeat of a Move to Reintroduce the Death Penalty

Proposed amendments to the Criminal Justice and Public Order Bill that would have restored the death penalty for murder or for the murder of a police officer acting in the execution of his duty were defeated in the House of Commons of the United Kingdom on February 21, 1994, by 403 votes to 159 and 383 votes to 186 respectively. The majorities of 244 and 197 were larger than in the last previous debate on the death penalty in 1990, when similar motions for reintroduction were defeated by majorities of 185 and 135 respectively. During the debate, Michael Howard, Secretary of State for Home Affairs (the cabinet minister responsible for law and order), said that until the 1990 debate he had voted consistently in favor of restoring the death penalty for certain categories of murder, believing that the deterrent effect would be greatest for those categories and that the appeals process would effectively eliminate the risk of a miscarriage of justice. Several recent miscarriages of justice, however, had caused him to change his mind. He said,

> Miscarriages of justice are a blot on a civilized society. For someone to spend years in prison for a crime he or she did not commit is both a terrible thing and one for which release from prison and financial recompense cannot make amends. But even that injustice cannot be compared with the icy comfort of a posthumous pardon. When we consider the plight of those who have been wrongly convicted, we cannot but be relieved that the death penalty was not available. We should not fail to consider the irreparable damage that would have been inflicted on the criminal justice system had innocent people been executed.[6]

Expansion of the Scope of the Death Penalty

The scope of the death penalty has recently been expanded in several countries.

In Lebanon, following the bombing of a church on February 27, 1994, in which at least ten people died, the parliament on March 10 approved government proposals to extend the death penalty to a further category of murder and to politically motivated killings. On April 23, judicial executions resumed for the first time in eleven years when Bassam Saleh al-Muslah was hanged; he had been convicted of murder and sentenced to death in 1993. Three further executions were carried out in the course of the year.

In Nigeria, the Civil Disturbances Tribunal set up in April 1994 by Rivers State Authority under the Special Tribunal (Offences Relating to Civil Disturbances) Edict, 1994 was reportedly given the power to impose the death penalty for crimes not previously punishable by death, including attempted murder.

In the United States of America, the death penalty was introduced for some sixty new offenses under federal civilian law under the Federal Death Penalty Act of 1994. The legislation consists of Title VI of the Violent Crime Control Act of 1994. The death penalty is introduced under a new chapter 228 of title 18 of the U.S. Code. The relevant sections are 18 U.S. Code 3591–3598. The Federal Death Penalty Act of 1994 was adopted by the Congress in August and signed by President Bill Clinton on September 13, 1994. New offenses punishable by death include the murder of federal officials and certain nonhomicidal offenses such as treason and espionage. Among the crimes made punishable by death under the act are felonious drug offenses committed as part of a "continuing criminal enterprise" and involving specified large gross receipts or specified large quantities of heroin, cocaine, marijuana, LSD, amphetamines, or certain other synthetic drugs.

The act also provides for the death penalty for attempted killings committed or ordered by a leader of a "continuing criminal enterprise" of drug trafficking in order to obstruct an investigation or prosecution.

Also in the United States of America, Kansas in April 1994 reinstated the death penalty for murder, becoming the thirty-seventh state to authorize its use. The governor of Kansas, Joan Finney, who personally opposed the death penalty, allowed the reinstatement bill to become law without her signature. The law, which came into effect on July 1, 1994, provides for the death penalty as an optional punishment for seven types of intentional, premeditated murder, including the killing of a rape victim or a police officer. It establishes lethal injection as the method of execution. The last execution carried out in Kansas was in 1965.

New York State reintroduced the death penalty, effective September 1, 1995. The new legislation was promised by Governor George E. Pataki in his 1994 election campaign against outspokenly abolitionist incumbent Governor Mario Cuomo. Although New York legislators have been attempting to reintroduce the death penalty since 1977, the bills had been systematically vetoed by the governor, first Hugh L. Carey and then Mario Cuomo. Interestingly, the incidence of violent crime and murder in particular has dropped dramatically since 1990, confirming the irrelevance of the issue of deterrence. In March 1996, Pataki took the unprecedented step of removing a district attorney from a capital case because of a commitment not to use the death penalty.

New York's last execution dates to 1963, when Eddie Lee Mays was put to death. Executions in New York hit a peak in the 1930s, although the number declined consistently through the 1940s and 1950s. During the 1950s, New York executed approximately five persons per year. In 1963, New York became the last jurisdiction in the United States to put an end to mandatory capital punishment for murder.

Public Opinion Polls

According to a poll of more than 3,000 adults conducted by the prime minister's office in Japan and published on November 25, 1994, 73.8 percent of respondents said that the death penalty was unavoidable in certain circumstances. Among the reasons given were that felons should compensate with their own lives and that the death penalty helps to deter felonies.

However, 13.6 percent said that the death penalty should be abolished, a 7 percent increase over a similar survey in 1989, and a high proportion of those who considered the death penalty unavoidable in certain circumstances agreed that it could be abolished if circumstances changed in the future. The total number of abolitionists together with these "conditional" abolitionists was higher than the number of people who thought the death penalty could never be abolished.

Following the publication of the poll, two Japanese prisoners, Ajima Yukio and Sasaki Kazumitsu, were executed in secret on December 1, 1994. Both had been convicted of murder; Ajima Yukio had been under sentence of death for sixteen years. The executions were the first in more than a year. In line with its established policy, the Japanese government refused to confirm that the executions had taken place. Amnesty International expressed concern that the results of the opinion poll might be used to justify further executions.

New Parties to International Treaties on the Death Penalty

During 1994 and 1995, Croatia, Denmark, Hungary, Italy, Macedonia, Malta, Namibia, the Seychelles, Slovenia, and Switzerland became parties to the Second Optional Protocol to the International Covenant on Civil and Political Rights, aiming at the abolition of the death penalty, bringing the number of states parties to twenty-nine. Ireland, Romania, and Slovenia became parties to Protocol No. 6 to the European Convention for the Protection of Human Rights and Fundamental Freedoms ("European Convention on Human Rights") concerning the abolition of the death penalty, bringing the number of states parties to twenty-three. Uruguay became a party to the Protocol to the American Convention on Human Rights to Abolish the Death Penalty, bringing the number of states parties to three; Brazil signed the Protocol, signifying its intention to become a party at a later date.

Developments in Intergovernmental Organizations

There have been important developments or discussions on the death penalty in several intergovernmental organizations.

In his report to the fiftieth session of the United Nations Commission on Human Rights (January 31–March 11, 1994), the U.N. Special Rapporteur on extrajudicial, summary, or arbitrary executions, Bacre Wady Ndiaye, expressed concern about reports of the extension of the scope of the death penalty in several countries during 1993 (paragraph 676). In the conclusions and recommendations of the report, he emphasized that "the abolition of capital punishment is most desirable" and stated, "The scope of application of the death penalty should never be extended and the Special Rapporteur invites those States which have done so to reconsider" (paragraph 677).

The Special Rapporteur drew attention to reports from twenty-three countries in 1993 of legislation and practice leading to the imposition and carrying out of death sentences when the defendants did not fully benefit from international guarantees for a fair trial (paragraph 680). The countries cited were Algeria, Azerbaijan,

Bangladesh, China, Comoros, Egypt, Iran, Kuwait, Kyrgyzstan, Malawi, Malaysia, Nigeria, Pakistan, Peru, Saudi Arabia, Sierra Leone, South Africa, Syria, Tadjikistan, Turkmenistan, United States of America, Uzbekistan, and Yemen.

He also cited reports of death sentences imposed on people despite their serious mental retardation in the United States, and of people under the age of eighteen at the time of the offense being sentenced to death in Pakistan and executed in the United States of America (paragraphs 472, 620, 628, 685–686). The Special Rapporteur called on the governments in question to conform to the relevant international standards providing for fair trials in death penalty cases (paragraph 684) and "to consider which measures may be more suitable than the death penalty to promote rehabilitation and reinsertion into society of juvenile or mentally retarded offenders" (paragraph 687).[7]

In its resolution 1994/82, adopted without a vote on March 9, 1994, the Commission on Human Rights requested the Special Rapporteur "to continue monitoring the implementation of existing international standards on safeguards and restrictions relating to the imposition of capital punishment, bearing in mind the comments made by the Human Rights Committee in its interpretation of article 6 of the International Covenant on Civil and Political Rights, as well as the Second Optional Protocol thereto."

The Commission also requested the Special Rapporteur "to respond effectively to information which comes before him, in particular when an extrajudicial, summary or arbitrary execution is imminent or threatened or when such an execution has occurred" and requested the United Nations Secretary-General "to continue to use his best endeavors in cases where the minimum standard of legal safeguards provided for in articles 6, 9, 14, and 15 of the International Covenant on Civil and Political Rights appears not to be respected." The language of the resolution on these points was nearly identical to that of the resolution on extrajudicial, summary, or arbitrary executions adopted by the Commission on Human Rights the previous year.

On October 4, 1994, the Parliamentary Assembly of the thirty-two-member Council of Europe adopted a recommendation, No. 1246 (1994), calling for the creation of a further protocol to the European Convention on Human Rights on the abolition of the death penalty. Unlike Protocol No. 6 to the Convention, which provides for the abolition of the death penalty but allows for its retention in time of war or imminent threat of war, the protocol envisaged in the recommendation would constitute an agreement among states parties to it to abolish the death penalty in all circumstances with no exceptions.

In recommendation 1246 the Parliamentary Assembly also recommended that the Committee of Ministers of the Council of Europe set up a control mechanism whereby states that retain the death penalty would be obliged to inform the Secretary-General of the Council of Europe without delay of any death sentences passed, and that would bind any country that schedules an execution to halt it for a period of six months, during which time the Secretary-General could send a delegation to conduct an investigation and make a recommendation to the country concerned. States retaining the death penalty would be obliged to set up national commissions with a view to abolishing the penalty and would be called on to implement a moratorium on executions immediately while the commissions fulfilled their tasks. These provisions for a control mechanism would apply both to member states of the Council of Europe and to states whose legislative assemblies enjoy special guest status with the Parliamentary Assembly.

The Parliamentary Assembly also recommended that "in accordance with the established case-law of the European Court of Human Rights," the Committee of Ministers "not allow the extradition of any person to a country in which he or she risks being sentenced to death and subjected to the extreme conditions on 'death row'"; that the committee organize a conference on the abolition of the death penalty, with the participation of all member states and states holding special guest status; and that the committee "consider the attitude of applicant states towards the death penalty when deciding on their admission as full members to the Council of Europe."

On January 16, 1996, the Committee of Ministers of the Council of Europe adopted an interim reply to recommendation 1246, which stated that the proposals from the Parliamentary Assembly contained in recommendation 1246 were being examined by the committee within the framework of its Rapporteur Group on Human Rights. The interim reply stated further that "the Committee of Ministers has encouraged member States which have not abolished the death penalty to operate *de facto* or *de jure* a moratorium on the execution of death sentences."

The Parliamentary Assembly also adopted a resolution (No. 1044 (1994)) on the abolition of capital punishment on October 4, 1994. In the resolution, the assembly called for the total abolition of the death penalty in all member states of the Council of Europe and all states holding special guest status. It invited all member states which have not done so to sign and ratify Protocol No. 6, and stated that "the willingness to ratify the protocol [should] be made a prerequisite for membership of the Council of Europe." In the resolution the assembly also "calls upon all the parliaments in the world which have not yet abolished the death penalty to do so promptly, following the example of the majority of Council of Europe member states" and "urges all heads of state and all parliaments in whose countries death sentences are passed to grant clemency to the convicted."

The recommendation and the resolution had been proposed in a report prepared by Hans Göran Franck, a Swedish member of the Parliamentary Assembly.[8] The report was based on the results of a questionnaire sent to the chairpersons of national parliamentary delegations. Replies were received from thirty of the thirty-two Council of Europe member states and eight of the nine states holding special guest status. (The information conveyed in the replies is summarized in Parliamentary Assembly, Committee on Legal Affairs and Human Rights, The Abolition of Capital Punishment: Answers to the Questionnaire, document No. AS/Jur [1994] 48, September 5, 1994.)

In response to an initiative led by Italy, the Third Committee (Social, Humanitarian, and Cultural) of the United Nations General Assembly on December 9, 1994, considered a draft resolution, cosponsored by forty-nine countries, whereby the General Assembly would have encouraged all states that have not yet abolished the death penalty "to consider the opportunity of instituting a moratorium on pending executions with a view to ensuring that the principle that no State should dispose of the life of any human being be affirmed in every part of the world by the year 2000."

As listed in a United Nations press release, the forty-nine cosponsors were Andorra, Argentina, Australia, Austria, Belgium, Bolivia, Cambodia, Cape Verde, Chile, Colombia, Costa Rica, Cyprus, Czech Republic, Denmark, Dominican Republic, Ecuador, El Salvador, Finland, France, Germany, Greece, Haiti, Honduras, Hungary, Iceland, Ireland, Italy, Liechtenstein, Luxembourg, Malta, Marshall Islands, Micronesia, Monaco, New Zealand, Nicaragua, Norway, Panama, Paraguay, Portugal, Romania, San Marino, São Tomé and Principe, Slovak Republic, Solomon Islands, Spain, Sweden, Uruguay, Vanuatu, and Venezuela.[9]

Singapore proposed an amendment introducing a preambular paragraph affirming "the sovereign right of States to determine the legal measures and penalties which are appropriate in their societies to combat serious crimes effectively." Representatives of Singapore and Egypt, speaking in favor of the proposed amendment, emphasized the importance of state sovereignty, while speakers against it called for adherence to international standards. The German representative, for example, said (according to the account of the debate issued by the U.N. Department of Public Information) that the amendment would indicate that in the future the standard to determine the legitimacy of a legal measure or penalty would involve only its application in a single society. That should not be the case, since there were further standards by which to measure penalties. Penalties should not be cruel, inhuman, or degrading. International provisions that were widely accepted could not be ignored. The international standards could not be the standard of a single state. Were that to be the case, if one country considered torture to be appropriate, the international community would have to accept that practice. Clearly, this would be very dangerous.

The Singaporean amendment was adopted by a vote of seventy in favor to sixty-five against, with twenty-one abstentions. All cosponsors of the resolution then withdrew their cosponsorship, and the draft resolution was rejected by a vote of thirty-six in favor to forty-four against, with seventy-four abstentions.

The initiative at the General Assembly was similar to an initiative at the Eighth United Nations Congress on the Prevention of Crime and the Treatment of Offenders (Havana, August 27–September 7,

1990), also led by Italy, for the adoption of a resolution inviting states that retain the death penalty to consider imposing a three-year moratorium on its use in order to permit a study of the effects of abolition. That resolution failed to secure the required two-thirds majority for adoption, although forty-eight votes were cast in favor of it, with twenty-nine against and sixteen abstentions.[10]

Death Sentences and Executions

During 1994, 2,331 prisoners are known to have been executed in thirty-seven countries and 4,032 sentenced to death in seventy-five countries. These figures include only cases known to Amnesty International; the true figures are certainly higher.

As in previous years, a small number of countries accounted for the vast majority of executions recorded. Amnesty International received reports of 1,791 executions in China, 139 executions in Iran, and at least 100 in Nigeria. These three countries alone accounted for 87 percent of all executions recorded by Amnesty International worldwide in 1994. Amnesty International received reports of several hundred executions in Iraq but was unable to confirm most of these reports or to give an exact figure.[11]

The increase over the number of executions recorded worldwide in 1993 (1,831) reflected an increase in executions recorded in China (1,419 in 1993). Until 1994, the annual number of executions recorded had seldom been higher than 2,100 or lower than 1,500 (it reached 3,278 in 1981, when Iran was carrying out large numbers of executions at a time of political conflict; it decreased to the 700s in 1986 and 1987, when reported executions in Iran declined; and it rose again in 1988, when Iran executed over 1,200 political prisoners). The number of countries known to have carried out executions each year since 1980 has ranged from twenty-six (in 1990) to forty-four (in 1985); since 1988 it has not exceeded thirty-seven. The number of countries known to have carried out 100 or more executions per year since 1984 has ranged from one (in 1993) to four (in 1984), and the proportion of executions recorded in those countries to the total executions recorded worldwide has varied from 56 percent to 89 percent over the same period.

Mass Commutations

Historically, death sentences have been commuted not only in individual cases but also in groups, often in connection with general amnesties marking some special occasion.[12]

In March 1994, King Hassan of Morocco commuted 196 death sentences to life imprisonment on the occasion of the thirty-third year since his accession to the throne. Up to ten other people sentenced to death reportedly awaited a review of their cases by the Supreme Court. No executions were carried out during that year.

After the election of a new government in Malawi in the first multiparty elections in the country for over thirty years, the new president, Bakili Muluzi, announced in his inauguration speech on May 21, 1994, the commutation of all outstanding death sentences—about 120—to life imprisonment. During the year, trials of death penalty cases, which until October 1993 had been heard in "Traditional Courts" that did not provide fair trials, were transferred to the High Court. By the end of the year at least two people had been sentenced to death for murder. No executions were carried out during 1994.

Notes

Eric Prokosch is Theme Research Coordinator, Amnesty International, London. A.B. 1962, Harvard University; M.A. 1965, University of London; Ph.D., 1969, Stanford University. Some additional information for 1995 and 1996 has been contributed by the editors.

1. AMNESTY INTERNATIONAL, *When the State Kills ... The Death Penalty v. Human Rights*, London: Amnesty International Publications, 1989, pp. 72, 155.

2. La peine de mort: Travaux de la Conférence Internationale" (1987), 58 *Revue internationale de droit pénal*.

3. AMNESTY INTERNATIONAL, "List of Abolitionist and Retentionist Countries," issued periodically.

4. ANTONIO MARCHESI, "The Death Penalty in Wartime: Arguments for Abolition," AI Index: ACT 50/01/94, January 1994.

5. General Framework Agreement for Peace in Bosnia and Herzegovina, Annex 4: Constitution of Bosnia and Herzegovina, art. II§2, Annex I, §7; General Framework Agreement for Peace in Bosnia and Herzegovina, Annex 6: Agreement on Human Rights, art. 1.

6. Parliamentary Debates (Hansard), House of Commons, Official Report, February 21, 1994, column 45.

7. Extrajudicial, summary, or arbitrary executions; report by the Special Rapporteur, U.N. Doc. E/CN.4/1994/7, December 7, 1993, and U.N. Doc. E/CN.4/1997/7/Corr.2, March 14, 1994.

8. Report on the Abolition of Capital Punishment, Parliamentary Assembly document No. 7154, September 15, 1994.

9. U.N. DEPARTMENT OF PUBLIC INFORMATION, "Draft Resolution on Capital Punishment Rejected by Third Committee," press release, U.N. Doc. GA/SHC/3287, December 9, 1994, pp. 2–3.

10. Report of the Eighth United Nations Congress on the Prevention of Crime and the Treatment of Offenders, Havana, Cuba, August 27–September 7, 1990, U.N. Doc. A/CONF.144/28, ¶¶ 335–359.

11. AMNESTY INTERNATIONAL, "Death Sentences and Executions in 1994," AI Index: ACT 51/01/95, March 1995.

12. See *When the State Kills, supra* note 1, at p. 74, for examples.

BOOK REVIEWS

HUGO ADAM BEDAU

The Death Penalty: Longhorn Style

JAMES W. MARQUART, SHELDON EKLAND-OLSON, and JONATHAN R. SORENSEN, *The Rope, the Chair, and the Needle: Capital Punishment in Texas, 1923–1990* (Austin: University of Texas Press, 1994).

Throughout this century the death penalty in the United States has been virtually a monopoly of *state* governments. As of the end of 1993, for example, six prisoners were on death row after sentencing in federal courts; another 2,710 prisoners—99.779 percent of the total—were under death sentences issued by state courts. Thanks to congressional death penalty legislation enacted in 1994 and 1995, the years ahead may show a slightly greater percentage of prisoners under a federal death sentence—but only slightly greater.

Just as the men (and the few women) on the nation's death row are there as a result of state criminal proceedings, the laws, regulations, and practices affecting the administration of the death penalty in the United States are entirely in the hands of state governments, except for the sporadic interference by the federal courts imposing on state criminal procedures the requirements of national constitutional law. However, such national uniformity as results from this constraint has to be weighed against the latitude that the federal courts grant to the states under the federalism compact. The death penalty in America, in short, is a matter of the history, politics, public morality, and law of state governments—yesterday, today, and tomorrow.

It is all the more surprising, therefore, that the scrutiny of the death penalty by scholars from various relevant disciplines (history, sociology, law, political science, American studies) has to date produced so little in the way of close investigations of capital punishment in any of the many state jurisdictions with a history of executions.[1] Anyone seriously interested in information about the past, recent, and current death penalty law and practices in this or that state is bound to go away disappointed. Thanks to *The Rope, the Chair, and the Needle,* this situation is no longer true for Texas. In this book there is, for the first time, a full-scale scholarly study of the death penalty in a particular American state jurisdiction covering the bulk of this century.

Nor is Texas just any death penalty jurisdiction; it is at the top among those that use capital punishment. Since 1930, Texas has executed more persons than any other state;[2] moreover, since the death penalty was revived in the late 1970s, Texas has executed more prisoners than any other state;[3] and today, Texas has more persons under death sentence than any other state (with the intermittent exception of California—the two states jockey for leadership in this category).[4] One could do worse than argue for the centrality of Texas in any study of the death penalty in the United States.

The authors of this important book are from three different Texas universities: James W. Marquart is an associate professor of criminal justice at Sam Houston State University (less than an hour's drive south from the Ellis Unit near Huntsville, Texas, where the state houses its death row prisoners); Sheldon Ekland-Olson is a professor of sociology at the University of Texas in Austin; and Jonathan R. Sorensen is an assistant professor of criminal justice at the Pan American branch of the University of Texas. Their collaboration has resulted in a truly pioneering volume that can and, one hopes, will prove to be the first of several similar studies devoted to major western (e.g., California), eastern (e.g., New York), and other southern (e.g., Georgia) states with a history of capital punishment as long or longer than that of Texas.

The title of the book marks out the three eras into which the death penalty can be conveniently (albeit unevenly) divided: from statehood (1845) through 1923, when executions were carried out in local communities by hanging, and when lynchings rivaled lawful executions; from February 1924 through July 1977, when the electric chair was used to carry out executions; and from August 1977 until mid-1992, during which time the method of execution became lethal injection. Eight photographs, fourteen figures, and twenty-three tables, plus the usual footnotes, bibliography, and index complete the apparatus.

While the three-era division of the subject by reference to the modes of carrying out the death penalty (the rope, the chair, and the needle), which constitutes the hooks on which the authors choose to hang their story, has a certain useful precision about it, there are apparently no important or interesting issues involving the use or rationale of the death penalty that are brought to prominence by this division. What is true in Texas on this point is true elsewhere. One can argue that the shift from hanging to electrocution and then to lethal injection marks a move—self-deceiving in some cases, earnest and sincere in others—to ever more humane methods of carrying out the death penalty.[5] However, it should not go unremarked (though it is by the authors) that the introduction of a new method of execution is typically unaccompanied by any other statutory changes in the direction of making the death penalty "more humane." Instead, the new mode of execution is superimposed on the prevailing practices that define and regulate the death penalty system, practices themselves that go unchanged (except as other, independent factors arise).

The book disposes of the first and longest phase, the hanging era, in a dozen pages (Chapter 1). The forty or so footnotes to this part of the book suggest that there is more historical research to be done on this period of Texas's history with the death penalty, though whether if done it would shed any interesting light on the subject, apart from a wealth of anecdotes about particular cases, is doubtful. The rest of the book is divided between the two remaining eras, with rather more emphasis given (as it should be) to the half century with the electric chair (four chapters) than to the fifteen years with lethal injection (three chapters). The authors list all fifty persons executed by lethal injection during the years covered by the book, beginning with Charlie Brooks in 1982 and ending with Robert Black in May 1992; a thumbnail sketch of each of these fifty cases is also provided. The 361 prisoners executed in the electric chair are listed in chronological sequence in Appendix B (along with all persons sentenced to death in Texas since 1924), but these cases are only selectively discussed in the text. A photo is reproduced of "Old Sparky," Texas's electric chair, in whose oaken embrace a prisoner died on average every six weeks for forty years. Another photograph shows the gurney (actually, that's a misnomer, since the bed has no wheels and is bolted to the floor) on which prisoners are now executed by lethal injection. No photograph of a Texas scaffold from earlier days is included.

The book is based in part on data concerning the lives (and in many cases, the deaths) of nearly a thousand Texas death row prisoners (923, to be exact) sentenced between 1923 and 1988. The tables and figures scattered through the book are largely based either in whole or in part on these cases. Demographic and other information about the death row prisoners has been compared with nearly 12,000 other Texas inmates convicted of capital crimes (murder, rape, armed robbery) but not sentenced to death during the same period. The book is by no means dedicated to interpretations of the tabular and graphic data, however. It is a true history of the subject, full of comparative commentary on parallel experience in other southern states and the nation, as well as anecdotal information about death row prisoners that enlivens what might otherwise be (as the authors themselves note) "a rather bloodless story" (p. xii).

Perhaps the flavor of the book's findings can be most easily revealed by commenting on five different topics, each of which reveals something important about the death penalty in Texas.

Race. The authors leave no doubt that they think the history of capital punishment in Texas is the history of one of the state's and the nation's leading racist (or, if you prefer, race-sensitive) practices. This theme shows up in many ways, but in none better than the history of the death penalty for rape (discussed in Chapter 3). Virtually everyone in Texas sentenced to death for rape in the pre-*Furman* era was executed (p. 40); about 75 percent were African American males (p. 56); in only one case of black-on-black rape was the offender executed (p. 58). When an African American male was convicted of raping a white woman, he was thirty-five times more likely to be sentenced to death than a white male similarly convicted (p. 56).

When one considers that during these years more than 2,000 men were convicted of rape in Texas but that only 5 percent of them were sentenced to death (p. 64), the use of the death penalty for rape as a racist practice seems beyond doubt. The race of the victim turns out to be paramount (p. 65), "a residual expression of the legacy of slavery" (p. 97).

Commutations. During the electric chair era, nearly one-fifth (92 of 510) of all persons sentenced to death had their sentences commuted to imprisonment (p. 106). During the current era of lethal injection, the story is somewhat confusing because of the number of judicially ordered commutations; one might even go so far as to call them pseudocommutations, because in these cases the resentencing to prison was ordered by the courts rather than being true exercises of executive clemency. Unfortunately, the authors do not attempt to identify which (and how many) of the commutations during this period were of each sort. Not only that: there is radical confusion over just how many commutations are under discussion. Marquart, Ekland-Olson, and Sorenson report that "80" commutations occurred subsequent to the *Furman* decision on June 29, 1972 (p. 137); but their own inventory of death penalty cases (Appendix B) shows that, as of June 1992, there were 141 commutations subsequent to *Furman*. Other investigators have previously reported only 36 commutations between 1972 and 1990.[6] Even if we subtract the 47 commutations of persons whose death sentences preceded *Furman* , that still leaves 94 post-*Furman* death sentence commutations. These discrepancies to one side, the authors show that all the death sentences for women (3) were commuted (p. 107) and that Hispanics were more likely than Anglos or African Americans to have a death sentence commuted (p. 117). Commuting the death sentences issued to women is commonplace and needs little or no explanation; why Hispanics under death sentence in Texas should be more likely to be commuted than others does need an explanation. Could it be an artifact of the crimes, not the race, of those on death row when court-ordered commutations took effect?

Recidivism. Of particular interest is the natural experiment that resulted from the 47 persons on death row in June 1972 whose sentences were commuted under court order following the *Furman* decision: What was the recidivism record of these prisoners? The authors report that they discovered no record of any homicide in prison from this cohort (p. 125) and that the majority of the infractions and felonies this cohort committed were done by about one-fourth of all those commuted (p. 124). In two cases, *Furman*-commuted murderers were found guilty of homicidal recidivism after release. In one, the homicide was immediately followed by the recidivist's own suicide (pp. 125–126). In the other, after more than two decades in prison, the offender was released in 1989 only to commit another murder a year later; he is back on Texas's death row (p. 126). A comparison of the postrelease recidivism between these *Furman*-released death row prisoners and a control group of convicted murderers in Texas sentenced to prison shows virtually no significantly greater dangerousness in either group (p. 127).

The moral of the story (which the authors do not draw) is surely this: to prevent recidivist homicide altogether, we must execute every convicted murderer. To prevent recidivist victimization outside prison walls, we must at least keep all convicted murderers behind bars for their natural lives (life without possibility of parole, or LWOP in the current jargon). Neither of these policies will withstand scrutiny. That situation leaves us with the unending task of using our best judgment in incarcerating and releasing selected offenders, knowing that some (but not knowing which) will cause further harm to the innocent. Only the third alternative—the dominant practice in all death penalty jurisdictions throughout this century—really makes sense. The growing national love affair with LWOP for capital offenders, like "Three Strikes and You're Out!" for lesser felons, guarantees that our prisons will slowly become geriatric wards, whether or not public safety or reasonable retribution requires it.

Death Row. Today, life for a Texas prisoner under death sentence is quite different from that experienced by his counterparts in neighboring jurisdictions. Whereas in most other states death row convicts spend all but a few hours a week locked up in their cells, Texas since 1986 has operated a garment factory in which most of the prisoners choose to work a four-hour shift without pay, cutting and stitching bedding, uniforms, and the like (pp. 138–140). If we can trust the authors, it looks as if for all its many flaws, the death penalty system in Texas has at least one feature that death row prisoners in other jurisdictions might well envy.

The Current Scene. Of the three statutory patterns of death sentencing ratified by the Supreme Court in 1976, the new death penalty laws in Texas (upheld in *Jurek* v. *Texas*) were arguably the worst. A prominent feature of the Texas death penalty statute was the requirement that the sentencer find that "there is a probability that the defendant would commit criminal acts of violence that would constitute a continuing threat to society." No sooner was the ink dry on this revision of the Texas penal code than the folly of such a requirement was fully exposed.[7] Still, no one could reasonably foresee how outrageously this clause would be interpreted and applied. The career of "Dr. Death," James Grigson, M.D., has become notorious for the way in which he has testified in case after case that the convicted defendant awaiting sentencing would commit further crimes of violence (pp. 176–177). Such testimony reached a ludicrous extreme both in those cases when Dr. Grigson made his predictions on the basis of no examination of the defendant whatever, and in those when he made it of defendants (such as Randall Dale Adams) who turned out to be completely innocent (a point not mentioned in this book). Dare one say that only in Texas such a farce could be tolerated?

The book ends with a brief account (pp. 195–196) of the plight of Leonel Herrera. The Texas law governing introduction of new evidence in a postconviction proceeding requires a defendant who seeks a new trial on that ground to file the evidence in question within thirty *days* of his sentence. As the records of persons wrongly convicted clearly reveal,[8] it is a rare case in which such evidence is uncovered so promptly. Not uncommonly, several years may go by before the defendant's attorney, family, or friends learn of exculpating evidence. In *Herrera* v. *Collins* (1993), the Supreme Court denied Herrera's federal habeas corpus petition for a new trial on the basis of evidence offered eight years after his conviction, thereby effectively upholding the Texas statute of limitations. *The Rope, the Chair, and the Needle* ends on the laconic note that Herrera was duly executed.

With the collapse of the federally funded death penalty resource centers around the nation, including the Texas Resource Center in Austin and Houston, in October 1995,[9] it is likely that innocent defendants in Texas will be convicted of murder, sentenced to death, and executed, thanks in no small part to erroneous predictions of future dangerousness and the statute of limitations on new evidence.

Yet the purpose of this book is not, at least not directly, persuasion;

The Rope, the Chair, and the Needle is not an abolitionist tract. It is an exercise in the "dispassionate analysis" (p. xii) of historical sociology, and as such requires us to consider what the authors regard as the proper focus of any serious scientific study of the death penalty in America. It "must address this basic question: Why [is] there such a concentration of executions in a single region of the country" (p. x), the Old Confederacy that runs from Texas in the West to the Florida-Virginia coast in the East? Their answer begins with the "legacy of slavery" (p. 16), a euphemism for antiblack racism. This legacy shows up in what the authors call "a logic of exclusion" (p. 17), a legitimated marginalization by the majority of certain minority groups from the norms that protect the majority. The relevant marginalized groups for the purpose of this book are defined by race and color: the African American and Hispanic minorities in Texas.

What do these authors see as the changes of note that have taken place during this century? They cite the post–Civil War practice of white mobs lynching helpless black males—a criminal justice system that operated in the streets—which slowly gave way to state-sanctioned practices (Jim Crow laws) designed to keep blacks in their place and using the death penalty as the ultimate sanction, as setting the stage for three trends, each the result of "legal reforms" within living memory (pp. 187–189).

The first trend is a decreasing tendency over the decades to sentence to death and execute mainly nonwhites. The second, ushered in by the Supreme Court in *Furman*, is a shift in the focus of racial prejudice from the jury box to the prosecutor's office, from sentencing decisions to prosecutorial decisions, from unfocused to "focused bias" (p. 147). The third is the steadily increasing delay in carrying out executions, manifesting "an increased reluctance to lethally cast persons outside the human community without first ensuring that all due process steps had been followed" (p. 188). Here, however, one must demur. No one can examine the death penalty in Texas since 1972 and believe that "all due process steps" have been followed; far from it. At best, only the most implausibly narrow reading of "due process of law" could vindicate current Texas death penalty practices.

No doubt the three trends identified above have occurred, but they are not unique to Texas; they are not unique even to the southern tier of death penalty states. Perhaps the best explanation of the "concentration of executions" in the Old Confederacy is not unique to Texas; nor have all southern states sentenced to death and executed prisoners at the rate that Texas has. So, before we can have unqualified confidence in the explanation offered in this volume, we need studies of Georgia, Alabama, Florida, and the other states in the nation's "death belt," as well as comparable studies of eastern, northern, and central states. Only such further historical and sociological investigations can confirm or modify the conclusions reached here.

Notes

Hugo A. Bedau is Austin Fletcher Professor of Philosophy, Tufts University, Medford, Massachusetts.

1. For example, Philip English MACKEY, *Hanging in the Balance: The Anti-Capital Punishment Movement in New York State, 1776–1861*, New York: Garland, 1982, contains little information on the actual use of the death penalty in New York state. There are, of course, many journal articles devoted to the death penalty in a given state jurisdiction, e.g., H. A. BEDAU, "Death Sentences in New Jersey, 1907–1960" (1964), 19 *Rutgers L. Rev.* 1.

2. U.S. Department of Justice, National Prisoner Statistics, "Capital Punishment 1971–72," December 1974, p. 17, Table 2; U.S. Department of Justice, Bureau of Justice Statistics, "Capital Punishment 1993," p. 11, Table 10; and NAACP LEGAL DEFENSE AND EDUCATIONAL FUND, INC., "Death Row, U.S.A.," Summer 1995, p. 10.

3. "Death Row, U.S.A.," *supra* note 2, p. 10.

4. As of August 31, 1995, California reported 418 persons under death sentence, compared with 401 in Texas. "Death Row, U.S.A.," *supra* note 2, at pp. 14, 38. According to the *New York Times*, September 20, 1995, Texas had carried out fourteen executions in 1995; the *New York Times*, October 5, 1995, reported another execution carried out in Texas on October 4.

5. See H. A. BEDAU, ed., *The Death Penalty in America*, New York: Doubleday Anchor, 1964, at pp. 15–20; H. A. BEDAU, ed., *The Death Penalty in America*, 3rd ed., New York, Oxford University Press, 1982, at pp. 14–18.

6. Michael L. RADELET, Barbara A. ZSEMBIK, "Executive Clemency in Post-*Furman* Capital Cases" (1993), 27 *U. Richmond L. Rev.* 289, at pp. 293–296.

7. Charles L. BLACK, Jr., *Capital Punishment: The Inevitability of Caprice and Mistake*, 2nd ed., New York: Norton, 1981, at pp. 111–134.

8. Michael L. RADELET, Hugo Adam BEDAU, and Constance E. PUTNAM, *In Spite of Innocence*, Boston: Northeastern University Press, 1992.

9. See Christy HOPPE, "Cuts to Close Law Center," *Dallas Morning News*, September 29, 1995, p. 39A; Richard C. DIETER, *With Justice for Few: The Growing Crisis in Death Penalty Representation*, Washington, D.C.: Death Penalty Information Center, October 1995.

MICHAEL RADELET

Deadly Innocence?

ROBERT PERSKE, *Deadly Innocence?* (Nashville, Tenn.: Abingdon Press, 1995).

Robert Perske is one of America's most forceful critics of the death penalty, particularly when it is used in the cases of mentally retarded or mentally ill inmates. His 1991 book, *Unequal Justice?* (Abingdon Press), is one of the best sources available for information on the various problems encountered by mentally retarded defendants who find themselves in the grips of the criminal justice system. Shortly after that book was published, one of Perske's friends sent him a poem about a prison warden who cried as he officiated over the execution of a mentally retarded inmate. The poem immediately sparked Perske's interest, and through Watt Espy, America's top death-penalty historian, Perske was soon able to identify the names of the defendant and the warden. Coincidentally, the case came from Perske's native state, Colorado, and he had actually briefly met the warden some forty years ago. Perske's interest grew and grew, and he eventually spent the next two years assembling every scrap of information he could find about the case. This book is the fruit of that research. It describes the life, conviction, and execution of Joe Arridy, a twenty-three-year old retarded man who was killed on January 6, 1939, in the gas chamber of the Colorado State Penitentiary in Canon City.

Arridy was born in Pueblo, Colorado, in 1915, shortly after his parents immigrated to the United States from Syria. When he was ten, he was labeled as "feebleminded" and sent to the Colorado State Home and Training School for Mental Defectives in Grand Junction. His father was able to secure his release ten months later. The boy spent the next three years at home but was reinstitutionalized when an enraged probation officer found him engaging in homosexual activities with some African American teens in Pueblo. Back at Grand Junction, he regularly was disciplined for public masturbation. After seven years, the twenty-two-year-old walked away from the institution, hopped on a freight train, and left town. Sixteen days later, on August 26, 1936, he was arrested for vagrancy in the railroad yards in Cheyenne, Wyoming.

Meanwhile, while Arridy was free, a gruesome murder occurred in his hometown of Pueblo. A fifteen-year-old girl, Dorothy Drain, was beaten, raped, and hacked to death with an axe in her bedroom. The pressure on the Pueblo police to find the killer was naturally intense, and although the newspapers did not know it, a few days after the murder the Pueblo authorities had arrested a key suspect named Frank Aguilar. Among other pieces of evidence that firmly tied Aguilar to the crime was the murder weapon, which was found in his home.

With Aguilar behind bars, the authorities were ready to make public the arrest and close the books on the murder. They were therefore astounded when the Cheyenne sheriff called to say that he had solved the crime: a "nut" named Joe Arridy had confessed. When told that another suspect had already been identified, the sheriff went back to Arridy, and before long his confession was modified to say that he had had a partner in the crime. Arridy also confessed to several other crimes, but subsequent investigations proved that he could not have committed them.

Both Aguilar and Arridy were eventually tried (separately), convicted, and sentenced to death. Arridy's court-appointed attorney rested the defense totally on insanity, not on innocence. When this tactic failed (despite expert testimony that "Arridy has a mind of a six-year-old"), little could be done in postconviction appeals to save his life. Not a speck of evidence, other than Arridy's "confession," tied him to Aguilar, placed him in Pueblo at the time of the crime, showed he had any interest in sexual activities with women, or hinted that he had ever harmed another person. Aguilar was quickly executed, but Arridy received nine stays of execution before exhausting his final appeals.

During Arridy's eighteen months on death row, Warden Roy Best took Arridy under his wing. Like other progressive wardens of his era, such as Lewis Lawes at Sing Sing in New York and Clinton Duffy at San Quentin in California, Best stood opposed to the death penalty. The warden was kind to Joe, and Perske tells us that "it is altogether conceivable that Joe's days in Roy Best's prison were by far the happiest days of his life." Best bought Arridy toys and picture books, always treating him with dignity and respect. During those months, although attorney Gail Ireland fought a valiant battle to prove that Joe was insane, the strength of the proof was pale in comparison to the strength of the political powers in Pueblo that wanted Arridy dead. In the end, Arridy passed his final days playing with a toy train that Warden Best had bought him as a Christmas present.

One leaves this book with a fuller appreciation of how easy it is to convict innocent defendants (particularly if retarded) in highly publicized cases, anger at the sheriff who induced what could very well have been a false confession, anger at the criminal justice system for railroading the child to the gas chamber, and admiration for the warden for sticking his neck out. Yet one also leaves wondering how the story remained untold for so long. How many other stories like this can be told? Unlike their British counterparts, American historians have done relatively little to reveal the untold mountains of sordid stories of how the death penalty has been practiced in the United States since its first execution four hundred years ago. Perske's book serves as both a model and an invitation for future work on stories of this ilk. Although old, this and similar cases can teach lessons that the public and political authorities in the United States have yet to learn.

One would hope that the United States is more "civilized" in the late 1990s than it was fifty years ago and that cases like Arridy's could not occur again. Yet, in January 1996, there were four executions in the United States: a man was hanged in Delaware; a mentally ill pedophile faced the firing squad in Utah; a team of medics spent thirty minutes trying to find a good vein in which to insert the catheter for a lethal injection in Virginia (eventually the needle was stuck through the man's foot); and, in the first execution of the year, an inmate with an I.Q. of 68, Walter Correll, was executed in Virginia. Correll's two crime partners blamed Correll and escaped the death penalty, and Correll confessed (without first consulting with an attorney). We will never know if Correll's confession was tainted. As long as we fail to learn the lessons taught by cases like Joe Arridy's, very few will ever care.

Note

Michael Radelet is Professor of Sociology, University of Florida, Gainesville.

PETER HODGKINSON

The Machinery of Death

ENID HARLOW, DAVID MATAS, JANE ROCAMORA, eds., *The Machinery of Death, A Shocking Indictment of Capital Punishment in the United States* (New York: Amnesty International, 1995).

In August 1993 Amnesty International in the United States organized a conference entitled "A Commission of Enquiry into the Death Penalty as Practiced in the United States." This book is a faithful account of the testimony heard by the commission and those who attended the conference. This reviewer attended the conference together with interns from the University of Westminster's Internship in Capital Punishment Studies project and will therefore reflect that dimension in his comments.

The jurists who gathered for this occasion reflected the wish to make this an international inquiry; they were Dr. Lloyd Barnet, President, Jamaican Bar Association; Dr. Roger Hood, Director, Centre for Criminological Research, University of Oxford; Gitobu Imanyara, Kenyan human rights attorney and editor-in-chief, *Nairobi Law Weekly;* Dr. Abdul Carimo Issa, Special Advisor to the Ministry of Justice, Republic of Mozambique; Florizelle O'Connor, Director, Jamaica Council for Human Rights; Dr. Belisario dos Santos, attorney and member of the Comissao Justica e Paz da Arquidiocese de São Paulo; and Francis Seow, Barrister-at-Law and Visiting Fellow, East Asian Legal Studies, Harvard Law School. If one assumes that they are all, in principle, opposed to the death penalty, or at least unsympathetic, it begs the question as to the impartiality of the commission, which presumably would have found the defendant guilty before hearing a scrap of evidence. This fact must, and did, detract from the rigor of the cross-examination of the witnesses.

This situation is pertinent because of the jaundiced view with which abolitionists in general and Amnesty International in particular are held within the United States, but more importantly within the membership of AIUSA, among which, it is rumored, some 25 percent are supporters of the death penalty. This last issue might just explain the apparent lack of support and cooperation offered by the organizers of the main event and the resulting tension experienced by those registered for the "Commission of Enquiry." The inspiration behind this event, Ashanti Chimurenga (former director of the Program to Abolish the Death Penalty of Amnesty International USA), employed all her diplomatic and negotiating skills to ameliorate the worst excesses of this tension.

As an abolitionist, this reviewer thinks that the "partiality" of the jurists and presenters was unfortunate. The very powerful testimony delivered fell upon the ears of those already converted, who needed no further evidence of the futile, unjust, and counterproductive nature of the death penalty. It meant, too, that this knowledgeable and high-profile audience received little or no media coverage and that the event itself went largely unreported. It is thus very important that this book has been published, and the editors are to be congratulated for bringing the fruits of this conference to a wider audience.

The book itself, which runs to some 216 pages, incorporates forty presentations consisting of the "testimony" of witnesses and the decisions of the jurists. The evidence was delivered in panels and encompassed the following topics and issues: overview of capital punishment in the United States; international legal and human rights issues; American legal and human rights issues; murder victims' family members; public attitudes towards the death penalty; juveniles and the death penalty; mental retardation and the death penalty; innocence and the death penalty; the role of law enforcement and the death penalty and the question of deterrence; racism, poverty and the death penalty; political repression and the death penalty; foreign nationals on U.S. death rows; the question of clemency; death row survivors; the executioner's perspective; the jurists' decisions. The appendix includes extracts from the Universal Declaration of Human Rights; the European Convention on Human Rights; the International Covenant on Civil and Political Rights; the American Convention on Human Rights; resolutions of the United Nations Economic and Social Council on "Implementation of the safeguards guaranteeing protection of the rights of those facing the death penalty"; and a list of those countries that are signatories to the above documents. The United States has ratified (with reservations) the International Covenant on Civil and Political Rights, but not the Second Optional Protocol thereto or the American Convention of Human Rights. The reservations formulated by the United States to the International Covenant were recently the subject of scrutiny by the United Nations Human Rights Committee. The response of the United States to the findings is awaited.

This conference and therefore this book differ from standard academic conferences and publications in that they provide an exceptional opportunity for commentators who would not normally have been able to share their views and experiences with such an informed audience. Unfortunately, however, the conference did not attract those who either support the death penalty or are undecided, as they would have heard reports from the "fringe" rather than the well-documented views of the mainstream "professional" abolitionists.

Walter McMillian was sentenced to death in 1987 for the murder of a young woman in Monroe County, Alabama. McMillian is black, the victim is white, a situation that makes a difference in the United States, especially in the south. He was arrested six months after the offense had been committed, charged initially with sodomy, and then languished a year on death row awaiting his trial, which lasted two days—two whole days! The evidence against him was provided by Ralph Myers and Bill Hooks; both men had been convicted on serious offenses. Aside from his color, McMillian was guilty of another offense: his girlfriend was a white woman and, furthermore, his son had married a white woman. The irrefutable alibi evidence of his respectable family and friends counted for nothing when compared with the testimony of the distinguished citizens mentioned above. Four and a half years and seven Alabama executions later, Bryan Stevenson, attorney and director of the former Alabama Post-Conviction Defender Organization, took on McMillian's case and, in so doing, the whole of the Alabama legal community. For McMillian, this was like winning the "lottery": the "lottery" is an appropriate label to describe access to effective legal representation in capital cases in the United States; the losers outnumber the winners. While McMillian was giving his shy, humble, barely audible but nonetheless powerful account, Stevenson was sitting alongside him in silence; McMillian, not Stevenson, was center stage ("Death Row Survivors," p. 156).

Here is the story of another survivor. "My name is Sonia Jacobs. I am called 'Sunny.' I am a death row survivor. I was on death row for five years and in prison for sixteen years, 233 days. It took all that time for the truth to come out and for me to be free because I was innocent of the crime for which I was convicted and sentenced to death." When Jacobs arrived on Florida's death row, she was the first woman since *Furman* in 1972 to be sentenced to death. She came to death row as a wife, a mother, and a daughter. When she was released in October 1992, she was a widow, a grandmother, and an orphan. Her husband, her co-accused, was executed in one of Florida's many celebrated botched electrocutions. "His head caught fire, and smoke and flames came out of it. He was innocent." Of course, those employed to defend the legal process in Florida will point to Jacobs's eventual release as an illustration of the effective nature of the system. The report of the Senate House Judiciary Committee on erroneous convictions identified over forty cases in which sentences of death were overturned, of which nineteen were from Florida's death row. If this is evidence that the process for scrutinizing capital sentences in Florida is a very effective one, then it would also seem to be evidence that the prosecution and trial of capital defendants is somewhat wanting for so many errors to have been uncovered. The reader must consider the emotional cost to the defendant, the financial cost to the taxpayer, and the humiliation and degradation of the Eighth and Fourteenth Amendments.

Jacobs's telling account lays bare the inadequacies of the system and the systematic abuse of process. "Falsified evidence and uncorroborated statements were used. Exculpatory evidence remained hidden until many, many years later. Testimony of a co-defendant was bargained for and used. My husband and I had a co-defendant who immediately pled to three life sentences and then testified against us. Later on, he confessed. They would not hear his confession. We found, accidentally, that his polygraph test was hidden from us. Years later when I was on death row, I discovered it myself and brought it to my attorney's attention. We had a hearing. It was considered harmless error—harmless error that evidence showing our innocence was withheld" ("Death Row Survivors," p. 152).

It is not just those who are innocent of any crime or of a capital crime that are affected by this manifestly flawed process. The procedures spawned by *Furman* and given legitimacy by *Gregg* remain as inconsistent, disparate, discriminatory, and capricious as they were at the time that the United States Supreme Court delivered its decision in *Furman*.

So much for the experiences of those whom we would kill; now for the killer. Donald Cabana, former warden of Mississippi State Penitentiary, presented "The Executioner's Perspective" (p. 163). "I suppose every camp has its clandestine enemy or adversary, depending on one's perception. I suppose I constitute that role because I am the executioner. I am probably the only witness to this Tribunal who has suffered the anguish and torture of carrying out the execution of other human beings." Having introduced himself thus, Cabana went on to please some and annoy others by explaining just how it was that he became enmeshed in the process of state killing while maintaining a principled opposition to capital punishment. Those whom he annoyed asked how he could take part in the ritual killing of his fellow citizens when he was opposed to the death penalty—they were not satisfied with the explanation that it was part of his job specification and that one could not pick and choose which parts of one's duties to perform. This annoyance and frustration were exacerbated when Cabana went on to reveal that there were many wardens in executing states who held similar views. If so, why didn't they have the courage of their convictions and say so, he was asked? They had families to raise and mortgages to pay, was part of the answer. If I didn't do it then they would find someone else who would carry out the executions with less sympathy. In his presentation Cabana very courageously laid himself open to scrutiny and criticism, commenting that he believed that it was better for him and the cause of abolition that he make his "conversion" public rather than vanish into quiet retirement.

His "coming out" may have been too late for his critics, but the very candid analysis of his experiences continues to make powerful reading and listening; his testimony is the more compelling because of his direct experience, not only with the mechanics of execution but also with the personalities drawn into the process and the effect it has on them all: death row inmates, prison guards, families of the condemned, and the victims. The demonized become human through his words. There is some evidence, albeit anecdotal, that his decision to go public is giving succor to others in the corrections field and may possibly encourage them to make career moves before retirement or at least make cautious attempts at civilizing the route to the death chamber.

Finally, this reviewer returns to his earlier comments about the "partiality" of the jurists and how that might have prejudiced the outcome of this inquiry. I was at the time convinced, and remain so having read the trial transcript, that the weight of evidence was so compelling that the verdict of guilty was never in dispute. However, many people continue to be sentenced to death in the face of equally compelling evidence of their innocence. This book should be required reading for prosecutors, judges, politicians, and all others who feel comfortable about capital punishment and the capital litigation process.

Note

Peter Hodgkinson is Senior Lecturer in Law, University of Westminster, London, and Director, Center for Capital Punishment Studies, London.

KENNETH BOLTON, JR.

Live from Death Row

Mumia Abu-Jamal, *Live from Death Row* (Reading, Mass.: Addison-Wesley Publishing Company, 1995).

Live from Death Row, Mumia Abu-Jamal's collection of essays, turns the prison system inside out, exposing its corrupt soul. From a tiny cell awaiting execution Abu-Jamal shouts his warning, "Wake Up! Time is short." As the rich and powerful continue to accumulate vast sums of capital, the poor are being surrounded with walls of brick, mortar, and ideology. Members of different social classes, people of various races, men and women, all are separated from one another, being prevented from questioning, analyzing, and redefining their world.

In this setting, Mumia Abu-Jamal's voice is dangerous and subversive. His writing is censored because he refuses to dwell in self-pity and because he doesn't place his case at the center of the universe or wallow in biographical narrative. Abu-Jamal is a revolutionary, his voice heard beyond walls, crossing boundaries, exposing injustices, shattering illusions, and building hope.

From the first prison command ("Yard in!"), *Live from Death Row* transports the reader to a world of hopeless desperation. Through the power of the narrative, the reader can hear the gates clang shut and smell the stench of sweat, stale urine, and blood. The nightmare of oppression and the shock of violence are so powerful as to make the reader hope that all this is but an illusion, that the surveillance and total control of all the aspects of a prisoner's life cannot be possible, cannot be real. As the reader aches to return to that freedom, Abu-Jamal taunts his audience by asking, "What does it mean to be free again?"

Abu-Jamal effectively reveals the inside-the-prison-wall reality of societal injustices, a place that is a mosaic of suffering: "CRACK! . . . Another dawn, another beating, another shackled inmate pummeled into the concrete by a squadron of guards" (p. 80). The reader is exposed to a bizarre, banal, contradictory world in which quasi-military guards enforce a life regimented by rule and regulation. Correctional officers beat, humiliate, and control the prisoners in the name of the state. The prisoners are either too young to know life's possibilities, too old to care about the future, too sick to live, too crazy to comprehend, or too black to elicit empathy. In isolation, on death row, locked in, locked down, the prisoners are deteriorating, comatose, drowning in "a stressful psychic stew" (p. 29), their humanity eroding.

Compassion has forsaken these walls. "Why can't we touch?" a tiny girl asks as she slams her fists against a Plexiglas barrier that prevents her from contact with her father. Prison experiences continue to assault the reader as the author describes the legalized degradation of humanity within the steel and concrete walls. The prisoners are forced to undergo body-cavity searches: "Turn around. Bend over. Spread your cheeks. Get dressed" (p. 10).

Abu-Jamal shows his audience that their outside-the-wall lives are inexorably linked to those lives within the walls. He whispers, "Don't drink the water." The warden finally announces that "an oil based substance has washed its way into institutional springs, due to heavy rains" (p. 61). The reader is reminded that "the white, well-fed families" of the areas surrounding the outside walls receive the same polluted water and are forced to look for alternative sources of water as well.

Abu-Jamal forcefully illustrates that the world inside prison and the world outside are analogous. That the outside can be incarcerating is revealed by relating the experience of the disintegration of homes by the "potent, mind-sucking, soul-ripping poison" of "crystalline crack wreaking havoc on poor black life" (p. 97). He argues that the "floodgates of drugs drown out the black revolutionary fires of urban resistance" (p. 97), effectively sealing the community away from hope. Blacks are socialized into oppression, learning that justice, law, civil rights, and freedom all have elastic meanings when applied to different groups of people.

Though blacks make up only 11 percent of the population, they make up 40 percent of those on death row. Education is underfunded, jobs are scarce, welfare is slashed, while Abu-Jamal and others like him wait to die in overcrowded prisons. These facts are dynamically related. Not only does the United States lead the world in the number of citizens imprisoned, but also it has recently passed a $30 billion bill to get "tougher" on crime. Tougher? Abu-Jamal lays bare the process by which prisons are transformed into "special housing units (SHU)" that strip prisoners of their humanity. He tells of juries that are not "of your peers," of expert witnesses who lie and fabricate evidence, of Supreme Court justices who wait until retirement to proclaim that they are against the death penalty. Abu-Jamal asserts that "prisons are where America's jobs programs, housing programs, and social control programs merge into a dark whole; and where those outside of the game can be exploited and utilized to keep the game going" (p. 127).

The reader is told that the "get tough on crime" ideology of the 1990s clearly makes life more costly for everyone. "It will drive public bankruptcy; it will fuel greater violence; it will create prisoners who are dumber, more alienated, but more desperate in life's scuffle for survival" (p. 130). The act of a "faceless" cop in kicking Abu-Jamal in his face drove him into the Black Panther Party.

The author demonstrates that social scientists can't interpret the world by looking through the lens of quantitative analysis. He therefore uses a montage of subjective horrors from the depths of hell to illuminate the crimes of society. The reader comes away from this narrative deeply troubled by the condemned man's brutalizing experiences but also enlightened by the author's attempt to "spark a renewal in revolutionary consciousness." Mumia Abu-Jamal is wise enough to understand that for blacks and for the poor, freedom is more than release from prison. Liberation is collective and not individual. Perhaps this is why Abu-Jamal doesn't dwell on his case; even were he to be released from prison, its walls would still incarcerate him as they do millions of Americans, perpetuating a cycle of violence that threatens all members of society.

Abu-Jamal's narrative ultimately inspires hope; from the obscurity of his cell he clearly sees deliverance where few others do: "the solution is not in the courts but in an awake, aware people" (p. 102); "the people themselves must organize for their own defense, or it won't get done" (p. 148). He remains optimistic for the youth, maintaining that the current generation is "far from lost, they are probably the most aware generation since Nat Turner's; they are not so much lost as they are mislaid, discarded by this increasingly racist system that undermines their inherent worth" (p. 165).

The youth, like Abu-Jamal, aren't dead yet, and as long as they fight for freedom, hope survives. *Live from Death Row* is a powerful revelation of brutality perpetuated by lack of understanding. The book perceives violence as institutionally based and views the outside-the-wall world as a diseased reflection of the savagery occurring within the walls. Abu-Jamal maintains that relief can be obtained only by collective revolutionary action, not through individual middle-class notions of liberty.

Notes

Kenneth Bolton, Jr., is a Ph.D. candidate in the Department of Sociology, University of Florida.

DOCUMENTS

International Tribunal for Rwanda

[Note: The Security Council Resolution creating the International Tribunal for the Former Yugoslavia (S/RES/827) formally excluded the death penalty from the applicable sanctions in cases of convictions for genocide, crimes against humanity, war crimes, and grave breaches. There was, apparently, no controversy about the matter when the resolution was adopted, in May 1993. Eighteen months later, the Security Council decided to establish a second ad hoc tribunal, this time for Rwanda. Rwanda was, at the time, an elected member of the Security Council, and it insisted that the death penalty be applicable.]

Security Council Meeting of November 8, 1994
(U.N. Doc. S/PV.3453)

[p. 5] Mr. Keating (New Zealand):—[. . .] We recall that the Government of Rwanda requested the Tribunal. That is a fact. We are disappointed that it has not supported this resolution. We understand that this is principally because of its desire that those convicted of genocide should be executed. As a State party to the Optional Protocol to the International Covenant on Civil and Political Rights [*sic*], New Zealand could never support an international tribunal that could impose the death penalty. For over three decades the United Nations has been trying progressively to eliminate the death penalty. It would be entirely unacceptable—and a dreadful step backwards—to introduce it here. Indeed, it would also go against the spirit of the Arusha Agreement, which the Government of Rwanda has said it will honor and which commit all parties in Rwanda to accept international human rights standards.

We do not believe that following the principle of "an eye for an eye" is the path to establishing a civilized society, no matter how horrendous the crimes the individuals concerned may have committed. The objective in Rwanda must be to establish a just and fair society based on respect for life and fundamental human rights. [...]

It may be that the lesser perpetrators will have to be dealt with by the Rwandan courts. This is likely because of the numbers involved. We can only say that our expectation is that in the domestic courts weight must be given to the Arusha human rights commitments. [...]

[p. 14] Mr. Bakuramutsa (Rwanda)—[...] In spite of many meetings with the sponsors of the draft resolution, and despite some amendments to the initial text, my Government is still not satisfied with the resolution or with the statute of the International Tribunal for Rwanda as it stands today, for the following reasons. [...]

[p. 16] The sixth reason is that the International Tribunal as designed in the resolution, establishes a disparity in sentences since it rules out capital punishment, which is nevertheless provided for in the Rwandese penal code. Since it is foreseeable that the Tribunal will be dealing with suspects who devised, planned and organized the genocide, these may escape capital punishment whereas those who simply carried out their plans would be subjected to the harshness of this sentence. That situation is not conducive to national reconciliation in Rwanda.

Security Council Resolution 955 (U.N. Doc. S/RES/955 [1994])

Annex

Statute of the International Tribunal for Rwanda

Article 23

penalties

1. The penalty imposed by the Trial Chamber shall be limited to imprisonment. [...]

[Note: The draft resolution (U.N. Doc. S/1994/1168) was adopted November 8, 1994, at the 3453rd meeting of the Security Council by thirteen votes to one, with one abstention.

In favor: Argentina, Brazil, Czech Republic, Djïbouti, France, New Zealand, Nigeria, Oman, Pakistan, Russian Federation, Spain, United Kingdom of Great Britain and Northern Ireland, United States of America

Against: Rwanda.

Abstaining: China.]

General Assembly Resolution Calling for a Moratorium on the Death Penalty

[Note:At the autumn 1994 session of the General Assembly, Italy presented a resolution dealing with the death penalty.]

Draft Resolution Proposed by Italy (U.N. Doc. A/49/234)

The General Assembly,

Recalling article 3 of the Universal Declaration of Human Rights which affirms everyone's right to life, article 6 of the International Covenant on Civil and Political Rights, articles 6 and 37(a) of the Convention on the Rights of the Child.

Recalling its resolutions 2857 (XXVI) of 20 December 1971, 32/61 of 8 December 1977, and 44/128 of 15 December 1989, the latter adopting and opening for signature the Second Optional Protocol to the International Covenant on Civil and Political Rights, aiming at the abolition of the death penalty.

Recalling also Economic and Social Council resolutions 1574(L) of 20 May 1971, 1745 (LIV) of 16 May 1973, 1930 (LVIII) of 6 May 1975, 1984/50 of 25 May 1984, 1985/33 of 29 May 1985, 1990/29 of 24 May 1990, and 1990/51 of 24 July 1990.

Deeply concerned about the fact that in some countries which have not yet abolished the death penalty, sentence of death is also imposed for other than the most serious crimes.

Also concerned that several countries impose the death penalty on juveniles, pregnant women and insane persons, in disregard of the limitations provided for in the International Covenant on Civil and Political Rights, in the Convention on the Rights of the Child, and in the Annex to ECOSOC resolution 1984/50.

Welcoming that in the Statutes of the ad hoc International Tribunals for the crimes committed in the former Yugoslavia and in Rwanda and in the draft statute for an International Criminal Court elaborated by the International Law Commission, capital punishment is excluded from the penalties that these Courts are authorized to impose.

Noting that abolition of the death penalty contributes to enhancement of human dignity and progressive development of human rights.

Reaffirming the sovereign right of states to determine in accordance with the international law, including the Charter of the United Nations, the legal measure and penalties which are appropriate to deal with the most serious crimes.

Invites all States parties that still maintain the death penalty to fully comply with their obligations under the International Covenant on Civil and Political Rights and the Convention on the Rights of the Child, and in particular to exclude pregnant women and juveniles from capital executions.

Invites all States which have not yet abolished the death penalty to consider the progressive restriction of the number of offenses for which the death penalty may be imposed and to exclude insane persons from capital executions.

Encourages all States which have not yet abolished the death penalty to consider the opportunity of instituting a moratorium on pending executions with a view to ensuring that the principle that no State should dispose of the life of any human being be affirmed in every part of the world by the year 2000.

[Note: Italy requested the Office of the Presidency of the General Assembly to add the item "capital punishment" to the agenda so that the draft resolution could be debated. Pakistan, speaking on behalf of the Organization of the Islamic Conference, argued that capital punishment was "a highly

sensitive and complicated issue, and warranted further and thorough consideration." Pakistan opposed modification of the agenda to include the item, adding that if the resolution was to be considered, this should be in the Sixth Committee, dealing with legal issues, and not the Third Committee, dealing with human rights issues [U.N. Doc. A/BUR/49/SR.6, §2]. The representative of Sudan described capital punishment as "a divine right according to some religions, in particular Islam" [U.N. Doc. A/BUR/49/SR.5, §13]; Iran, Malaysia, and Egypt also opposed discussing the draft resolution, while Uruguay, Malta, Cambodia, Austria, Burundi, Guinea-Bissau, Nicaragua, France, Ukraine, and Andorra urged it be included on the agenda of the Third Committee [U.N. Doc. A/BUR/49/SR.5-6]. The item "capital punishment" was added to the agenda of the Third Committee on a vote of the General Assembly, with seventy states in favor, twenty-four opposed, and forty-two abstentions [U.N. Doc. A/49/610, §2]. The draft resolution was subsequently debated in the Third Committee of the General Assembly.]*

Debates in the Third Committee of the General Assembly

U.N. DOC. A/C.3/49/SR.39

[. . .] 20. Mr. KEATING (New Zealand), speaking on the subject of capital punishment, said that the current initiative under sub-item (e) was modest in its ambitions. New Zealand rejected the arguments put forward by critics of the initiative that the death penalty was the prerogative of States and that systems of justice must reflect their national circumstances and that efforts towards universal abolition thus constituted a challenge to national sovereignty.

21. It had been firmly established that the death penalty did not come solely within domestic jurisdiction; it was governed by an international human rights instrument which had been adopted by the General Assembly and had entered into force. The Second Optional Protocol to the International Covenant on Civil and Political Rights established the principle that the abolition of the death penalty contributed to the enhancement of human dignity and the development of human rights. New Zealand was proud to be the first country to have ratified the Second Optional Protocol, as it considered that the

death penalty was a punishment which could not be reconciled with respect for human rights. His country had removed all provisions for capital punishment from its domestic law and believed that a discussion in the present forum on the need for steps towards the universal implementation of the Second Optional Protocol was fully in keeping with the Charter of the United Nations.

22. His delegation was therefore disappointed at the expressions of support for capital punishment, but was even more disappointed at the arguments put forward by those who opposed it. The issue should be discussed on its merits; there was no justification for resorting to questions of sovereignty and domestic jurisdiction. He recalled that, not so long ago, the propagandists of various tyrannical regimes had resisted discussion in the United Nations on torture and other cruel and inhuman forms of punishment on similar grounds, and United Nations efforts to eradicate racism, colonialism, and even apartheid had also been opposed on such grounds.

23. New Zealand was not seeking to impose its position on any other country, but it rejected the suggestion that it was not appropriate to discuss the issue in the General Assembly or to seek to persuade others to reconsider their positions and, progressively and voluntarily, to bring their systems of justice into line with international human rights standards. As to the proposals put forward in the draft resolution contained in document A/49/234, his delegation considered that there was no need for the issue to come before the General Assembly year after year. It would be sufficient for the issue to be raised periodically during the General Assembly, for all human rights standards were best achieved through persuasion and encouragement.

24. Mr. MINOVES-TRIQUELL (Andorra) said that the sponsors of the draft resolution contained in document A/49/234 had no desire to impose their ideas on others or to infringe, as some had suggested, on the national sovereignty of States, respect for which was one of the underlying principles of the Organization. They wished only to advance the rational debate on what was an issue of human rights. It had taken two murderous world wars and the prospect of a final one to make the international community understand the principle that

war itself was wrong. The question of capital punishment, too, involved a matter of principle; it was not simply an aspect of a particular set of societal or religious values.

25. Because of centuries of bloody conflict, his country had been quick to recognize the evils of war and had outlawed it in 1278. Similarly, because of Andorra's small size, on the occasions when the death penalty had been imposed, significant numbers of the population had been directly involved in the execution or had witnessed it. His people had eventually been thus forced to acknowledge the degrading effect of the death penalty on human dignity. No death sentence had been passed in Andorra since 1943, and the penalty itself had been abolished in 1990.

26. "A life for a life" seemed to be a reasonable equation. However, in practice, by legalizing the killing of another human being under certain circumstances, the existence of the death penalty made murder more justifiable in the eyes of the potential criminal. Not surprisingly, no statistical or comparative study showed any correlation between the imposition of the death penalty and the murder rate. The only true deterrent to murder was absolute respect of the right to life.

U.N. DOC. A/C.3/49/SR.43

[. . .] 43. Mr. AL-RASSI (Saudi Arabia) said that the inclusion of capital punishment as an item on the agenda was a further attempt to give currency to so-called "universal concepts" without taking account of the cultural and religious features or domestic laws of different countries. With reference to the penultimate preambular paragraph of the draft resolution contained in document A/49/234, he wondered whether the sponsors of the draft resolution had forgotten that ethnic cleansing was among the human rights violations committed in Bosnia and Herzegovina. Decisive measures were needed to deal with such crimes, which threatened the survival of the human race. Far from promoting full respect for human rights, the draft resolution conflicted with those rights by giving criminals the right to life and withdrawing that same right from their innocent victims, thereby encouraging further killing and human rights violations.

44. The draft resolution should be referred to the Sixth Committee, with the request that it recommend the establishment of an expert committee to make an analytical study of the issue, for submission to the General Assembly at its fifty-first session. In his own country, the capital punishment provided for under Islamic law was intended simply as a powerful deterrent to serious crime, which was fortunately rare. Any capital punishment imposed, however, was implemented according to specific conditions, the details of which were beyond the scope of the present discussion.

45. Mr. CASSAR (Malta) said that it was only natural that the discussion of capital punishment should arouse some emotion on the part of delegations, since opinions on the issue were influenced by millennial cultural conditions, moral values, and concerns about the powers of the State in ensuring law and order. These factors had been taken into consideration by the sponsors of the draft resolution contained in document A/49/234, rather than seeking to impose a set of values, simply invited Member States to reflect on the issue. . . .

50. It was twenty years since Malta had abolished capital punishment for ordinary crimes. Current legislation provided for the application of the death penalty to persons subject to the Malta Armed Forces Act, but only in exception and serious cases in times of war. His Government was looking at the possibility of ratifying the Second Optional Protocol and therefore understood the serious consideration which other States might give to the matter. Rather than impose views, the aim was to seek codes of behavior which would bring peace of mind, given the intrinsic value of the life of each individual and the fact that no society was infallible.

51. Mr. HAMIDA (Libyan Arab Jamahiriya) said that while the international human rights instruments provided the foundation for the universal promotion and protection of all human rights, no progress could be made until those right were respected by States and international organizations. It was therefore regrettable that some United Nations bodies were adopting resolutions that flagrantly violated fundamental human rights, demonstrating the absence of democracy within the United Nations and the dominance of certain States

therein. Such resolutions would remain without credibility until democracy prevailed within the Organization, together with respect for its Charter and for the international human rights instruments. In that connection, although respect for the sovereignty of States was a cornerstone of international law, human rights were often used as a pretext for interference in their internal affairs and for waging political campaigns against the developing countries in particular. No country had the right to claim superiority and impose its values and traditions on others. . . .

53. On the subject of capital punishment, his country was seeking to arrive at a society free of poverty, oppression, and other social ills, in which imposition of the death penalty would be unnecessary. With a view to its eventual abolition, capital punishment was imposed, in accordance with Islamic law, only as retribution or on persons who endangered or corrupted society. There should be no attempt to impose the abolition of capital punishment, which was still the sole deterrent to serious crimes such as murder. Libya believed that the matter should be left to the discretion of each individual society and therefore disagreed with the draft resolution in document A/49/234 and hoped that its sponsors would not insist on its consideration.

54. Mr. CATARINO (Portugal) said that his country had been a pioneer in the abolition of capital punishment. Its Constitution specified that in no case would the death penalty be applicable, and public opinion was clearly opposed to it. His delegation supported the view that capital punishment should be dealt with in a human rights framework, and attached particular importance to the Second Optional Protocol to the International Covenant on Civil and Political Rights.

55. Experience showed that resorting to the death penalty did not generally achieve the deterrent effect that was the main justification for its use. It should also be borne in mind that decision-making in criminal courts was subject to errors of judgment which could have tragic and irreversible consequences. Those countries which applied the death penalty should not see the current discussion as a tool to divide States or an attempt to interfere in their internal affair. Prog-

ress on the subject depended on the will to engage in a full and unconstrained dialogue.

56. He appealed to those States which had not yet done so to become signatories to the relevant human rights instruments, and to those which still applied the death penalty to consider the progressive restriction of the number of offenses for which it could be imposed, as well as the possibility of a moratorium on pending executions.

57. Mr. ELARBY (Egypt) emphasized the need for all States to accede to the major international human rights instruments, which Egypt had already ratified. . . .

58. Capital punishment was intended not only to deter crime, but to compensate victims who had been deprived of the basic right to life. Any restriction of the State's role in exacting retribution on behalf of such victims would be a breach of the social contract under which individuals relinquished certain rights and freedoms in return for guarantees of material and spiritual welfare from the State. Punishment should also fit the crime, in which case the death penalty was the appropriate punishment for crimes which could not be compensated, such as those involving killing. His country was not alone in believing that the type of penalty which a country imposed should not be used as a measure of its respect for human rights. It was, moreover, illogical to recognize self-defense against an attacker as a fundamental right, even if the attacker died as a result, while simultaneously arguing that an attacker should not receive the death penalty if his attack led to the death of his victim.

59. Capital punishment in Egypt was subject to clear controls and safeguards. First, the death penalty was mandatory only for certain crimes and only if the court was unanimous in its verdict, which had to be delivered in the presence of the accused. Second, even in the absence of an appeal, all death sentences were referred to the Court of Cassation with a view to ascertaining that the law had been properly applied. Third, criminal courts were bound to seek the opinion of the Grand Mufti before delivering a death sentence, which was then subject to approval by the President, who could grant pardon or

commute the sentence. Fourth, the death sentence was not imposed on persons aged under eighteen or on pregnant or nursing women. Lastly, due process of law was observed, in that criminal courts were legally bound to appoint a defense lawyer for the accused and to pay his fees.

60. He appreciated the views of those countries which had abolished capital punishment, but called on them to respect the position of States such as Egypt which still retained the death penalty. Egypt's position merely reflected another approach to human rights, in which the victim's right to retribution was recognized. Besides, capital punishment was a preventive measure and its ultimate objective was to protect the right to life.

61. Mr. REZVANI (Islamic Republic of Iran) said that the use of the death penalty had always aroused emotions of compassion and mercy which were deeply rooted in the Islamic system of criminal justice. However, Islam also recognized the legitimacy of applying capital punishment to a restricted number of the most serious crimes. Iran therefore imposed the death penalty for such crimes, in conformity with article 6(2) of the International Covenant on Civil and Political Rights, and provided appropriate safeguards to ensure that its application was subject to due process of law.

62. It was the sovereign right of every State to choose the most appropriate penal system, taking into account its society's cultural, religious and historical characteristics. His Government was unconvinced by the argument that capital punishment did not have a deterrent effect, believed that deterrence and retribution played a significant role in a complex world, and unequivocally opposed any effort to impose a particular system of justice. . . .

66. Mr. OK (Cambodia) After much debate, Cambodia's Constituent Assembly had concluded that the death penalty should be abolished, because of the risks of judicial error or abuse of power and because there had also been a tendency in the past to apply the death penalty to the poor and to ethnic minorities and to use it as an instrument of political repression. Besides, Cambodia's experience showed that the crime rate stayed the same after abolition. His dele-

gation hoped that, by the twenty-first century, the death penalty would have been eliminated throughout the world. . . .

68. Ms. DE WET (Namibia) The historical perspective and the social, cultural, and political reality of Namibia prior to independence had played a major role in shaping its Constitution. Her people believed the right to life to be the most fundamental human right. Capital punishment was therefore clearly and expressly banned by the Constitution. Namibia was also in the process of acceding to the Second Optional Protocol.

69. Mr. HORIUCHI (Japan) said that the question of whether to retain or abolish the death penalty should be carefully considered by each State, taking into account the sentiments of its people and the state of crime and criminal policy. In Japan, capital punishment was applied only to the most heinous crimes, such as mass murder, and always in accordance with the strictest judicial procedures. It was inappropriate to make universal decisions on the issue, which was why Japan had raised objections to the Second Optional Protocol to the International Covenant on Civil and Political Rights. In fact, it was because opinions were divided that the Protocol had not been incorporated into the Covenant: there had been no prospect that the international community would reach a consensus. His delegation would oppose any draft resolution which encouraged all Member States to consider abolition of the death penalty and the institution of a moratorium on pending executions.

70. Mr. OBEIDAT (Jordan) said that while the right of the human being to life—a fundamental, divine right on which all other human rights depended—must be preserved, a delicate balance must be struck between that right and the right of society to rid itself of crime and its perpetrators.

71. Islam guaranteed all human rights, particularly the right to life, but also provided strict penalties for aggression against the lives of others. Legislation differed from country to country, however, and no society had the right to impose its views on another. His country did not agree that abolishing capital punishment would enhance human dignity; otherwise, the same reasoning would apply to the abo-

lition of arrest and imprisonment. It felt that capital punishment should be applied in the case of the most serious crimes, for that served as a deterrent.

72. The CHAIRMAN said that the Committee had concluded its general discussions of . . . sub-item 100 (e) entitled "Capital punishment." . . .

74. With regard to sub-item 100 (e), the Committee had clearly been divided into two camps: those favoring the abolition of capital punishment and those wishing to retain it. Arguments in favor of abolishing the death penalty had been the following: States could not impose the death penalty as a means of reducing crime because there was no evidence that it had a deterrent effect; the right to life was the most basic human right and, consequently, States did not have the right to take the life of any individual; the death penalty sometimes veiled a desire for vengeance or provided an easy way of eliminating political opponents; the death penalty, once applied, could not be reversed in the event of judicial error; and capital punishment was excluded from the penalties used by international tribunals, including those established to deal with the situations in the former Yugoslavia and Rwanda, and should consequently become less prevalent in national legislation.

75. Arguments in support of maintaining the death penalty had been the following: certain legislative systems were based on religious laws; it was not possible to impose the ethical standards of a single culture on all countries; there was a need to discourage extremely serious crimes; and, in some countries, capital punishment was a constitutional or even a religious obligation.

76. At the same time, all members had agreed on certain fundamental points: the death penalty should be applied only in exceptional circumstances and subject to strict preconditions; and its scope of application should be extremely limited.

U.N. DOC. A/C.3/49/SR.57
[. . .] 14. The CHAIRMAN announced that Bolivia, Germany, Micronesia, and Venezuela had become sponsors of draft resolution

A/C.3/49/L.32, entitled "Capital punishment," which had no program budget implications.

15. Mr. FULCI (Italy) said that the following delegations had become sponsors: Argentina, Cyprus, Dominican Republic, El Salvador, New Zealand, São Tomé and Principe, Slovakia, and Solomon Islands.

16. Mr. CHEW (Singapore) proposed a motion, under rule 116 of the rules of procedure, that no action should be taken on the item. The Committee had thoroughly debated capital punishment and it was clear that there was no consensus on the issue. Action on the draft resolution could only widen the breach between those who supported it and those who opposed it. Those in favor had exercised their sovereign right to accede to the Second Optional Protocol to the International Covenant on Civil and Political Rights. The drafters of that Protocol had acted wisely in making it optional, showing that they realized there was no consensus on the issue and refraining from attempting to impose their views on other sovereign States.

17. Capital punishment was not a human rights issue. No other human rights instruments characterized capital punishment as a violation of human rights. Indeed, the International Covenant explicitly recognized the right of Governments to impose capital punishment, and the sovereign right of Governments to determine legal measures and penalties which were appropriate in their countries to combat serious crime was enshrined in Article 2(7) of the Charter of the United Nations.

18. Mr. SAHRAOUI (Algeria) said that the harmonization of national laws was not a matter of concealing the particularities of different judicial systems but rather of taking advantage of their common features. The work of the United Nations in the codification and progressive development of international law had shown that universal adherence to norms, particularly norms which did not derive from customary law, was always determined by the degree to which those norms were compatible, or at any rate not incompatible, with the broad principles on which national legislation was based. The current status of the issue of capital punishment was, in fact, a result of

that approach and reflected the objective limits to harmonization of laws on the subject at the international level.

19. Although the sponsors of the draft resolution might not have intended to force a choice on Member States, any vote on the subject of capital punishment would have that effect. Those States whose legislation incorporated capital punishment would have no option but to vote against the draft resolution if they were not to betray their own constitutions or laws. The way for States to make a choice in that regard was by exercising their sovereign right to ratify, or not to ratify, the Second Optional Protocol to the International Covenant. His delegation therefore supported the motion for no action on the draft resolution.

20. Mr. FULCI (Italy) said that his delegation was opposed to the motion proposed by Singapore and had hoped that the Committee would be able to vote on the draft resolution without becoming engaged in procedural manoeuvres. The motion called for the fifth procedural vote on sub-item 100(e), on capital punishment. In the past few weeks, there had been two procedural votes in the General Committee and two in plenary meetings of the General Assembly on that question. A further attempt had been made to prevent even a discussion of the issue. The motion was, in reality, designed to eliminate the draft resolution, without giving delegations a chance to state their positions on it.

21. If the motion was adopted, it would set a negative precedent, since the request for inclusion of the item had been supported by 34 countries belonging to all the regional groups and draft resolution A/C.3/49/L.32 had been sponsored by almost 50 countries, again from all regions of the world. It would be wrong to conclude that those numbers were insufficient to allow the General Assembly to take a decision on a proposal, or that the draft resolution had to be submitted by a majority of the Member States.

22. There was no need to resort to such a motion in the Third Committee. Human rights questions were of such fundamental importance that artificial obstacles to a debate on the issue could not be justified. It was precisely in the highly sensitive area of human rights

that the rules of procedure of the General Assembly should not be used to prevent or delay the decision-making process. The sponsors of the draft resolution realized that the issue of capital punishment was controversial and divisive and, for that very reason, had submitted a balanced, mild, and non-intrusive text, focusing on the need to guarantee respect for basic humanitarian principles.

[Note: Singapore proposed an amendment that eliminated the phrase "in accordance with the international law, including the Charter of the United Nations," found in the eighth preambular paragraph of the draft. The amendment was adopted, seventy-one to sixty-five, with twenty-one abstentions:

In favor: Afghanistan, Algeria, Antigua-Barbuda, Bahamas, Bahrain, Bangladesh, Barbados, Belize, Bhutan, Brunei, Burkina Faso, Burundi, Cameroon, China, Cuba, Korea, Egypt, Eritrea, Grenada, Guinea, Guyana, India, Indonesia, Iran, Iraq, Ivory Coast, Jamaica, Japan, Jordan, Kenya, Kuwait, Kyrgyzstan, Laos, Lebanon, Lesotho, Libya, Malaysia, Maldives, Mauritania, Mongolia, Morocco, Myanmar, Namibia, Nigeria, Oman, Pakistan, Papua New Guinea, Peru, Philippines, Qatar, Republic of Korea, Saudi Arabia, Senegal, Sierra Leone, Singapore, Sri Lanka, Sudan, Suriname, Swaziland, Syria, Thailand, Trinidad and Tobago, Tunisia, Uganda, United Arab Emirates, Tanzania, Uzbekistan, Vietnam, Yemen, Zambia, Zimbabwe.

Against: Andorra, Angola, Argentina, Armenia, Australia, Austria, Belgium, Brazil, Bulgaria, Cambodia, Canada, Cape Verde, Chile, Colombia, Costa Rica, Cyprus, Czech Republic, Denmark, El Salvador, Estonia, Finland, France, Germany, Greece, Haiti, Honduras, Hungary, Iceland, Ireland, Israel, Italy, Latvia, Liechtenstein, Lithuania, Luxembourg, Macedonia, Malta, Marshall Islands, Micronesia, Monaco, Mozambique, Nepal, Netherlands, New Zealand, Nicaragua, Norway, Panama, Paraguay, Poland, Portugal, Moldova, Romania, Russian Federation, San Marino, Slovakia, Slovenia, Solomon Islands, South Africa, Spain, Sweden, United Kingdom of Great Britain and Northern Ireland, United States of America, Uruguay, Vanuatu, Venezuela.

Abstaining: Albania, Azerbaijan, Belarus, Benin, Bolivia, Croatia, Ecuador, Ethiopia, Fiji, Gabon, Gambia, Georgia, Ghana, Guatemala, Kazakhstan, Mali, Mauritius, Mexico, Niger, Togo, Ukraine.

The entire resolution, as amended, was then defeated, thirty-six voted in favor, and forty-four voted against, with seventy-four abstentions:

In favor: Argentina, Armenia, Cambodia, Cape Verde, Chile, Colombia, Costa Rica, Croatia, Cyprus, Ecuador, El Salvador, Fiji, Gambia, Georgia, Greece, Haiti, Ireland, Israel, Italy, Kyrgyzstan, Macedonia, Malta, Marshall Islands, Mexico, Mozambique, Namibia, Nepal, Nicaragua, Panama, Paraguay, Portugal, San Marino, Slovenia, Uzbekistan, Venezuela.

Against: Afghanistan, Algeria, Antigua-Barbuda, Bahamas, Bahrain, Bangladesh, Barbados, Belize, Brunei, Cameroon, China, Comoros, Egypt, Guinea, Guyana, India, Indonesia, Iran, Iraq, Jamaica, Japan, Jordan, Kuwait, Lebanon, Libya, Malaysia, Maldives, Morocco, Myanmar, Nigeria, Oman, Pakistan, Qatar, Republic of Korea, Saudi Arabia, Senegal, Sierra Leone, Singapore, Sudan, Syria, Trinidad and Tobago, United Arab Emirates, United States of America, Yemen.

Abstaining: Albania, Andorra, Australia, Austria, Azerbaijan, Belarus, Belgium, Benin, Bolivia, Botswana, Brazil, Bulgaria, Burkina Faso, Burundi, Canada, Cuba, Czech Republic, Denmark, Estonia, Ethiopia, Finland, France, Gabon, Germany, Grenada, Guatemala, Honduras, Hungary, Iceland, Ivory Coast, Kazakhstan, Kenya, Korea, Latvia, Lesotho, Liechtenstein, Lithuania, Luxembourg, Madagascar, Malawi, Mali, Mauritius, Micronesia, Moldova, Monaco, Mongolia, Netherlands, New Zealand, Niger, Norway, Papua New Guinea, Peru, Philippines, Poland, Romania, Russian Federation, Slovakia, South Africa, Spain, Sri Lanka, Suriname, Swaziland, Sweden, Tanzania, Thailand, Togo, Tunisia, Uganda, Ukraine, United Kingdom of Great Britain and Northern Ireland, Vanuatu, Vietnam, Zambia, Zimbabwe.]

Constitutional Court of the Republic of South Africa: State *v.* Makwanyane and Mchunu

[Note: On June 8, 1995, the South African Constitutional Court ruled that the death penalty, as provided for in the country's Criminal Procedure Act, was contrary to provisions of its new interim constitution enshrining the right to life (section 9) and prohibiting the use of cruel, inhuman, or degrading treatment or punishment (section 11(2)). The eleven-member court was unanimous in striking down the death penalty. The lead judgment was drafted by the president of the court, Arthur Chaskalson. President Chaskalson addressed only the issue of cruel, inhuman, or degrading punishment, preferring not to pronounce himself on the subject of the right to life. Nine of the justices, however, concluded that South Africa's capital punishment provisions also breach the right to life. The Sourcebook *reproduces some important excerpts from President Chaskalson's reasons for judgment.]*

Section 11(2)—Cruel, Inhuman, or Degrading Punishment

Death is the most extreme form of punishment to which a convicted criminal can be subjected. Its execution is final and irrevocable. It puts an end not only to the right to life itself, but to all other personal rights which had vested in the deceased under Chapter Three of the *Constitution.* It leaves nothing except the memory in others of what has been and the property that passes to the deceased's heirs. In the ordinary meaning of the words, the death sentence is undoubtedly a cruel punishment. Once sentenced, the prisoner waits on death row in the company of other prisoners under sentence of death, for the processes of their appeals and the procedures for clemency to be carried out. Throughout this period, those who remain on death row are uncertain of their fate, not knowing whether they will ultimately be reprieved or taken to the gallows. Death is a cruel penalty and the legal processes which necessarily involve waiting in uncertainty for the sentence to be set aside or carried out, add to the cruelty. It is also an inhuman punishment for it ". . . involves, by its very nature, a denial of the executed person's humanity,"[34] and it is degrading because it strips the convicted person of all dignity and treats him or her as an object to be eliminated by the state. The question is not, however, whether the death sentence is a cruel, inhuman, or degrading punishment in the ordinary meaning of these words but whether it is a cruel, inhuman, or degrading punishment within the meaning of section 11(2) of our *Constitution*.[35] The accused, who rely on section 11(2) of the *Constitution*, carry the initial onus of establishing this proposition.[36]

The Contentions of the Parties

The principal arguments advanced by counsel for the accused in support of their contention that the imposition of the death penalty for murder is a "cruel, inhuman, or degrading punishment," were that the death sentence is an affront to human dignity, is inconsistent with the unqualified right to life entrenched in the *Constitution*, cannot be corrected in case of error or enforced in a manner that is not arbitrary, and that it negates the essential content of the right to life and the other rights that flow from it. The Attorney General argued that the death penalty is recognized as a legitimate form of punishment in many parts of the world, it is a deterrent to violent crime, it meets society's need for adequate retribution for heinous offenses, and it is regarded by South African society as an acceptable form of punishment. He asserted that it is, therefore, not cruel, inhuman or degrading within the meaning of section 11(2) of the *Constitution*. These arguments for and against the death sentence are well known and have been considered in many of the foreign authorities and cases to which we were referred. We must deal with them now in the light of the provisions of our own *Constitution*.

The Effect of the Disparity in the Laws Governing Capital Punishment

One of the anomalies of the transition initiated by the *Constitution* is that the *Criminal Procedure Act* does not apply throughout South Africa. This is a consequence of section 229 of the *Constitution* which provides:

> Subject to this Constitution, all laws which immediately before the commencement of this Constitution were in force in any area which forms part of the national territory, shall continue in force in such area, subject to any repeal or amendment of such laws by a competent authority.

Prior to the commencement of the *Constitution*, the *Criminal Procedure Act* was in force only in the old Republic of South Africa. Its operation did not extend to the former Transkei, Bophuthatswana, Venda or Ciskei, which were then treated by South African law as independent states and had their own legislation. Although their respective criminal procedure statutes were based on the South African legislation, there were differences, including differences in regard to the death penalty. The most striking difference in this regard was in Ciskei, where the death sentence was abolished on June 8, 1990, by the military regime,[37] the *de facto* government of the territory, and it ceased from that date to be a competent sentence.[38] These differences still exist,[39] which means that the law governing the imposition of the death sentence in South Africa is not uniform. The greatest disparity is in the Eastern Cape Province. A person who commits murder and is brought to trial in that part of the province which was formerly Ciskei, cannot be sentenced to death, whilst a person who commits murder and is brought to trial in another part of the same province, can be sentenced to death. There is no rational reason for this distinction, which is the result of history, and we asked for argument to be addressed to us on the question whether this difference has a bearing on the constitutionality of section 277(1)(a) of the *Criminal Procedure Act*.

Counsel for the accused argued that it did. They contended that in the circumstances section 277 was not a law of general application (which is a requirement under section 33(1) for the validity of any law which limits a Chapter Three right), and that the disparate application of the death sentence within South Africa discriminates unfairly between those prosecuted in the former Ciskei and those prosecuted elsewhere in South Africa, and offends against the right to "equality before the law and to equal protection of the law."[40]

If the disparity had been the result of legislation enacted after the *Constitution* had come into force the challenge to the validity of section 277 on these grounds may well have been tenable. Criminal law and procedure is a national competence and the national government could not without very convincing reasons have established a "safe haven" in part of one of the provinces in which the death penalty would not be enforced. The disparity is not, however, the result of the legislative policy of the new Parliament, but a consequence of the *Constitution* which brings together again in one country the parts that had been separated under apartheid. The purpose of section 229 was to ensure an orderly transition, and an inevitable consequence of its provisions is that there will be disparities in the law reflecting pre-existing regional variations, and that this will continue until a uniform system of law has been established by the national and provincial legislatures within their fields of competence as contemplated by Chapter Fifteen of the *Constitution*.

The requirement of section 229 that existing laws shall continue to be in force subject to the *Constitution*, makes the *Constitution* applicable to existing laws within each of the geographic areas. These laws have to meet all the standards prescribed by Chapter Three, and this no doubt calls for consistency and parity of laws within the boundaries of each of the different geographic areas. It does not, however, mean that there has to be consistency and parity between the laws of the different geographic areas themselves.[41] Such a construction would defeat the apparent purpose of section 229, which is to allow different legal orders to exist side by side until a process of rationalization has been carried out, and would inappropriately expose a substantial part if not the entire body of our statutory law to challenges under section 8 of the *Constitution*. It follows that disparities between the legal orders in different parts of the country, consequent upon the provisions of section 229 of the *Constitution*, cannot for that reason alone be said to constitute a breach of the equal protection provisions of section 8, or render the laws such that they are not of general application.

International and Foreign Comparative Law

The death sentence is a form of punishment which has been used throughout history by different societies. It has long been the subject of controversy.[42] As societies became more enlightened, they restricted the offences for which this penalty could be imposed.[43] The movement away from the death penalty gained momentum during the second half of the present century with the growth of the abolitionist movement. In some countries it is now prohibited in all circumstances, in some it is prohibited save in times of war, and in most countries that have retained it as a penalty for crime, its use has been restricted to extreme cases. According to Amnesty International, 1,831 executions were carried out throughout the world in 1993 as a result of sentences of death, of which 1,419 were in China, which means that only 412 executions were carried out in the rest of the world in that year.[44] Today, capital punishment has been abolished as a penalty for murder either specifically or in practice by almost half the countries of the world including the democracies of Europe and our neighboring countries, Namibia, Mozambique and Angola.[45] In most of those countries where it is retained, as the Amnesty International statistics show, it is seldom used.

In the course of the arguments addressed to us, we were referred to books and articles on the death sentence, and to judgments dealing with challenges made to capital punishment in the courts of other countries and in international tribunals. The international and foreign authorities are of value because they analyze arguments for and against the death sentence and show how courts of other jurisdictions have dealt with this vexed issue. For that reason alone they require our attention. They may also have to be considered because of their relevance to section 35(1) of the *Constitution*, which states:

> In interpreting the provisions of this Chapter a court of law shall promote the values which underlie an open and democratic society based on freedom and equality and shall, where applicable, have

regard to public international law applicable to the protection of the rights entrenched in this Chapter, and may have regard to comparable foreign case law.

Customary international law and the ratification and accession to international agreements is dealt with in section 231 of the *Constitution* which sets the requirements for such law to be binding within South Africa. In the context of section 35(1), public international law would include non-binding as well as binding law.[46] They may both be used under the section as tools of interpretation. International agreements and customary international law accordingly provide a framework within which Chapter Three can be evaluated and understood, and for that purpose, decisions of tribunals dealing with comparable instruments, such as the United Nations Committee on Human Rights,[47] the Inter-American Commission on Human Rights,[48] the Inter-American Court of Human Rights,[49] the European Commission on Human Rights,[50] and the European Court of Human Rights,[51] and in appropriate cases, reports of specialized agencies such as the International Labour Organization may provide guidance as to the correct interpretation of particular provisions of Chapter Three.

Capital punishment is not prohibited by public international law, and this is a factor that has to be taken into account in deciding whether it is cruel, inhuman or degrading punishment within the meaning of section 11(2). International human rights agreements differ, however, from our *Constitution* in that where the right to life is expressed in unqualified terms they either deal specifically with the death sentence, or authorize exceptions to be made to the right to life by law.[52] This has influenced the way international tribunals have dealt with issues relating to capital punishment, and is relevant to a proper understanding of such decisions.

Comparative "bill of rights" jurisprudence will no doubt be of importance, particularly in the early stages of the transition when there is no developed indigenous jurisprudence in this branch of the law on which to draw. Although we are told by section 35(1) that we "may" have regard to foreign case law, it is important to appreciate that this will not necessarily offer a safe guide to the interpretation of Chapter Three of our *Constitution*.[53] This has already been pointed out in a number of decisions of the Provincial and Local Divisions of the Supreme Court,[54] and is implicit in the injunction given to the Courts in section 35(1), which in permissive terms allows the Courts to "have regard to" such law. There is no injunction to do more than this.

When challenges to the death sentence in international or foreign courts and tribunals have failed, the constitution or the international instrument concerned has either directly sanctioned capital punishment or has specifically provided that the right to life is subject to exceptions sanctioned by law. The only case to which we were referred in which there were not such express provisions in the *Constitution*, was the decision of the Hungarian Constitutional Court. There the challenge succeeded and the death penalty was declared to be unconstitutional.[55]

Our *Constitution* expresses the right to life in an unqualified form, and prescribes the criteria that have to be met for the limitation of entrenched rights, including the prohibition of legislation that negates the essential content of an entrenched right. In dealing with comparative law, we must bear in mind that we are required to construe the South African Constitution, and not an international instrument or the constitution of some foreign country, and that this has to be done with due regard to our legal system, our history and circumstances, and the structure and language of our own *Constitution*.[56] We can derive assistance from public international law and foreign case law, but we are in no way bound to follow it.

Capital Punishment in the United States of America

The earliest litigation on the validity of the death sentence seems to have been pursued in the courts of the United States of America. It has been said there that the "Constitution itself poses the first obstacle to [the] argument that capital punishment is *per se* unconstitutional."[57] From the beginning, the United States *Constitution* recognized capital punishment as lawful. The Fifth Amendment (adopted in 1791) refers in specific terms to capital punishment and impliedly recognizes its validity. The Fourteenth Amendment (adopted in 1868) obliges the states, not to "deprive any person of life, liberty, or property, without due process of law" and it too impliedly recognizes the right of the states to make laws for such purposes.[58] The argument that capital punishment is unconstitutional was based on the Eighth Amendment, which prohibits cruel and unusual punishment.[59] Although the Eighth Amendment "has not been regarded as a static concept"[60] and as drawing its meaning "from the evolving standards of decency that mark the progress of a maturing society,"[61] the fact that the Constitution recognizes the lawfulness of capital punishment has proved to be an obstacle in the way of the acceptance of this argument, and this is stressed in some of the judgments of the United States Supreme Court.[62]

Although challenges under state constitutions to the validity of the death sentence have been successful,[63] the federal constitutionality of the death sentence as a legitimate form of punishment for murder was affirmed by the United States Supreme Court in *Gregg* v. *Georgia*.[64] Both before and after *Gregg's case*, decisions upholding and rejecting challenges to death penalty statutes have divided the Supreme Court, and have led at times to sharply-worded judgments.[65] The decisions ultimately turned on the votes of those judges who considered the nature of the discretion given to the sentencing authority to be the crucial factor.

Statutes providing for mandatory death sentences, or too little discretion in sentencing, have been rejected by the Supreme Court because they do not allow for consideration of factors peculiar to the convicted person facing sentence, which may distinguish his or her case from other cases.[66] For the same reason, statutes which allow too wide a discretion to judges or juries have also been struck down on the grounds that the exercise of such discretion leads to arbitrary results.[67] In sum, therefore, if there is no discretion, too little discretion, or an unbounded discretion, the provision authorizing the death sentence has been struck down as being contrary to the Eighth Amendment; where the discretion has been "suitably directed and limited so as to minimize the risk of wholly arbitrary and capricious action,"[68] the challenge to the statute has failed.[69]

Arbitrariness and Inequality

Basing his argument on the reasons which found favour with the majority of the United States Supreme Court in *Furman* v. *Georgia*, Mr. Trengove contended on behalf of the accused that the imprecise language of section 277, and the unbounded discretion vested by it in the Courts, make its provisions unconstitutional.

Section 277 of the Criminal Procedure Act provides:

Sentence of death

(1) The sentence of death may be passed by a superior court only and only in the case of a conviction for—(a) murder; (b) treason committed when the Republic is in a state of war; (c) robbery or attempted robbery, if the court finds aggravating circumstances to have been present; (d) kidnapping; (e) child-stealing; (f) rape.

(2) The sentence of death shall be imposed—

(a) after the presiding judge conjointly with the assessors (if any), subject to the provisions of s 145(4)(a), or, in the case of a trial by a special superior court, that court, with due regard to any evidence and argument on sentence in terms of section 274, has made a finding on the presence or absence of any mitigating or aggravating factors; and

(b) if the presiding judge or court, as the case may be, with due regard to that finding, is satisfied that the sentence of death is the proper sentence.

(3) (a) The sentence of death shall not be imposed upon an accused who was under the age of 18 years at the time of the commission of the act which constituted the offence concerned.

(b) If in the application of paragraph (a) the age of an accused is placed in issue, the onus shall be on the State to show beyond reasonable doubt that the accused was 18 years of age or older at the relevant time.

Under our court system questions of guilt and innocence, and the proper sentence to be imposed on those found guilty of crimes, are not decided by juries. In capital cases, where it is likely that the death sentence may be imposed, judges sit with two assessors who have an equal vote with the judge on the issue of guilt and on any mitigating or aggravating factors relevant to sentence; but sentencing is the prerogative of the judge alone. The *Criminal Procedure Act* allows a full right of appeal to persons sentenced to death, including a right to dispute the sentence without having to establish an irregularity or misdirection on the part of the trial judge. The Appellate Division is empowered to set the sentence aside if it would not have imposed such sentence itself, and it has laid down criteria for the exercise of this power by itself and other courts.[70] If the person sentenced to death does not appeal, the Appellate Division is nevertheless required to review the case and to set aside the death sentence if it is of the opinion that it is not a proper sentence.[71]

Mitigating and aggravating factors must be identified by the Court, bearing in mind that the onus is on the State to prove beyond reasonable doubt the existence of aggravating factors, and to negative beyond reasonable doubt the presence of any mitigating factors relied on by the accused.[72] Due regard must be paid to the personal circumstances and subjective factors which might have influenced the accused person's conduct,[73] and these factors must then be weighed up with the main objects of punishment, which have been held to be: deterrence, prevention, reformation, and retribution.[74] In this process "[e]very relevant consideration should receive the most scrupulous care and reasoned attention,"[75] and the death sentence should only be imposed in the most exceptional cases, where there is no reasonable prospect of reformation and the objects of punishment would not be properly achieved by any other sentence.[76]

There seems to me to be little difference between the guided discretion required for the death sentence in the United States, and the criteria laid down by the Appellate Division for the imposition of the death sentence. The fact that the Appellate Division, a court of experienced judges, takes the final decision in all cases is, in my view, more likely to result in consistency of sentencing, than will be the case where sentencing is in the hands of jurors who are offered statutory guidance as to how that discretion should be exercised.

The argument that the imposition of the death sentence under section 277 is arbitrary and capricious does not, however, end there. It also focuses on what is alleged to be the arbitrariness inherent in the application of section 277 in practice. Of the thousands of persons put on trial for murder, only a very small percentage are sentenced to death by a trial court, and of those, a large number escape the ultimate penalty on appeal.[77] At every stage of the process there is an element of chance. The outcome may be dependent upon factors such as the way the case is investigated by the police, the way the case is presented by the prosecutor, how effectively the accused is defended, the personality and particular attitude to capital punishment of the trial judge and, if the matter goes on appeal, the particular judges who are selected to hear the case. Race[78] and poverty are also alleged to be factors.

Most accused facing a possible death sentence are unable to afford legal assistance, and are defended under the *pro deo* system. The defending counsel is more often than not young and inexperienced, frequently of a different race to his or her client, and if this is the case, usually has to consult through an interpreter. *Pro deo* counsel are paid only a nominal fee for the defense, and generally lack the financial resources and the infrastructural support to undertake the necessary investigations and research, to employ expert witnesses to give advice, including advice on matters relevant to sentence, to assemble witnesses, to bargain with the prosecution, and generally to conduct an effective defense. Accused persons who have the money to do so, are able to retain experienced attorneys and counsel, who are paid to undertake the necessary investigations and research, and as a result they are less likely to be sentenced to death than persons similarly placed who are unable to pay for such services.[79]

It needs to be mentioned that there are occasions when senior members of the bar act *pro deo* in particularly difficult cases—indeed the present case affords an example of that, for Mr. Trengove and his juniors have acted *pro deo* in the proceedings before us, and the Legal Resources Centre who have acted as their instructing attorneys, have done so without charge. An enormous amount of research has gone into the preparation of the argument and it is highly doubtful that even the wealthiest members of our society could have secured a better service than they have provided. But this is the exception and not the rule. This may possibly change as a result of the provisions of section 25(3)(e) of the *Constitution*, but there are limits to the available financial and human resources, limits which are likely to exist for the foreseeable future, and which will continue to place poor accused at a significant disadvantage in defending themselves in capital cases.

It cannot be gainsaid that poverty, race and chance play roles in the outcome of capital cases and in the final decision as to who should live and who should die. It is sometimes said that this is understood by the judges, and as far as possible, taken into account by them. But in itself this is no answer to the complaint of arbitrariness; on the contrary, it may introduce an additional factor of arbitrariness that would also have to be taken into account. Some, but not all accused persons may be acquitted because such allowances are made, and others who are convicted, but not all, may for the same reason escape the death sentence.[80]

In holding that the imposition and the carrying out of the death penalty in the cases then under consideration constituted cruel and unusual punishment in the United States, Justice Douglas, concurring in *Furman* v. *Georgia*, said that "[a]ny law which is nondiscriminatory on its face may be applied in such a way as to violate the Equal Protection Clause of the Fourteenth Amendment." Discretionary statutes are:

> . . . pregnant with discrimination and discrimination is an ingredient not compatible with the idea of equal protection of the laws that is implicit in the ban on "cruel and unusual" punishments.[81]

It was contended that we should follow this approach and hold that the factors to which I have referred, make the application of section 277, in practice, arbitrary and capricious and, for that reason, any resulting death sentence is cruel, inhuman and degrading punishment.

The differences that exist between rich and poor, between good and bad prosecutions, between good and bad defense, between severe and lenient judges, between judges who favor capital punishment and those who do not, and the subjective attitudes that might be brought into play by factors such as race and class, may in similar ways affect any case that comes before the courts, and is almost certainly present to some degree in all court systems. Such factors can be mitigated, but not totally avoided, by allowing convicted persons to appeal to a higher court. Appeals are decided on the record of the case and on findings made by the trial court. If the evidence on record and the findings made have been influenced by these factors, there may be nothing that can be done about that on appeal. Imperfection inherent in criminal trials means that error cannot be excluded; it also means that persons similarly placed may not necessarily receive similar punishment. This needs to be acknowledged. What also needs to be acknowledged is that the possibility of error will be present in any system of justice and that there cannot be perfect equality as between accused persons in the conduct and outcome of criminal trials. We have to accept these differences in the ordinary criminal cases that come before the courts, even to the extent that some may go to gaol when others similarly placed may be acquitted or receive non-custodial sentences. But death is different, and the question is, whether this is acceptable when the difference is between life and death. Unjust imprisonment is a great wrong, but if it is discovered, the prisoner can be released and compensated; but the killing of an innocent person is irremediable.[82]

In the United States, the Supreme Court has addressed itself primarily to the requirement of due process. Statutes have to be clear and discretion curtailed without ignoring the peculiar circumstances of each accused person. Verdicts are set aside if the defense has not been adequate,[83] and persons sentenced to death are allowed wide rights of appeal and review. This attempt to ensure the utmost procedural fairness has itself led to problems. The most notorious is the "death row phenomenon" in which prisoners cling to life, exhausting every possible avenue of redress, and using every device to put off the date of execution, in the natural and understandable hope that there will be a reprieve from the Courts or the executive. It is common for prisoners in the United States to remain on death row for many years, and this dragging out of the process has been characterized as being cruel and degrading.[84] The difficulty of implementing a system of capital punishment which on the one hand avoids arbitrariness by insisting on a high standard of procedural fairness, and on the other hand avoids delays that in themselves are the cause of impermissible cruelty and inhumanity, is apparent. Justice Blackmun, who sided with the majority in *Gregg's case*, ultimately came to the conclusion that it is not possible to design a system that avoids arbitrariness.[85] To design a system that avoids arbitrariness and delays in carrying out the sentence is even more difficult.

The United States jurisprudence has not resolved the dilemma arising from the fact that the Constitution prohibits cruel and unusual punishments, but also permits, and contemplates that there will be capital punishment. The acceptance by a majority of the United States Supreme Court of the proposition that capital punishment is not *per se* unconstitutional, but that in certain circumstances it may be arbitrary, and thus unconstitutional, has led to endless litigation. Considerable expense and interminable delays result from the exceptionally high standard of procedural fairness set by the United States courts in attempting to avoid arbitrary decisions. The difficulties that have been experienced in following this path, to which Justice Blackmun and Justice Scalia have both referred,[86] but from which they have drawn different conclusions, persuade me that we should not follow this route.

The Right to Dignity

Although the United States Constitution does not contain a specific guarantee of human dignity, it has been accepted by the United States Supreme Court that the concept of human dignity is at the core of the prohibition of "cruel and unusual punishment" by the Eighth and Fourteenth Amendments.[87] For Justice Brennan this was decisive of the question in *Gregg* v. *Georgia*. The fatal constitutional infirmity in the punishment of death is that it treats "members of the human race as nonhumans, as objects to be toyed with and discarded. [It is] thus inconsistent with the fundamental premise of the Clause that even the vilest criminal remains a human being possessed of common human dignity."[88]

Under our constitutional order the right to human dignity is specifically guaranteed. It can only be limited by legislation which passes the stringent test of being 'necessary.' The weight given to human dignity by Justice Brennan is wholly consistent with the values of our Constitution and the new order established by it. It is also consistent with the approach to extreme punishments followed by courts in other countries.

In Germany, the Federal Constitutional Court has stressed this aspect of punishment. Respect for human dignity especially requires the prohibition of cruel, inhuman, and degrading punishments. [The state] cannot turn the offender into an object of crime prevention to the detriment of his constitutionally protected right to social worth and respect.[89]

That capital punishment constitutes a serious impairment of human dignity has also been recognized by judgments of the Canadian Supreme Court. *Kindler* v. *Canada*[90] was concerned with the extradition from Canada to the United States of two fugitives, Kindler, who had been convicted of murder and sentenced to death in the United States, and Ng, who was facing a murder charge there and a possible death sentence. Three of the seven judges who heard the cases expressed the opinion that the death penalty was cruel and unusual:

> It is the supreme indignity to the individual, the ultimate corporal punishment, the final and complete lobotomy and the absolute and irrevocable castration. [It is] the ultimate desecration of human dignity.[91]

Three other judges were of the opinion that:

> [t]here is strong ground for believing, having regard to the limited extent to which the death penalty advances any valid penological objectives and the serious invasion of human dignity it engenders, that the death penalty cannot, except in exceptional circumstances, be justified in this country.[92]

In the result, however, the majority of the Court held that the validity of the order for extradition did not depend upon the constitutionality of the death penalty in Canada, or the guarantee in its Charter of Rights against cruel and unusual punishment. The Charter was concerned with legislative and executive acts carried out in Canada, and an order for extradition neither imposed nor authorized any punishment within the borders of Canada.

The issue in *Kindler's case* was whether the action of the Minister of Justice, who had authorized the extradition without any assurance that the death penalty would not be imposed, was constitutional. It was argued that this executive act was contrary to section 12 of the Charter which requires the executive to act in accordance with fundamental principles of justice. The Court decided by a majority of four to three that in the particular circumstances of the case the decision of the Minister of Justice could not be set aside on these grounds. In balancing the international obligations of Canada in respect of extradition, and another purpose of the extradition legislation—to prevent Canada from becoming a safe haven for criminals, against the likelihood that the fugitives would be executed if returned to the United States, the view of the majority was that the decision to return the fugitives to the United States could not be said to be contrary to the fundamental principles of justice. In their view, it would not shock the conscience of Canadians to permit this to be done.

The International Covenant on Civil and Political Rights

Ng and Kindler took their cases to the Human Rights Committee of the United Nations, contending that Canada had breached its obligations under the *International Covenant on Civil and Political Rights*. Once again, there was a division of opinion within the tribunal. In *Ng's case* it was said:

> The Committee is aware that, by definition, every execution of a sentence of death may be considered to constitute cruel and inhuman treatment within the meaning of article 7 of the covenant.[93]

There was no dissent from that statement. But the *International Covenant* contains provisions permitting, with some qualifications, the imposition of capital punishment for the most serious crimes. In view of these provisions, the majority of the Committee were of the opinion that the extradition of fugitives to a country which enforces the death sentence in accordance with the requirements of the *International Covenant*, should not be regarded as a breach of the obligations of the extraditing country. In *Ng's case*, the method of execution which he faced if extradited was asphyxiation in a gas chamber. This was found by a majority of the Committee to involve unnecessary physical and mental suffering and, notwithstanding the sanction given to capital punishment, to be cruel punishment within the meaning of article 7 of the *International Covenant*. In *Kindler's case*, in which the complaint was delivered at the same time as that in the *Ng's case*, but the decision was given earlier, it was held that the method of execution which was by lethal injection was not a cruel method of ex-

ecution, and that the extradition did not in the circumstances constitute a breach of Canada's obligations under the *International
Covenant.*[94]

The Committee also held in *Kindler's case* that prolonged judicial
proceedings giving rise to the death row phenomenon does not *per se*
constitute cruel, inhuman or degrading treatment. There were dis-
sents in both cases. Some Commissioners in *Ng's case* held that asphyxiation was not crueller than other forms of execution. Some in
Kindler's case held that the provision of the International Covenant
against the arbitrary deprivation of the right to life took priority over
the provisions of the *International Covenant* which allow the death
sentence, and that Canada ought not in the circumstances to have
extradited Kindler without an assurance that he would not be executed.

It should be mentioned here that although articles 6(2) to (5) of
the *International Covenant* specifically allow the imposition of the
death sentence under strict controls "for the most serious crimes" by
those countries which have not abolished it, it provides in article 6(6)
that "[n]othing in this article shall be invoked to delay or to prevent
the abolition of capital punishment by any State Party to the present
Covenant". The fact that the International Covenant sanctions capital punishment must be seen in this context. It tolerates but does not
provide justification for the death penalty.

Despite these differences of opinion, what is clear from the decisions of the Human Rights Committee of the United Nations is that
the death penalty is regarded by it as cruel and inhuman punishment
within the ordinary meaning of those words, and that it was because
of the specific provisions of the *International Covenant* authorizing
the imposition of capital punishment by member States in certain
circumstances, that the words had to be given a narrow meaning.

The European Convention on Human Rights

Similar issues were debated by the European Court of Human
Rights in *Soering* v. *United Kingdom.*[95] This case was also concerned
with the extradition to the United States of a fugitive to face murder
charges for which capital punishment was a competent sentence. It
was argued that this would expose him to inhuman and degrading

treatment or punishment in breach of article 3 of the *European Convention on Human Rights*. Article 2 of the *European Convention* protects the right to life but makes an exception in the case of "the execution of a sentence of a court following [the] conviction of a crime for which this penalty is provided by law". The majority of the Court held that article 3 could not be construed as prohibiting all capital punishment, since to do so would nullify article 2. It was, however, competent to test the imposition of capital punishment in particular cases against the requirements of article 3—the manner in which it is imposed or executed, the personal circumstances of the condemned person and the disproportionality to the gravity of the crime committed, as well as the conditions of detention awaiting execution, were capable of bringing the treatment or punishment received by the condemned person within the proscription.

On the facts, it was held that extradition to the United States to face trial in Virginia would expose the fugitive to the risk of treatment going beyond the threshold set by article 3. The special factors taken into account were the youth of the fugitive (he was 18 at the time of the murders), an impaired mental capacity, and the suffering on death row which could endure for up to eight years if he were convicted. Additionally, although the offense for which extradition was sought had been committed in the United States, the fugitive who was a German national was also liable to be tried for the same offense in Germany. Germany, which has abolished the death sentence, also sought his extradition for the murders. There was accordingly a choice in regard to the country to which the fugitive should be extradited, and that choice should have been exercised in a way which would not lead to a contravention of article 3. What weighed with the Court was the fact that the choice facing the United Kingdom was not a choice between extradition to face a possible death penalty and no punishment, but a choice between extradition to a country which allows the death penalty and one which does not. We are in a comparable position. A holding by us that the death penalty for murder is unconstitutional, does not involve a choice between freedom and death; it involves a choice between death in the very few cases which would otherwise attract that penalty under section 277(1)(a), and the severe penalty of life imprisonment.

Capital Punishment in India

In the amicus brief of the South African Police, reliance was placed on decisions of the Indian Supreme Court, and it is necessary to refer briefly to the way the law has developed in that country.

Section 302 of the Indian *Penal Code* authorizes the imposition of the death sentence as a penalty for murder. In *Bachan Singh* v. *State of Punjab,*[96] the constitutionality of this provision was put in issue. Article 21 of the Indian *Constitution* provides that:

> No person shall be deprived of his life or personal liberty except according to procedure established by law.

The wording of this article presented an obstacle to a challenge to the death sentence, because there was a "law" which made provision for the death sentence. Moreover, article 72 of the *Constitution* empowers the President and Governors to commute sentences of death, and article 134 refers to the Supreme Court's powers on appeal in cases where the death sentence has been imposed. It was clear, therefore, that capital punishment was specifically contemplated and sanctioned by the framers of the Indian *Constitution*, when it was adopted by them in November 1949.[97]

Counsel for the accused in *Bachan Singh's case* sought to overcome this difficulty by contending that article 21 had to be read with article 19(1), which guarantees the freedoms of speech, of assembly, of association, of movement, of residence, and the freedom to engage in any occupation. These fundamental freedoms can only be restricted under the Indian Constitution if the restrictions are reasonable for the attainment of a number of purposes defined in sections 19(2) to (6). It was contended that the right to life was basic to the enjoyment of these fundamental freedoms, and that the death sentence restricted them unreasonably in that it served no social purpose, its deterrent effect was unproven and it defiled the dignity of the individual.

The Supreme Court analyzed the provisions of article 19(1) and came to the conclusion, for reasons that are not material to the present case, that the provisions of section 302 of the Indian *Penal Code* did "not have to stand the test of article 19(1) of the Constitution."[98]

It went on, however, to consider "arguendo" what the outcome would be if the test of reasonableness and public interest under article 19(1) had to be satisfied.

The Supreme Court had recognized in a number of cases that the death sentence served as a deterrent, and the Law Commission of India, which had conducted an investigation into capital punishment in 1967, had recommended that capital punishment be retained. The court held that in the circumstances it was "for the petitioners to prove and establish that the death sentence for murder is so outmoded, unusual or excessive as to be devoid of any rational nexus with the purpose and object of the legislation."[99]

The Court then dealt with international authorities for and against the death sentence, and with the arguments concerning deterrence and retribution.[100] After reviewing the arguments for and against the death sentence, the court concluded that:

> ... the question whether or not [the] death penalty serves any penological purpose is a difficult, complex and intractable issue [which] has evoked strong, divergent views. For the purpose of testing the constitutionality of the impugned provisions as to death penalty ... on the grounds of reasonableness in the light of Articles 19 and 21 of the Constitution, it is not necessary for us to express any categorical opinion, one way or another, as to which of these antithetical views, held by the Abolitionists and the Retentionists, is correct. It is sufficient to say that the very fact that persons of reason, learning and light are rationally and deeply divided in their opinion on this issue, is ground among others, for rejecting the petitioners' argument that retention of death penalty in the impugned provision, is totally devoid of reason and purpose.[101]

It accordingly held that section 302 of the Indian *Penal Code* "violates neither the letter nor the ethos of Article 19."[102]

The Court then went on to deal with article 21. It said that if article 21 were to be expanded in accordance with the interpretative principle applicable to legislation limiting rights under Article 19(1), article 21 would have to be read as follows:

> No person shall be deprived of his life or personal liberty except according to fair, just and reasonable procedure established by a valid law.

And thus expanded, it was clear that the State could deprive a person of his or her life, by "fair, just and reasonable procedure." In the circumstances, and taking into account the indications that capital punishment was considered by the framers of the constitution in 1949 to be a valid penalty, it was asserted that "by no stretch of the imagination can it be said that death penalty . . . either *per se* or because of its execution by hanging constitutes an unreasonable, cruel or unusual punishment" prohibited by the *Constitution*.[103]

The wording of the relevant provisions of our *Constitution* are different. The question we have to consider is not whether the imposition of the death sentence for murder is "totally devoid of reason and purpose," or whether the death sentence for murder "is devoid of any rational nexus" with the purpose and object of section 277(1)(a) of the *Criminal Procedure Act*. It is whether in the context of our *Constitution*, the death penalty is cruel, inhuman or degrading, and if it is, whether it can be justified in terms of section 33.

The Indian *Penal Code* leaves the imposition of the death sentence to the trial judge's discretion. In *Bachan Singh's case* there was also a challenge to the constitutionality of the legislation on the grounds of arbitrariness, along the lines of the challenges that have been successful in the United States. The majority of the Court rejected the argument that the imposition of the death sentence in such circumstances is arbitrary, holding that a discretion exercised judicially by persons of experience and standing, in accordance with principles crystallized by judicial decisions, is not an arbitrary discretion.[104] To complete the picture, it should be mentioned that long delays in carrying out the death sentence in particular cases have apparently been held in India to be unjust and unfair to the prisoner, and in such circumstances the death sentence is liable to be set aside.[105]

The Right to Life

The unqualified right to life vested in every person by section 9 of our *Constitution* is another factor crucially relevant to the question whether the death sentence is cruel, inhuman or degrading punishment within the meaning of section 11(2) of our *Constitution*. In this respect our *Constitution* differs materially from the Constitutions of the United States and India. It also differs materially from the *European Convention* and the *International Covenant.* Yet in the cases decided under these constitutions and treaties there were judges who dissented and held that notwithstanding the specific language of the constitution or instrument concerned, capital punishment should not be permitted.

In some instances the dissent focused on the right to life. In *Soering's case* before the European Court of Human Rights, Judge de Meyer, in a concurring opinion, said that capital punishment is "not consistent with the present state of European civilization"[106] and for that reason alone, extradition to the United States would violate the fugitive's right to life.

In a dissent in the United Nations Human Rights Committee in *Kindler's case,* Committee member B. Wennergren also stressed the importance of the right to life.

> The value of life is immeasurable for any human being, and the right to life enshrined in article 6 of the Covenant is the supreme human right. It is an obligation of States [P]arties to the Covenant to protect the lives of all human beings on their territory and under their jurisdiction. If issues arise in respect of the protection of the right to life, priority must not be accorded to the domestic laws of other countries or to (bilateral) treaty articles. Discretion of any nature permitted under an extradition treaty cannot apply, as there is no room for it under Covenant obligations. It is worth repeating that no derogation from a State's obligations under article 6, paragraph 1, is permitted. This is why Canada, in my view, violated article 6, paragraph 1, by consenting to extradite Mr. Kindler to the United States, without having secured assurances that Mr. Kindler would not be subjected to the execution of the death sentence.[107]

An individual's right to life has been described as "[t]he most fundamental of all human rights,"[108] and was dealt with in that way in the judgments of the Hungarian Constitutional Court declaring capital punishment to be unconstitutional.[109] The challenge to the death sentence in Hungary was based on section 54 of its *Constitution* which provides:

(1) In the Republic of Hungary everyone has the inherent right to

life and to human dignity, and no one shall be arbitrarily deprived of these rights.

(2) No one shall be subjected to torture or to cruel or inhuman or degrading punishment.

Section 8, the counterpart of section 33 of our *Constitution*, provides that laws shall not impose any limitations on the essential content of fundamental rights. According to the finding of the Court, capital punishment imposed a limitation on the essential content of the fundamental rights to life and human dignity, eliminating them irretrievably. As such it was unconstitutional. Two factors are stressed in the judgment of the Court. First, the relationship between the rights of life and dignity, and the importance of these rights taken together. Secondly, the absolute nature of these two rights taken together. Together they are the source of all other rights. Other rights may be limited, and may even be withdrawn and then granted again, but their ultimate limit is to be found in the preservation of the twin rights of life and dignity. These twin rights are the essential content of all rights under the *Constitution*. Take them away, and all other rights cease. I will deal later with the requirement of our *Constitution* that a right shall not be limited in ways which negate its essential content. For the present purposes it is sufficient to point to the fact that the Hungarian Court held capital punishment to be unconstitutional on the grounds that it is inconsistent with the right to life and the right to dignity.

Our *Constitution* does not contain the qualification found in section 54(1) of the Hungarian constitution, which prohibits only the arbitrary deprivation of life. To that extent, therefore, the right to life in section 9 of our *Constitution* is given greater protection than it is by the Hungarian *Constitution*.

The fact that in both the United States and India, which sanction capital punishment, the highest courts have intervened on constitutional grounds in particular cases to prevent the carrying out of death sentences, because in the particular circumstances of such cases, it would have been cruel to do so, evidences the importance attached to the protection of life and the strict scrutiny to which the imposition and carrying out of death sentences are subjected when a constitutional challenge is raised. The same concern is apparent in the decisions of the European Court of Human Rights and the United Nations Committee on Human Rights. It led the Court in *Soering's case* to order that extradition to the United States, in the circumstances of that case, would result in inhuman or degrading punishment, and the Human Rights Committee to declare in *Ng's case* that he should not be extradited to face a possible death by asphyxiation in a gas chamber in California.

Public Opinion

The Attorney General argued that what is cruel, inhuman or degrading depends to a large extent upon contemporary attitudes within society, and that South African society does not regard the death sentence for extreme cases of murder as a cruel, inhuman or degrading form of punishment. It was disputed whether public opinion, properly informed of the different considerations, would in fact favor the death penalty. I am, however, prepared to assume that it does and that the majority of South Africans agree that the death sentence should be imposed in extreme cases of murder. The question before us, however, is not what the majority of South Africans believe a proper sentence for murder should be. It is whether the Constitution allows the sentence.

Public opinion may have some relevance to the enquiry, but in itself, it is no substitute for the duty vested in the Courts to interpret the *Constitution* and to uphold its provisions without fear or favor. If public opinion were to be decisive there would be no need for constitutional adjudication. The protection of rights could then be left to Parliament, which has a mandate from the public, and is answerable to the public for the way its mandate is exercised, but this would be a return to parliamentary sovereignty, and a retreat from the new legal order established by the 1993 *Constitution*. By the same token the issue of the constitutionality of capital punishment cannot be referred to a referendum, in which a majority view would prevail over the wishes of any minority. The very reason for establishing the new legal order, and for vesting the power of judicial review of all legislation in the courts, was to protect the rights of minorities and others who cannot protect their rights adequately through the democratic process. Those who are entitled to claim this protection include the social outcasts and marginalized people of our society. It is only if there is a willingness to protect the worst and the weakest amongst us, that all of us can be secure that our own rights will be protected.

This Court cannot allow itself to be diverted from its duty to act as an independent arbiter of the *Constitution* by making choices on the basis that they will find favor with the public.[110] Justice Powell's comment in his dissent in *Furman* v. *Georgia* bears repetition:

> . . . the weight of the evidence indicates that the public generally has not accepted either the morality or the social merit of the views so passionately advocated by the articulate spokesmen for abolition. But however one may assess amorphous ebb and flow of public opinion generally on this volatile issue, this type of inquiry lies at the periphery—not the core—of the judicial process in constitutional cases. The assessment of popular opinion is essentially a legislative, and not a judicial, function.[111]

So too does the comment of Justice Jackson in *West Virginia State Board of Education* v. *Barnette*:

> The very purpose of a Bill of Rights was to withdraw certain subjects from the vicissitudes of political controversy, to place them beyond the reach of majorities and officials and to establish them as legal principles to be applied by the courts. One's right to life, liberty, and property, to free speech, a free press, freedom of worship and assembly and other fundamental rights may not be submitted to vote; they depend on the outcome of no elections.[112]

Cruel, Inhuman and Degrading Punishment

The United Nations Committee on Human Rights has held that the death sentence by definition is cruel and degrading punishment. So has the Hungarian Constitutional Court, and three judges of the Canadian Supreme Court. The death sentence has also been held to be cruel or unusual punishment and thus unconstitutional under the state constitutions of Massachusetts and California.[113]

The California decision is *People* v. *Anderson*.[114] Capital punishment was held by six of the seven judges of the Californian Supreme

Court to be "impermissibly cruel"[115] under the California Constitution which prohibited cruel or unusual punishment. Also, it degrades and dehumanizes all who participate in its processes. It is unnecessary to any legitimate goal of the state and is incompatible with the dignity of man and the judicial process.[116]

In the Massachusetts decision in *District Attorney for the Suffolk District* v. *Watson*,[117] where the Constitution of the State of Massachusetts prohibited cruel or unusual punishment, the death sentence was also held, by six of the seven judges, to be impermissibly cruel.[118]

In both cases the disjunctive effect of "or" was referred to as enabling the Courts to declare capital punishment unconstitutional even if it was not "unusual." Under our Constitution it will not meet the requirements of section 11(2) if it is cruel, or inhuman, or degrading.

Proportionality is an ingredient to be taken into account in deciding whether a penalty is cruel, inhuman or degrading.[119] No Court would today uphold the constitutionality of a statute that makes the death sentence a competent sentence for the cutting down of trees or the killing of deer, which were capital offenses in England in the 18th Century.[120] But murder is not to be equated with such "offenses." The wilful taking of an innocent life calls for a severe penalty, and there are many countries which still retain the death penalty as a sentencing option for such cases. Disparity between the crime and the penalty is not the only ingredient of proportionality; factors such as the enormity and irredeemable character of the death sentence in circumstances where neither error nor arbitrariness can be excluded, the expense and difficulty of addressing the disparities which exist in practice between accused persons facing similar charges, and which are due to factors such as race, poverty, and ignorance, and the other subjective factors which have been mentioned, are also factors that can and should be taken into account in dealing with this issue. It may possibly be that none alone would be sufficient under our *Constitution* to justify a finding that the death sentence is cruel, inhuman or degrading. But these factors are not to be evaluated in isolation. They must be taken together, and in order to decide whether the threshold set by section 11(2) has been crossed[121] they must be evaluated with other relevant factors, including the two fundamental rights on which the accused rely, the right to dignity and the right to life.

The carrying out of the death sentence destroys life, which is protected without reservation under section 9 of our *Constitution*, it annihilates human dignity which is protected under section 10, elements of arbitrariness are present in its enforcement and it is irremediable. Taking these factors into account, as well as the assumption that I have made in regard to public opinion in South Africa, and giving the words of section 11(2) the broader meaning to which they are entitled at this stage of the enquiry, rather than a narrow meaning,[122] I am satisfied that in the context of our *Constitution* the death penalty is indeed a cruel, inhuman and degrading punishment.

Is Capital Punishment for Murder Justifiable?

The question that now has to be considered is whether the imposition of such punishment is nonetheless justifiable as a penalty for murder in the circumstances contemplated by sections 277(1)(a), 316A and 322(2A) of the *Criminal Procedure Act*.

It is difficult to conceive of any circumstances in which torture, which is specifically prohibited under section 11(2), could ever be justified. But that does not necessarily apply to capital punishment. Capital punishment, unlike torture, has not been absolutely prohibited by public international law. It is therefore not inappropriate to consider whether the death penalty is justifiable under our Constitution as a penalty for murder. This calls for an enquiry similar to that undertaken by Justice Brennan in *Furman's case*[123] in dealing with the contention that "death is a necessary punishment because it prevents the commission of capital crimes more effectively than any less severe punishment."[124] The same question is addressed and answered in the negative in the judgment of Chief Justice Wright in *People v. Anderson*.[125] Under the United States *Constitution* and the Californian *Constitution*, which have no limitation clauses, this enquiry had to be conducted within the larger question of the definition of the right. With us, however, the question has to be dealt with under section 33(1).

Section 33(1) of the *Constitution* provides, in part, that:

> The rights entrenched in this Chapter may be limited by law of general application, provided that such limitation—(a) shall be permissible only to the extent that it is—(i) reasonable; and (ii) justifiable in

an open and democratic society based on freedom and equality; and (b) shall not negate the essential content of the right in question.

Section 33(1)(b) goes on to provide that the limitation of certain rights, including the rights referred to in section 10 and section 11 "shall, in addition to being reasonable as required in paragraph (a)(I), also be necessary."

The Two-Stage Approach

Our Constitution deals with the limitation of rights through a general limitations clause. As was pointed out by Acting Justice Kentridge in *Zuma's case*,[126] this calls for a "two-stage" approach, in which a broad rather than a narrow interpretation is given to the fundamental rights enshrined in Chapter Three, and limitations have to be justified through the application of section 33. In this it differs from the *Constitution* of the United States, which does not contain a limitation clause, as a result of which courts in that country have been obliged to find limits to constitutional rights through a narrow interpretation of the rights themselves. Although the "two-stage" approach may often produce the same result as the "one-stage" approach,[127] this will not always be the case.

The practical consequences of this difference in approach are evident in the present case. In *Gregg* v. *Georgia*, the conclusion reached in the judgment of the plurality was summed up as follows:

> In sum, we cannot say that the judgment of the Georgia legislature that capital punishment may be necessary in some cases is clearly wrong. Considerations of federalism, as well as respect for the ability of a legislature to evaluate, in terms of its particular state the moral consensus concerning the death penalty and its social utility as a sanction, require us to conclude in the absence of more convincing evidence, that the infliction of death as a punishment for murder is not without justification, and is thus not unconstitutionally severe.[128]

Under our *Constitution*, the position is different. It is not whether the decision of the State has been shown to be clearly wrong; it is whether the decision of the State is justifiable according to the criteria prescribed by section 33. It is not whether the infliction of death as a punishment for murder "is not without justification," it is whether the infliction of death as a punishment for murder has been shown to be both reasonable and necessary, and to be consistent with the other requirements of section 33. It is for the legislature, or the party relying on the legislation, to establish this justification, and not for the party challenging it to show that it was not justified.[129]

The Application of Section 33

The criteria prescribed by section 33(1) for any limitation of the rights contained in section 11(2) are that the limitation must be justifiable in an open and democratic society based on freedom and equality, it must be both reasonable and necessary and it must not negate the essential content of the right.

The limitation of constitutional rights for a purpose that is reasonable and necessary in a democratic society involves the weighing up of competing values, and ultimately an assessment based on proportionality.[130] This is implicit in the provisions of section 33(1). The fact that different rights have different implications for democracy, and in the case of our *Constitution*, for "an open and democratic society based on freedom and equality," means that there is no absolute standard which can be laid down for determining reasonableness and necessity. Principles can be established, but the application of those principles to particular circumstances can only be done on a case by case basis. This is inherent in the requirement of proportionality, which calls for the balancing of different interests. In the balancing process, the relevant considerations will include the nature of the right that is limited, and its importance to an open and democratic society based on freedom and equality; the purpose for which the right is limited and the importance of that purpose to such a society; the extent of the limitation, its efficacy, and particularly where the limitation has to be necessary, whether the desired ends could reasonably be achieved through other means less damaging to the right in question. In the process regard must be had to the provisions of section 33(1), and the underlying values of the *Constitution*, bearing in mind that, as a Canadian Judge has said, "the role of the Court is not to second-guess the wisdom of policy choices made by legislators."[131]

Limitation of Rights in Canada

In dealing with this aspect of the case, Mr. Trengove placed considerable reliance on the decision of the Canadian Supreme Court in *R. v. Oakes.*[132] The *Canadian Charter of Rights*, as our *Constitution* does, makes provision for the limitation of rights through a general clause. Section 1 of the *Charter* permits such reasonable limitations of *Charter* rights "as can be demonstrably justified in a free and democratic society." In *Oakes' case* it was held that in order to meet this requirement a limitation of a Charter right had to be directed to the achievement of an objective of sufficient importance to warrant the limitation of the right in question, and that there had also to be proportionality between the limitation and such objective. In a frequently-cited passage, Chief Justice Dickson described the components of proportionality as follows:

> There are, in my view, three important components of a proportionality test. First, the measures adopted must be carefully designed to achieve the objective in question. They must not be arbitrary, unfair or based on irrational considerations. In short, they must be rationally connected to the objective. Second, the means, even if rationally connected to the objective in this first sense, should impair "as little as possible" the right or freedom in question: *R. v. Big M Drug Mart Ltd.* at p. 352. Third, there must be a proportionality between the effects of the measures which are responsible for limiting the Charter right or freedom, and the objective which has been identified as of "sufficient importance."[133]

Although there is a rational connection between capital punishment and the purpose for which it is prescribed, the elements of arbitrariness, unfairness and irrationality in the imposition of the penalty, are factors that would have to be taken into account in the application of the first component of this test. As far as the second component is concerned, the fact that a severe punishment in the form of life imprisonment is available as an alternative sentence, would be relevant to the question whether the death sentence impairs the right as little as possible. And as I will show later, if all relevant considerations are taken into account, it is at least doubtful whether a sentence of capital punishment for murder would satisfy the third component of the *Oakes* test.

The second requirement of the *Oakes* test, that the limitation should impair the right "as little as possible" raises a fundamental problem of judicial review. Can, and should, an unelected court substitute its own opinion of what is reasonable or necessary for that of an elected legislature? Since the judgment in *R.* v. *Oakes*, the Canadian Supreme Court has shown that it is sensitive to this tension, which is particularly acute where choices have to be made in respect of matters of policy. In *Irwin Toy Ltd* v. *Quebec (Attorney General)*,[134] Chief Justice Dickson cautioned that courts, "must be mindful of the legislature's representative function." In *Reference re ss. 193 and 195 (1) (c) of the Criminal Code (Manitoba)*,[135] it was said that "the role of the Court is not to second-guess the wisdom of policy choices made by . . . legislators"; and in *R.* v. *Chaulk*, that the means must impair the right "as little as is reasonably possible."[136] Where choices have to be made between "differing reasonable policy options", the courts will allow the government the deference due to legislators, but "[will] not give them an unrestricted licence to disregard an individual's *Charter* rights. Where the government cannot show that it had a reasonable basis for concluding that it has complied with the requirement of minimal impairment in seeking to attain its objectives, the legislation will be struck down."[137]

Limitation of Rights in Germany

The German *Constitution* does not contain a general limitations clause but permits certain basic rights to be limited by law. According to Professor Grimm,[138] the Federal Constitutional Court allows such limitation "only in order to make conflicting rights compatible or to protect the rights of other persons or important community interests...any restriction of human rights not only needs constitutionally valid reasons but also has to be proportional to the rank and importance of the right at stake." Proportionality is central to the process followed by the Federal Constitutional Court in its adjudication upon the limitation of rights. The Court has regard to the purpose of the limiting legislation, whether the legislation is suitable for the achievement of such purpose, which brings into consideration whether it in fact achieves that purpose, is necessary therefor, and whether a proper balance has been achieved between the purpose enhanced by the limitation, and the fundamental right that has been limited.[139] The German *Constitution* also has a provision similar to section 33(1)(b) of our *Constitution*, but the Court apparently avoids making use of this provision,[140] preferring to deal with extreme limitations of rights through the proportionality test.

Limitation of Rights under the European Convention

The *European Convention* also has no general limitations clause, but makes certain rights subject to limitation according to specified criteria. The proportionality test of the European Court of Human Rights calls for a balancing of ends and means. The end must be a "pressing social need" and the means used must be proportionate to the attainment of such an end. The limitation of certain rights is conditioned upon the limitation being "necessary in a democratic society" for purposes defined in the relevant provisions of the *Convention*. The national authorities are allowed a discretion by the European Court of Human Rights in regard to what is necessary—a margin of appreciation—but not unlimited power. The "margin of appreciation" that is allowed varies depending upon the nature of the right and the nature and ambit of the restriction. A balance has to be achieved between the general interest, and the interest of the individual.[141] Where the limitation is to a right fundamental to democratic society, a higher standard of justification is required[142]; so too, where a law interferes with the "intimate aspects of private life."[143] On the other hand, in areas such as morals or social policy greater scope is allowed to the national authorities.[144] The jurisprudence of the European Court of Human Rights provides some guidance as to what may be considered necessary in a democratic society, but the margin of appreciation allowed to national authorities by the European Court must be understood as finding its place in an international agreement which has to accommodate the sovereignty of the member states. It is not necessarily a safe guide as to what would be appropriate under section 33 of our *Constitution*.

Is Capital Punishment for Murder Justifiable under the South African Constitution?

In *Zuma's case*, Acting Justice Kentridge pointed out that the criteria developed by the Canadian courts for the interpretation of section 1 of the *Canadian Charter of Rights* may be of assistance to our Courts, but that there are differences between our *Constitution* and the Canadian *Charter* which have a bearing on the way in which section 33 should be dealt with. This is equally true of the criteria developed by other courts, such as the German Constitutional Court and the European Court of Human Rights. Like Acting Justice Kentridge, "I see no reason in this case . . . to attempt to fit our analysis into the Canadian pattern,"[145] or for that matter to fit it into the pattern followed by any of the other courts to which reference has been made. Section 33 prescribes in specific terms the criteria to be applied for the limitation of different categories of rights and it is in the light of these criteria that the death sentence for murder has to be justified.

"Every person" is entitled to claim the protection of the rights enshrined in Chapter Three, and "no" person shall be denied the protection that they offer. Respect for life and dignity which are at the heart of section 11(2) are values of the highest order under our *Constitution*. The carrying out of the death penalty would destroy these and all other rights that the convicted person has, and a clear and convincing case must be made out to justify such action.

The Attorney General contended that the imposition of the death penalty for murder in the most serious cases could be justified according to the prescribed criteria. The argument went as follows. The death sentence meets the sentencing requirements for extreme cases of murder more effectively than any other sentence can do. It has a greater deterrent effect than life imprisonment; it ensures that the worst murderers will not endanger the lives of prisoners and warders who would be at risk if the "worst of the murderers" were to be imprisoned and not executed; and it also meets the need for retribution which is demanded by society as a response to the high level of crime. In the circumstances presently prevailing in the country, it is therefore a necessary component of the criminal justice system. This, he said, is recognized by the Appellate Division, which only confirms a death sentence if it is convinced that no other sentence would be a proper sentence.[146]

The Judgments of the Appellate Division

The decisions of the Appellate Division to which the Attorney General referred are only of limited relevance to the questions that have to be decided in the present case. The law which the Appellate Division has applied prescribes that the death sentence is a competent sentence for murder in a proper case. The Appellate Division has reserved this sentence for extreme cases in which the maximum punishment would be the appropriate punishment. Were it to have done otherwise, and to have refused to pass death sentences, it would in effect have been saying that the death sentence is never a proper sentence, and that section 277(1)(a) should not be enforced. This was not within its competence. The criteria set by the Appellate Division for the passing of a death sentence for murder are relevant to the argument on arbitrariness, and also provide a basis for testing the justifiability of such a penalty. They do not, however, do more than that.

The Judgment of the Tanzanian Court of Appeal

There is support for part of the Attorney General's argument in the judgment of the Tanzanian Court of Appeal in *Mbushuu and Another v. The Republic*.[147] It was held in this case that the death sentence amounted to cruel and degrading punishment, which is prohibited under the Tanzanian *Constitution*, but that despite this finding, it was not unconstitutional. The *Constitution* authorized derogations to be made from basic rights for legitimate purposes, and a derogation was lawful if it was not arbitrary, and was reasonably necessary for such purpose. The legitimate purposes to which the death sentence was directed was a constitutional requirement that "everyone's right to life shall be protected by law." The death sentence was a mandatory penalty for murder, but it was not considered by the Court to be arbitrary because decisions as to guilt or innocence are taken by judges. There was no proof one way or the other that the death sentence was necessarily a more effective punishment than a long period of imprisonment. In the view of the Court, however, it was for society and not the courts to decide whether the death sentence was a necessary punishment. The Court was satisfied that society favored the death sentence, and that in the circumstances "the reasonable and necessary" standard had been met. Accordingly, it held that the death sentence was a lawful derogation from the prohibition of cruel and degrading punishment, and thus valid.

The approach of the Tanzanian Court of Appeal to issues concerning the limitation of basic rights seems to have been influenced by the language of the Tanzanian *Constitution*,[148] and rules of interpretation developed by the Courts to deal with that language. The relevant provisions of our *Constitution* are different and the correct approach to the interpretation of the limitations clause must be found in the language of section 33 construed in the context of the *Constitution* as a whole. It is for the Court, and not society or Parliament, to decide whether the death sentence is justifiable under the provisions of section 33 of our *Constitution*.[149] In doing so we can have regard to societal attitudes in evaluating whether the legislation is reasonable and necessary, but ultimately the decision must be ours. If the decision of the Tanzanian Court of Appeal is inconsistent with this conclusion, I must express my disagreement with it.

Deterrence

The Attorney General attached considerable weight to the need for a deterrent to violent crime. He argued that the countries which had abolished the death penalty were on the whole developed and peaceful countries in which other penalties might be sufficient deterrents. We had not reached that stage of development, he said. If in years to come we did so, we could do away with the death penalty. Parliament could decide when that time has come. At present, however, so the argument went, the death sentence is an indispensable weapon if we are serious about combatting violent crime.

The need for a strong deterrent to violent crime is an end the validity of which is not open to question. The state is clearly entitled, indeed obliged, to take action to protect human life against violation by others. In all societies there are laws which regulate the behavior of people and which authorize the imposition of civil or criminal sanctions on those who act unlawfully. This is necessary for the preservation and protection of society. Without law, society cannot exist. Without law, individuals in society have no rights. The level of violent crime in our country has reached alarming proportions. It poses a threat to the transition to democracy, and the creation of development opportunities for all, which are primary goals of the *Constitution*. The high level of violent crime is a matter of common knowledge and is amply borne out by the statistics provided by the Commissioner of Police in his amicus brief. The power of the State to impose sanctions on those who break the law cannot be doubted. It is of fundamental importance to the future of our country that respect for the law should be restored, and that dangerous criminals should be apprehended and dealt with firmly. Nothing in this judgment should be understood as detracting in any way from that proposition. But the question is not whether criminals should go free and be allowed to escape the consequences of their anti-social behavior. Clearly they should not; and equally clearly those who engage in violent crime should be met with the full rigor of the law. The question is whether the death sentence for murder can legitimately be made part of that law. And this depends on whether it meets the criteria prescribed by section 33(1).

The Attorney General pointed to the substantial increase in the incidence of violent crime over the past five years during which the death sentence has not been enforced. He contended that this supported his argument that imprisonment is not a sufficient deterrent, and that we have not yet reached the stage of development where we can do without the death sentence. Throughout this period, however, the death sentence remained a lawful punishment, and was in fact imposed by the courts although the sentences were not carried out.[150] The moratorium was only announced formally on 27 March 1992.[151] A decision could have been taken at any time to terminate the moratorium on executions, and none of the criminals had any assurance that the moratorium would still be in place if they were to be caught, brought to trial, convicted and sentenced to death.

The cause of the high incidence of violent crime cannot simply be attributed to the failure to carry out the death sentences imposed by the courts. The upsurge in violent crime came at a time of great social change associated with political turmoil and conflict, particularly during the period 1990 to 1994. It is facile to attribute the increase in violent crime during this period to the moratorium on executions.[152] It was a progression that started before the moratorium was announced. There are many factors that have to be taken into account in looking for the cause of this phenomenon. It is a matter of common knowledge that the political conflict during this period, particularly in Natal and the Witwatersrand, resulted in violence and destruction of a kind not previously experienced. No-go areas, random killings on trains, attacks and counter attacks upon political opponents, created a violent and unstable environment, manipulated by political dissidents and criminal elements alike.

Homelessness, unemployment, poverty and the frustration consequent upon such conditions are other causes of the crime wave. And there is also the important factor that the police and prosecuting authorities have been unable to cope with this. The statistics presented in the police amicus brief show that most violent crime is not solved, and the Attorney General confirmed that the risk of a criminal being apprehended and convicted for such offenses is somewhere between 30 and 40 percent. Throughout the period referred to by the Attorney General the death sentence remained on the statute book and was imposed on convicted murderers when the Courts considered it appropriate to do so.

We would be deluding ourselves if we were to believe that the execution of the few persons sentenced to death during this period, and of a comparatively few other people each year from now onwards will provide the solution to the unacceptably high rate of crime. There will always be unstable, desperate, and pathological people for whom the risk of arrest and imprisonment provides no deterrent, but there is nothing to show that a decision to carry out the death sentence would have any impact on the behavior of such people, or that there will be more of them if imprisonment is the only sanction. No information was placed before us by the Attorney General in regard to the rising crime rate other than the bare statistics, and they alone prove nothing, other than that we are living in a violent society in which most crime goes unpunished—something that we all know.

The greatest deterrent to crime is the likelihood that offenders will be apprehended, convicted and punished. It is that which is presently lacking in our criminal justice system; and it is at this level and through addressing the causes of crime that the State must seek to combat lawlessness.

In the debate as to the deterrent effect of the death sentence, the issue is sometimes dealt with as if the choice to be made is between the death sentence and the murder going unpunished. That is of course not so. The choice to be made is between putting the criminal to death and subjecting the criminal to the severe punishment of a long term of imprisonment which, in an appropriate case, could be a sentence of life imprisonment.[153] Both are deterrents, and the question is whether the possibility of being sentenced to death, rather than being sentenced to life imprisonment, has a marginally greater deterrent effect, and whether the *Constitution* sanctions the limitation of rights affected thereby.

In the course of his argument the Attorney General contended that if sentences imposed by the Courts on convicted criminals are too lenient, the law will be brought into disrepute, and members of society will then take the law into their own hands. Law is brought into disrepute if the justice system is ineffective and criminals are not punished. But if the justice system is effective and criminals are apprehended, brought to trial and in serious cases subjected to severe sentences, the law will not fall into disrepute. We have made the commitment to "a future founded on the recognition of human rights, democracy and peaceful co-existence . . . for all South Africans."[154] Respect for life and dignity lies at the heart of that commitment. One of the reasons for the prohibition of capital punishment is "that allowing the State to kill will cheapen the value of human life and thus [through not doing so] the State will serve in a sense as a role model for individuals in society."[155] Our country needs such role models.

The Attorney General also contended that if even one innocent life should be saved by the execution of perpetrators of vile murders, this would provide sufficient justification for the death penalty.[156] The hypothesis that innocent lives might be saved must be weighed against the values underlying the *Constitution*, and the ability of the State to serve "as a role model." In the long run more lives may be saved through the inculcation of a rights culture, than through the execution of murderers.

The death sentence has been reserved for the most extreme cases, and the overwhelming majority of convicted murderers are not and, since extenuating circumstances became a relevant factor sixty years ago, have not been sentenced to death in South Africa. I referred earlier to the figures provided by the Attorney General which show that between the amendment of the *Criminal Procedure Act* in 1990, and January 1995, which is the date of his written argument in the present case, 243 death sentences were imposed, of which 143 were confirmed by the Appellate Division. Yet, according to statistics placed before us by the Commissioner of Police and the Attorney General, there were on average approximately 20,000 murders committed, and 9,000 murder cases brought to trial, each year during this period. Would the carrying out of the death sentence on these 143 persons have deterred the other murderers or saved any lives?

It was accepted by the Attorney General that this is a much disputed issue in the literature on the death sentence. He contended that it is common sense that the most feared penalty will provide the greatest deterrent, but accepted that there is no proof that the death sentence is in fact a greater deterrent than life imprisonment for a long period. It is, he said, a proposition that is not capable of proof, because one never knows about those who have been deterred; we know only about those who have not been deterred, and who have committed terrible crimes. This is no doubt true, and the fact that there is no proof that the death sentence is a greater deterrent than imprisonment does not necessarily mean that the requirements of section 33 cannot be met. It is, however, a major obstacle in the way of the Attorney General's argument, for he has to satisfy us that the penalty is reasonable and necessary, and the doubt which exists in regard to the deterrent effect of the sentence must weigh heavily against his argument. "A punishment as extreme and as irrevocable as death cannot be predicated upon speculation as to what the deterrent effect might be. . . ."[157] I should add that this obstacle would not be removed by the implementation of a suggestion in one of the amicus briefs, that section 277(1) of the *Criminal Procedure Act* should be made more specific, and should identify the extreme categories of murder for which the death sentence would be a permissible punishment.

Prevention

Prevention is another object of punishment. The death sentence ensures that the criminal will never again commit murders, but it is not the only way of doing so, and life imprisonment also serves this purpose. Although there are cases of gaol murders, imprisonment is regarded as sufficient for the purpose of prevention in the overwhelming number of cases in which there are murder convictions, and there is nothing to suggest that it is necessary for this purpose in the few cases in which death sentences are imposed.

Retribution

Retribution is one of the objects of punishment, but it carries less weight than deterrence.[158] The righteous anger of family and friends of the murder victim, reinforced by the public abhorrence of vile crimes, is easily translated into a call for vengeance. But capital punishment is not the only way that society has of expressing its moral outrage at the crime that has been committed. We have long outgrown the literal application of the biblical injunction of "an eye for an eye, and a tooth for a tooth." Punishment must to some extent be commensurate with the offense, but there is no requirement that it be equivalent or identical to it. The state does not put out the eyes of a person who has blinded another in a vicious assault, nor does it punish a rapist, by castrating him and submitting him to the utmost humiliation in gaol. The state does not need to engage in the cold and calculated killing of murderers in order to express moral outrage at their conduct. A very long prison sentence is also a way of expressing outrage and visiting retribution upon the criminal.

Retribution ought not to be given undue weight in the balancing process. The *Constitution* is premised on the assumption that ours will be a constitutional state founded on the recognition of human rights.[159] The concluding provision on National Unity and Reconciliation contains the following commitment:

> The adoption of this Constitution lays the secure foundation for the people of South Africa to transcend the divisions and strife of the past, which generated gross violations of human rights, the transgression of humanitarian principles in violent conflicts and a legacy of hatred, fear, guilt and *revenge*.
>
> These can now be addressed on the basis that there is a need for understanding but *not for vengeance*, a need for reparation but *not for retaliation*, a need for *ubuntu* but *not for victimization*. (Emphasis supplied)

Although this commitment has its primary application in the field of political reconciliation, it is not without relevance to the enquiry we are called upon to undertake in the present case. To be consistent with the value of ubuntu ours should be a society that "wishes to prevent crime . . . [not] to kill criminals simply to get even with them."[160]

The Essential Content of the Right

Section 33(1)(b) provides that a limitation shall not negate the essential content of the right. There is uncertainty in the literature concerning the meaning of this provision. It seems to have entered constitutional law through the provisions of the German *Constitution*, and in addition to the South African *Constitution*, appears, though not precisely in the same form, in the constitutions of Namibia, Hungary, and possibly other countries as well. The difficulty of interpretation arises from the uncertainty as to what the "essential content" of a right is, and how it is to be determined. Should this be determined subjectively from the point of view of the individual affected by the invasion of the right, or objectively, from the point of view of the nature of the right and its place in the constitutional order, or possibly in some other way? Professor Currie draws attention to the large number of theories which have been propounded by German scholars as to how the "essence" of a right should be discerned and how the constitutional provision should be applied.[161] The German

Federal Constitutional Court has apparently avoided to a large extent having to deal with this issue by subsuming the enquiry into the proportionality test that it applies and the precise scope and meaning of the provision is controversial.[162]

If the essential content of the right not to be subjected to cruel, inhuman or degrading punishment is to be found in respect for life and dignity, the death sentence for murder, if viewed subjectively from the point of view of the convicted prisoner, clearly negates the essential content of the right. But if it is viewed objectively from the point of view of a constitutional norm that requires life and dignity to be protected, the punishment does not necessarily negate the essential content of the right. It has been argued before this Court that one of the purposes of such punishment is to protect the life and hence the dignity of innocent members of the public, and if it in fact does so, the punishment will not negate the constitutional norm. On this analysis it would, however, have to be shown that the punishment serves its intended purpose. This would involve a consideration of the deterrent and preventative effects of the punishment and whether they add anything to the alternative of life imprisonment. If they do not, they cannot be said to serve a life protecting purpose. If the negation is viewed both objectively and subjectively, the ostensible purpose of the punishment would have to be weighed against the destruction of the individual's life. For the purpose of that analysis the element of retribution would have to be excluded and the "life saving" quality of the punishment would have to be established.

It is, however, not necessary to solve this problem in the present case. At the very least the provision evinces concern that, under the guise of limitation, rights should not be taken away altogether. It was presumably the same concern that influenced Chief Justice Dickson to say in *R. v. Oakes* that rights should be limited "as little as possible,"[163] and the German Constitutional Court to hold in the life imprisonment case that all possibility of parole ought not to be excluded.[164]

The Balancing Process

In the balancing process, deterrence, prevention and retribution must be weighed against the alternative punishments available to the state, and the factors which taken together make capital punishment cruel, inhuman and degrading: the destruction of life, the annihilation of dignity, the elements of arbitrariness, inequality and the possibility of error in the enforcement of the penalty.

The Attorney General argued that the right to life and the right to human dignity were not absolute concepts. Like all rights they have their limits. One of those limits is that a person who murders in circumstances where the death penalty is permitted by section 277, forfeits his or her right to claim protection of life and dignity. He sought to support this argument by reference to the principles of self-defense. If the law recognizes the right to take the life of a wrongdoer in a situation in which self-defense is justified, then, in order to deter others, and to ensure that the wrongdoer does not again kill an innocent person, why should it not recognize the power of the state to take the life of a convicted murderer? Conversely, if the death sentence negates the essential content of the right to life, how can the taking of the life of another person in self-defense, or even to protect the State itself during war or rebellion, ever be justified.

This argument is fallacious. The rights vested in every person by Chapter Three of the *Constitution* are subject to limitation under section 33. In times of emergency, some may be suspended in accordance with the provisions of section 34 of the *Constitution*.[165] But subject to this, the rights vest in every person, including criminals convicted of vile crimes. Such criminals do not forfeit their rights under the *Constitution* and are entitled, as all in our country now are, to assert these rights, including the right to life, the right to dignity and the right not to be subjected to cruel, inhuman or degrading punishment. Whether or not a particular punishment is inconsistent with these rights depends upon an interpretation of the relevant provisions of the *Constitution*, and not upon a moral judgment that a murderer should not be allowed to claim them.

Self-defense is recognized by all legal systems. Where a choice has to be made between the lives of two or more people, the life of the innocent is given preference over the life of the aggressor. This is consistent with section 33(1). To deny the innocent person the right to act in self-defense would deny to that individual his or her right to life. The same is true where lethal force is used against a hostage taker who threatens the life of the hostage. It is permissible to kill the hostage taker to save the life of the innocent hostage. But only if the hostage is in real danger. The law solves problems such as these through the doctrine of proportionality, balancing the rights of the aggressor against the rights of the victim, and favoring the life or lives of innocents over the life or lives of the guilty.[166] But there are strict limits to the taking of life, even in the circumstances that have been described, and the law insists upon these limits being adhered to. In any event, there are material respects in which killing in self-defense or necessity differ from the execution of a criminal by the State. Self-defense takes place at the time of the threat to the victim's life, at the moment of the emergency which gave rise to the necessity and, traditionally, under circumstances in which no less-severe alternative is readily available to the potential victim. Killing by the State takes place long after the crime was committed, at a time when there is no emergency and under circumstances which permit the careful consideration of alternative punishment.

The examples of war and rebellion are also not true analogies. War and rebellion are special cases which must be dealt with in terms of the legal principles governing such situations. It is implicit in any constitutional order that the State can act to put down rebellion and to protect itself against external aggression. Where it is necessary in the pursuit of such ends to kill in the heat of battle the taking of life is sanctioned under the *Constitution* by necessary implication, and as such, is permissible in terms of section 4(1).[167] But here also there are limits. Thus prisoners of war who have been captured and who are no longer a threat to the State cannot be put to death; nor can lethal force be used against rebels when it is not necessary to do so for the purposes of putting down the rebellion.

The case of a police officer shooting at an escaping criminal was also raised in argument. This is permitted under section 49(2) of the *Criminal Procedure Act* as a last resort if it is not possible to arrest the criminal in the ordinary way. Once again, there are limits. It would not, for instance, be permissible to shoot at point blank range at a criminal who has turned his or her back upon a police officer in order to abscond, when other methods of subduing and arresting the criminal are possible. We are not concerned here with the validity of section 49(2) of the *Criminal Procedure Act*, and I specifically refrain from expressing any view thereon. Greater restriction on the use of lethal force may be one of the consequences of the establishment of a constitutional state which respects every person's right to life. Shooting at a fleeing criminal in the heat of the moment, is not necessarily to be equated with the execution of a captured criminal. But, if one of the consequences of this judgment might be to render the provisions of section 49(2) unconstitutional, the legislature will have to modify the provisions of the section in order to bring it into line with the *Constitution*. In any event, the constitutionality of the death sentence for murder does not depend upon whether it is permissible for life to be taken in other circumstances currently sanctioned by law. It depends upon whether it is justifiable as a penalty in terms of section 33 of the *Constitution*. In deciding this question, the fact that the person sentenced to death is denied his or her right to life is of the greatest importance.

The Attorney General argued that all punishment involves an impairment of dignity. Imprisonment, which is the alternative to the death sentence, severely limits a prisoner's fundamental rights and freedoms. There is only the barest freedom of movement or of residence in prison, and other basic rights such as freedom of expression and freedom of assembly are severely curtailed.

Dignity is inevitably impaired by imprisonment or any other punishment, and the undoubted power of the state to impose punishment as part of the criminal justice system, necessarily involves the power to encroach upon a prisoner's dignity. But a prisoner does not lose all his or her rights on entering prison.

> [Prisoners retain] those absolute natural rights relating to personality, to which every man is entitled. True [their] freedom had been greatly impaired by the legal process of imprisonment but they were entitled to demand respect for what remained. The fact that their liberty had been legally curtailed could afford no excuse for a further legal encroachment upon it. [It was] contended that the [prisoners] once in prison could claim only such rights as the Ordinance and the regulations conferred. But the directly opposite view is surely the correct one. They were entitled to all their personal rights and personal dignity not temporarily taken away by law, or necessarily inconsistent with the circumstances in which they had been placed.[168]

A prisoner is not stripped naked, bound, gagged and chained to his or her cell. The right of association with other prisoners, the right to exercise, to write and receive letters and the rights of personality referred to by Justice Innes are of vital importance to prisoners and highly valued by them precisely because they are confined, have only limited contact with the outside world, and are subject to prison discipline. Imprisonment is a severe punishment; but prisoners retain all the rights to which every person is entitled under Chapter Three subject only to limitations imposed by the prison regime that are justifiable under section 33.[169] Of these, none are more important than the section 11(2) right not to be subjected to "torture of any kind . . . nor to cruel, inhuman or degrading treatment or punishment." There is a difference between encroaching upon rights for the purpose of punishment and destroying them altogether. It is that difference with which we are concerned in the present case.

Conclusion

The rights to life and dignity are the most important of all human rights, and the source of all other personal rights in Chapter Three. By committing ourselves to a society founded on the recognition of human rights we are required to value these two rights above all others. And this must be demonstrated by the State in everything that it does, including the way it punishes criminals. This is not achieved by objectifying murderers and putting them to death to serve as an example to others in the expectation that they might possibly be deterred thereby.

In the balancing process the principal factors that have to be weighed are on the one hand the destruction of life and dignity that is a consequence of the implementation of the death sentence, the elements of arbitrariness and the possibility of error in the enforcement of capital punishment, and the existence of a severe alternative punishment (life imprisonment) and, on the other, the claim that the death sentence is a greater deterrent to murder, and will more effectively prevent its commission, than would a sentence of life imprisonment, and that there is a public demand for retributive justice to be imposed on murderers, which only the death sentence can meet.

Retribution cannot be accorded the same weight under our *Constitution* as the rights to life and dignity, which are the most important of all the rights in Chapter Three. It has not been shown that the death sentence would be materially more effective to deter or prevent murder than the alternative sentence of life imprisonment would be. Taking these factors into account, as well as the elements of arbitrariness and the possibility of error in enforcing the death penalty, the clear and convincing case that is required to justify the death sentence as a penalty for murder, has not been made out. The requirements of section 33(1) have accordingly not been satisfied, and it follows that the provisions of section 277(1)(a) of the *Criminal Procedure Act, 1977* must be held to be inconsistent with section 11(2) of the *Constitution*. In the circumstances, it is not necessary for me to consider whether the section would also be inconsistent with sections 8, 9 or 10 of the *Constitution* if they had been dealt with separately and not treated together as giving meaning to section 11(2).

Notes

34. *Furman* v. *Georgia*, 408 U.S. 238, 290 (1972) (Brennan J., concurring).

35. This has been the approach of certain of the justices of the United States Supreme Court. Thus, White J., concurring, who said in *Furman* v. *Georgia, supra* note 34, at 312, that "[T]he imposition and execution of the death penalty are obviously cruel in the dictionary sense," was one of the justices who held in *Gregg* v. *Georgia, infra* note 60, that capital punishment was not per se cruel and unusual punishment within the meaning of the Fifth and Fourteenth Amendments of the United States Constitution. Burger CJ., dissenting, refers in *Furman's case* at 379, 380, and 382 to a punishment being cruel "in the constitutional sense." See also comments by Justice Stewart, concurring in *Furman's case* at 309, ". . . the death sentences now before us are the product of a legal system that brings them, I believe, within the very core of the . . . guarantee against cruel and unusual punishments. . . . it is clear that these sentences are 'cruel' in the sense that they excessively go beyond, not in degree but in kind, the punishments that the legislatures have determined to be necessary [citing *Weems* v. *United States*, 217 U.S. 349 (1910)]. . . . death sentences [imposed arbitrarily] are cruel and unusual in the same way that being struck by lightning is cruel and unusual."

36. *Matinkinca and Another* v. *Council of State, Ciskei and Another*, 1994 (1) B.C.L.R. 17 (Ck), at 34B–D; *Qozeleni* v. *Minister of Law and Order and Another*, 1994 (1) B.C.L.R. 75(E), at 87D–E. Cf. *Kindler* v. *Canada (Minister of Justice)*, (1992) 6 C.R.R. (2d) 193, at 214.

37. The *Criminal Procedure Second Amendment Decree, 1990*, Decree No. 16 of 1990 of the Council of State of the Republic of Ciskei, 8 June 1990, as amended.

38. *S.*v. *Qeqe and Another*, 1990 (2) S.A.C.R. 654 (CkAD).

39. In the former Transkei, Bophuthatswana, and Venda the death sentence was a competent verdict for murder but the provisions of the relevant statutes in Transkei and Bophuthatswana are not identical to section 277. For the purposes of this judgment it is not necessary to analyze the differences, which relate in the main to the procedure prescribed for appeals and the powers of the court on appeal, procedures that are now subject to the provisions of section 241(1) and (1A) of the *Constitution*, as amended by the *Constitution of the Republic of South Africa Third Amendment Act No. 13 of 1994.*

40. See section 8 of the *Constitution.*

41. *AK Entertainment CC* v. *Minister of Safety and Security and Others*, 1995 (1) S.A.C.L.R. 130 (E), at 135–136.

42. An account of the history of the death sentence, the growth of the abolitionist movement, and the application of the death sentence by South African courts is given by Prof. B. van Niekerk in "Hanged by the Neck Until You Are Dead" (1969) 86 S.A.L.J. 457; Professor E. Kahn in "The Death Penalty in South Africa" (1970) 33 T.H.R.H.R. 108; and by Professor G. Devenish in "The historical and jurisprudential evolution and background to the application of the death penalty in South Africa and its relationship with constitutional and political reform," S.A.C.J. (1992) 1. For analysis of trends in capital punishment internationally, see Amnesty International, *When the State Kills . . . The death penalty v. human rights* (1989).

43. See generally, Amnesty International, The Death Penalty: List of Abolitionist and Retentionist Countries (December 1, 1993), AI Index ACT 50/02/94.

44. Amnesty International, Update to Death Sentences and Executions in 1993, AI Index ACT 51/02/94.

45. *Supra* note 43.

46. J. Dugard in *Rights and Constitutionalism: the New South African Legal Order*, 192–195 (Dawid van Wyk et al., eds., Juta & Co., Ltd., 1994). Professor Dugard suggests, at 193–194, that section 35 requires regard to be had to "all the sources of international law recognized by article 38(1) of the *Statute of the International Court of Justice, i.e.*: (a) international conventions, whether general or particular, establishing rules expressly recognized by the contesting states; (b) international custom, as evidence of a general practice accepted as law; (c) the general principles of law recognized by civilized nations; [and] (d) . . . judicial decisions and the teachings of the most highly qualified publicists of the various nations, as subsidiary means for the determination of rules of law."

47. Established under article 28 of the *International Covenant on Civil and Political Rights (ICCPR* or *International Covenant)*, 1966.

48. Established in terms of article 33 of the *American Convention on Human Rights*, 1969.

49. *Ibid.*

50. Established in terms of article 19 of the *European Convention for the Protection of Human Rights and Fundamental Freedoms*, 1950 ("*European Convention*").

51. *Ibid.*

52. The pertinent part of article 6 of the *ICCPR* reads: 1. Every human being has the inherent right to life. This right shall be protected by law. No one shall be arbitrarily deprived of his life. 2. . . . sentence of death may be imposed only for the most serious crimes in accordance with the law in force at the time of the commission of the crime and not contrary to the provisions of the present covenant. . . . Article 4(2) of the *American Convention on Human Rights* and article 2 of the *European Convention of Human Rights* contain similar provisions. Article 4 of the *African Charter of Human and People's Rights* provides: Human beings are inviolable. Every human being shall be entitled to respect for his life and the integrity of his person. No one may be *arbitrarily* deprived of this right. (Emphasis supplied.)

53. See *S. v. Zuma and Two Others*, Case No. CCT/5/94 (5 April 1995).

54. See, e.g., *Qozeleni v. Minister of Law and Order and Another*, 1994 (1) B.C.L.R. 75(E), at 80B–C; *S. v. Botha and Others*, 1994 (3) B.C.L.R. 93 (W), at 110F–G.

55. Decision No. 23/1990 (X.31.) AB of the (Hungarian) Constitutional Court (George Feher trans.).

56. The judgment of Kentridge AJ. in *S. v. Zuma and Two Others*, *supra* note 53, discusses the relevance of foreign case law in the context of the facts of that case, and demonstrates the use that can be made of such authorities in appropriate circumstances.

57. *Furman* v. *Georgia*, *supra* note 34, at 418 (Powell J., joined by Burger CJ., Blackmun J. and Rehnquist J., dissenting).

58. See *Furman v. Georgia*, *supra* note 34.

59. *Ibid.*

60. *Gregg* v. *Georgia*, 428 U.S. 153, 173 (1976) (Stewart, Powell, and Stevens JJ.).

61. *Trop* v. *Dulles*, 356 U.S. 86, 101 (1958).

62. See *Furman* v. *Georgia*, *supra* note 34, at 380–384, and at 417–420 (Burger CJ. and Powell J., respectively, dissenting). See also *Gregg* v. *Georgia*, *supra* note 60, at 176–180; and *Callins* v. *Collins*, 114 S.Ct. 1127 (1994) (judgment denying cert.) (Scalia J., concurring). Those who take the contrary view say that these provisions do no more than recognize the existence of the death penalty at the time of the adoption of the Constitution, but do not exempt it from the cruel and unusual punishment clause. *Furman* v. *Georgia* at 283–284 (Brennan J., concurring); *People* v. *Anderson*, 493 P.2d 880, 886 (Cal. 1972) (Wright CJ.).

63. See *infra*.

64. *Supra* note 60, at 187.

65. See, *e.g.*, the concurring opinion of Scalia J., in *Callins* v. *Collins*, *supra* note 62; the opinions of Rehnquist J., concurring in part and dissenting in part, in *Lockett* v. *Ohio*, *infra* note 66, at 628 *et seq.*, and dissenting in *Woodson* v. *North Carolina*, *infra* note 66, at 308 *et seq.*

66. *Woodson* v. *North Carolina*, 428 U.S. 280 (1976); *Roberts* v. *Louisiana*, 428 U.S. 325 (1976), reh'g denied 429 U.S. 890 (1976); *Lockett* v. *Ohio*, 438 U.S. 586 (1978) (system for imposing death sentences invalid to the extent it precludes consideration by sentencing jury or judge of potentially mitigating factors).

67. See *Green* v. *Georgia*, 442 U.S. 95 (1979).

68. *Gregg* v. *Georgia*, *supra* note 60, at 189.

69. *Ibid.* See also, *Proffitt* v. *Florida*, 428 U.S. 242 (1976). The nature of the offense for which the sentence is imposed is also relevant. *Coker* v. *Georgia*, 433 U.S. 584 (1977).

70. *Criminal Procedure Act No. 51 of 1977*, section 322(2A) (as amended by section 13 of Act No. 107 of 1990).

71. *Ibid.*, section 316A(4)(a).

72. *S.* v. *Nkwanyana and Others*, 1990 (4) S.A. 735 (A), at 743E–745A.

73. *S.* v. *Masina and Others*, 1990 (4) S.A. 709 (A), at 718G–H.

74. *S.* v. *J.*, 1989 (1) S.A. 669 (A), at 682G. "Generally speaking, however, retribution has tended to yield ground to the aspects of correction and prevention, and it is deterrence (including prevention) which has been described as the 'essential,' 'all important,' 'paramount,' and 'universally admitted' object of punishment." *Ibid.*, at 682I–J (cited with approval in *S.* v. *P.*, 1991 (1) S.A. 517 (A), at 523G–H). Cf. *R* v. *Swanepoel*, 1945 A.D. 444, at 453–455.

75. Per Holmes JA. in *S.* v. *Letsolo*, 1970 (3) S.A. 476 (A), at 477B (cited with approval by Nicholas AJA. in *S.* v. *Dlamini*, 1992 (1) S.A. 18 (A), at 31I–32A, in the context of the approach to sentencing under section 322(2A)(b) of the *Criminal Procedure Act No. 51 of 1977*).

76. *S.* v. *Senonohi*, 1990 (4) S.A. 727 (A), at 734F–G; *S.* v. *Nkwanyana*, *supra* note 72, at 749A–D.

77. According to the statistics referred to in the amicus brief of the South African Police approximately 9,000 murder cases are brought to trial each year. In the more than 40,000 cases that have been heard since the amendment to section 277 of the *Criminal Procedure Act*, only 243 persons were sentenced to death, and of these sentences, only 143 were ultimately confirmed on appeal. See also Devenish, *supra* note 42, at 8 and 13.

78. In the amicus brief of Lawyers for Human Rights, Centre for Applied Legal Studies and the Society for the Abolition of the Death Penalty in South Africa, it is pointed out that the overwhelming majority of those sentenced to death are poor and black. There is an enormous social and cultural divide between those sentenced to death and the judges before whom they appear, who are presently almost all white and middle class. This in itself gives rise to prob-

lems which even the most meticulous judge cannot avoid. The formal trial proceedings are recorded in English or Afrikaans, languages which the judges understand and speak, but which many of the accused may not understand, or of which they may have only an imperfect understanding. The evidence of witnesses and the discourse between the judge and the accused often has to be interpreted, and the way this is done influences the proceedings. The differences in the backgrounds and culture of the judges and the accused also comes into the picture, and is particularly relevant when the personal circumstances of the accused have to be evaluated for the purposes of deciding upon the sentence. All this is the result of our history, and with the demise of apartheid this will change. Race and class are, however, factors that run deep in our society and cannot simply be brushed aside as no longer being relevant.

79. I do not want to be understood as being critical of the *pro deo* counsel who perform an invaluable service, often under extremely difficult conditions, and to whom the courts are much indebted. But the unpalatable truth is that most capital cases involve poor people who cannot afford and do not receive as good a defense as those who have means. In this process, the poor and the ignorant have proven to be the most vulnerable, and are the persons most likely to be sentenced to death.

80. See the comments of Curlewis J. in (1991) 7 *S.A.J.H.R.*, Vol. 7, p. 229, arguing that judges who do not impose the death sentence when they should do so are not doing their duty. "Let me return to the point that troubles the authors: 'that a person's life may depend upon who sits in judgment.' Of course this happens. I do not know why the authors are so hesitant in saying so. Their own reasoning, let alone their tables, proves this." *Ibid.*, at 230.

81. *Furman v. Georgia, supra* note 34, at 257.

82. "While this court has the power to correct constitutional or other errors retroactively . . . it cannot, of course, raise the dead." *Suffolk District v. Watson and Others*, 381 Mass. 648, 663 (1980) (Hennessy, CJ.) (plurality decision holding the death penalty unconstitutionally cruel under the Massachusetts State Constitution). "Death, in its finality, differs more from life imprisonment than a 100-year prison term differs from one of only a year or two. Because of the qualitative difference, there is a corresponding difference in the need for reliability in the determination that death is the appropriate punishment in a specific case." *Woodson v. North Carolina, supra* note 66, at 305 (Stewart, Powell and Stevens JJ.).

83. *Voyles v. Watkins*, 489 F.Supp 901 (D.D.C.: N.D.Miss. 1980). See also *People v. Frierson*, 599 P.2d. 587 (1979). Cf. *Powell v. Alabama*, 287 U.S. 45 (1932).

84. *Furman v. Georgia, supra* note 34, at 288–289 (Brennan J., concurring). Although in the United States prolonged delay extending even to more than ten years has not been held, in itself, a reason for setting aside a death sentence, *Richmond v. Lewis*, 948 F.2d 1473, 1491 (9th Cir. 1990) (rejecting a claim that exe-

cution after sixteen years on death row would constitute cruel and unusual punishment in violation of the Eighth and Fourteenth Amendments), in other jurisdictions a different view is taken. It is part of the human condition that a condemned man will take every opportunity to save his life through use of the appellate procedure. If the appellate procedure enables the prisoner to prolong the appellate hearings over a period of years, the fault is to be attributed to the appellate system that permits such delay and not to the prisoner who takes advantage of it. Appellate procedures that echo down the years are not compatible with capital punishment. The death row phenomenon must not become established as a part of our jurisprudence. *Pratt et al.* v. *Attorney General for Jamaica et al.*, [1993] 4 All.E.R. 769, [1993] 2 L.R.C. 349, [1994] 2 A.C. 1, [1993] 3 W.L.R. 995, 43 W.I.R. 340, 14 *H.R.L.J.* 338, 33 I.L.M. 364 (J.C.P.C.), at 1014 (W.L.R.).

85. *Callins* v. *Collins, supra* note 62 (Blackmun J., dissenting).

86. *Ibid.* (compare Scalia J., concurring, with Blackmun J., dissenting).

87. *Trop* v. *Dulles, supra* note 61, at 100. See also *Furman* v. *Georgia, supra* note 34, at 270–281 (Brennan J., concurring); *Gregg* v. *Georgia, supra* note 60, at 173; *People* v. *Anderson, supra* note 62, at 895 ("The dignity of man, the individual and the society as a whole, is today demeaned by our continued practice of capital punishment.").

88. *Gregg* v. *Georgia, supra* note 60, at 230 (Brennan J., dissenting) (quoting his opinion in *Furman* v. *Georgia*, at 273). See also *Furman* v. *Georgia, supra* note 34, at 296, where Brennan J., concurring, states: "The country has debated whether a society for which the dignity of the individual is the supreme value can, without a fundamental inconsistency, follow the practice of deliberately putting some of its members to death."

89. [1977] 45 BVerfGE 187, 228 (Life Imprisonment case) (as translated in Kommers, *The Constitutional Jurisprudence of the Federal Republic of Germany* (1987), at 316). The statement was made in the context of a discussion on punishment to be meted out in respect of murders of wanton cruelty. It was held that a life sentence was a competent sentence as long as it allowed the possibility of parole for a reformed prisoner rehabilitated during his or her time in prison.

90. *Kindler* v. *Canada*, [1991] 2 S.C.R. 779, 67 C.C.C. (3d) 1, 84 D.L.R. (4th) 438, 6 C.R.R. (2d) 193.

91. *Ibid.*, at 241 (C.R.R.) (*per* Cory J., dissenting with Lamer CJC., concurring). See also Sopinka J., dissenting (with Lamer CJC., concurring), at 220.

92. *Ibid.*, at 202 (per La Forest J.) (L'Heureux-Dube and Gonthier JJ., concurring).

93. *Reference: Re Ng Extradition (Can.)*, [1991] 2 S.C.R. 858, 84 D.L.R. (4th) 498, 67 C.C.C. (3d) 61.

94. *Kindler* v. *Canada* (No. 470/1991), U.N. Doc. A/48/40, Vol. II, p. 138, 14 *H.R.L.J.* 307, 6 *R.U.D.H.* 165.

95. (1989) 11 E.H.R.R. 439 at paras. 103, 105 and 111.

96. (1980) 2 S.C.C. 684.

97. *Ibid.*, at 730, para. 136.

98. *Ibid.*, at 709, para. 61.

99. *Ibid.*, at 712, para. 71.

100. I have not yet dealt specifically with the issues of deterrence, prevention and retribution, on which the Attorney General placed reliance in his argument. These are all factors relevant to the purpose of punishment and are present both in capital punishment, and in the alternative of imprisonment. Whether they serve to make capital punishment a more effective punishment than imprisonment is relevant to the argument on justification, and will be considered when that argument is dealt with. For the moment it is sufficient to say that they do not have a bearing on the nature of the punishment, and need not be taken into account at this stage of the enquiry.

101. *Supra* note 96, at 729, para. 132.

102. *Ibid.*

103. *Ibid.*, at 730–731, para. 136. For similar reasons, the death penalty was held not to be inconsistent with the *Constitution* of Botswana, or with the *Constitution* of the former Bophuthatswana. *S.* v. *Ntesang*, 1995 (4) B.C.L.R. 426 (Botswana); *S.* v. *Chabalala*, 1986 (3) S.A. 623 (B AD).

104. *Supra* note 96, at 740, para. 165. Bhagwati J. dissented. The dissenting judgment is not available to me, but according to Amnesty International, *When the State Kills*, *supra* note 42, at 147, Bhagwati J. asserted in his judgment that "[t]he prevailing standards of human decency are incompatible with [the] death penalty."

105. *Triveniben* v. *State of Gujarat*, [1992] L.R.C. (Const.) 425 (Sup. Ct. of India); *Daya Singh* v. *Union of India*, [1992] L.R.C. (Const.) 452 (Sup. Ct. of India).

106. *Soering* v. *United Kingdom*, *supra* note 95.

107. *Kindler* v. *Canada*, *supra* note 94, at 23.

108. Per Lord Bridge in *R.* v. *Home Secretary, Ex parte Bugdaycay*, [1987] A.C. 514, at 531G.

109. *Supra* note 55.

110. "The cruel or unusual punishment clause of the California Constitution, like other provisions of the Declaration of Rights, operates to restrain legislative and executive action and to protect fundamental individual and minority rights against encroachment by the majority. It is the function of the court to examine legislative acts in the light of such constitutional mandates to ensure that the promise of the Declaration of Rights is a reality to the individual (citations omitted). . . . Were it otherwise, the Legislature would ever be the sole judge of the permissible means and extent of punishment and article I, section 6, of the Constitution would be superfluous." *People* v. *Anderson*, *supra* note 62, at 888. This was also the approach of the President of the Hungarian Constitutional Court in his concurring opinion on the constitutionality of capital punishment,

where he said: "The Constitutional Court is not bound either by the will of the majority or by public sentiments." *Supra* note 55, at 12. See also *Gregg* v. *Georgia, supra* note 60, at 880. In the decisive judgment of the Court, Justices Stewart, Powell and Stevens, accepted that ". . . the Eighth Amendment demands more than that a challenged punishment be acceptable to contemporary society. The Court also must ask whether it comports with the basic concept of human dignity at the core of the Amendment" (citation omitted).

111. *Supra* note 34, at 443.

112. 319 U.S. 624, 638 (1943).

113. The Californian *Constitution* was subsequently amended to sanction capital punishment.

114. *Supra* note 62.

115. *Ibid.*, at 899. The cruelty lay ". . . not only in the execution itself and the pain incident thereto, but also in the dehumanizing effects of the lengthy imprisonment prior to the execution during which the judicial and administrative procedures essential to due process of law are carried out." *Ibid.*, at 894 (citations omitted).

116. *Ibid.*, at 899.

117. 381 Mass. 648 (1980).

118. ". . . [T]he death penalty is unacceptable under contemporary standards of decency in its unique and inherent capacity to inflict pain. The mental agony is, simply and beyond question, a horror." *Ibid.*, at 664. "All murderers are extreme offenders. Fine distinctions, designed to select a very few from the many, are inescapably capricious when applied to murders and murderers." *Ibid.*, at 665. ". . . [A]rbitrariness and discrimination . . . inevitably persist even under a statute which meets the demands of Furman." *Ibid.*, at 670. ". . . [T]he supreme punishment of death, inflicted as it is by chance and caprice, may not stand." *Ibid.*, at 671. "The death sentence itself is a declaration that society deems the prisoner a nullity, less than human and unworthy to live. But that negation of his personality carries through the entire period between sentence and execution." *Ibid.*, at 683 (Liacos J., concurring).

119. *E.g.*, *Coker* v. *Georgia*, 433 U.S. 782 (1977) (imposition of the death penalty for rape violates due process guarantees because the sentence is grossly disproportionate punishment for a nonlethal offense). See also *Gregg* v. *Georgia, supra* note 60, at 187 ("[W]e must consider whether the punishment of death is disproportionate in relation to the crime for which it is imposed"), and *Furman* v. *Georgia, supra* note 34, at 273 (". . . a punishment may be degrading simply by reason of its enormity").

120. The Black Act: 9 George I. C.22, as cited in E. P. Thompson, *Whigs and Hunters, The Origin of the Black Act* 211 (Pantheon). The author notes that these provisions were described by Lord Chief Justice Hardwicke as "necessary for the present state and condition of things and to suppress mischiefs, which were growing frequent among us."

121. This was the approach of Brennan J., in *Furman* v. *Georgia, supra* note 34, at 282 ("The test, then, will ordinarily be a cumulative one: If a punishment is unusually severe, if there is a strong probability that it is inflicted arbitrarily, if it is substantially rejected by contemporary society [a determination he makes based on the infrequency of use in relation to the number of offenses for which such punishment may apply], and if there is no reason to believe that it serves any penal purpose more effectively than some less severe punishment, then the continued infliction of that punishment violates the [clause prohibiting cruel and unusual punishment]").

122. *S.* v. *Zuma and Two Others, supra* note 53, para. 21.

123. *Furman* v. *Georgia, supra* note 34, at 300. Brennan J. was dealing here with the proposition that "an unusually severe and degrading punishment may not be excessive in view of the purposes for which it is inflicted."

124. *Ibid.*

125. "The People concede that capital punishment is cruel to the individual involved. They argue, however, that only unnecessary cruelty is constitutionally proscribed, and that if a cruel punishment can be justified it is not forbidden by article I, section 6, of the California Constitution." *Supra* note 62, at 895.

126. *S.* v. *Zuma and Two Others, supra* note 53.

127. *Attorney-General of Hong Kong* v. *Lee Kwong-Kut,* [1993] A.C. 951 (J.C.P.C.), at 970–972.

128. *Supra* note 60, at 186–187.

129. *S.* v. *Zuma and Two Others, supra* note 53.

130. A proportionality test is applied to the limitation of fundamental rights by the Canadian courts, the German Federal Constitutional Court and the European Court of Human Rights. Although the approach of these Courts to proportionality is not identical, all recognize that proportionality is an essential requirement of any legitimate limitation of an entrenched right. Proportionality is also inherent in the different levels of scrutiny applied by United States courts to governmental action.

131. *Reference re ss. 193 and 195(1)(c) of the Criminal Code of Manitoba, infra* note 135.

132. (1986) 19 C.R.R. 308.

133. *Ibid.,* at 337.

134. (1989) 39 C.R.R. 193, at 248.

135. (1990) 48 C.R.R. 1, at 62.

136. (1991) 1 C.R.R. (2d) 1, at 30.

137. Per La Forest J. in *Tetreault-Gadoury* v. *Canada (Employment and Immigration Commission),* (1991) 4 C.R.R.(2d) 12, at 26. See also *Rodriquez* v. *British Columbia* (AG), (1994) 17 C.R.R.(2d) 192, at 222 and 247.

138. Dieter Grimm, Human Rights and Judicial Review in Germany, in *Human Rights and Judicial Review: A Comparative Perspective* 267, 275 (David H.

Beatty, ed., Martinus Nijhoff publ.) (1994). Prof. Grimm is presently a member of the German Federal Constitutional Court.

139. *Ibid.* For a discussion of the application of the principle of proportionality in German Constitutional jurisprudence, see Currie, *The Constitution of the Federal Republic of Germany* 18–20, 307–310 (Univ. of Chicago Press)(1994). Prof. Currie outlines the genesis of proportionality, intimated in the Magna Carta and generally described by Blackstone, and notes that it was further developed by Carl Gottleib Svarez, a celebrated thinker of the German Enlightenment. "Svarez insisted on proportionality both between ends and means and between costs and benefits; both aspects of the principle are reflected in the jurisprudence of the Constitutional Court." Currie at 307.

140. Currie, *ibid.*, at 178, note 15 and accompanying text. See also *infra* note 161.

141. *R.* v. *France*, (1993) 16 E.H.R.R. 1, para. 63.

142. *Handyside* v. *United Kingdom*, (1979–80) 1 E.H.R.R. 737, para. 49.

143. *Dudgeon* v. *United Kingdom*, (1981) 4 E.H.R.R. 149, para. 52; *Norris* v. *Ireland*, (1988) 13 E.H.R.R. 186, para. 46; *Modinos* v. *Cyprus*, (1993) 16 E.H.R.R. 485.

144. ". . . [T]he margin of appreciation available to the legislature in implementing social and economic policies should be a wide one. . . ." *James* v. *United Kingdom*, (1986) 8 E.H.R.R. 123, para. 46. See also, *Lithgow* v. *United Kingdom*, (1986) 8 E.H.R.R. 329, para. 122.

145. *S.* v. *Zuma and Two Others, supra* note 53, para. 35.

146. *S.* v. *Senonohi, supra* note 76, at 734F–G.

147. Criminal Appeal No. 142 of 1994; 30 January 1995.

148. *Ibid.*, wherein Ramadhani JA. highlights with respect to the Republic of Tanzania Constitution, that article 30(2) provides that laws, and actions taken in accordance with such laws, shall not be invalidated under the Constitution if such laws (or actions) make provision, *inter alia*, for "ensuring that the rights and freedom of other or the public interest are not prejudiced by the misuse of the individual rights and freedom." *Ibid.*, at p. 23. The judgment refers to "derogations" and not to "limitations."

149. See discussion on public opinion *supra*.

150. *S.* v. *W.*, 1993(2) S.A.C.R. 74, at 76H–I.

151. In the Statement of Minister of Justice dated 27 March 1992, South African Government Heads of Argument, Vol. 1, authorities, para. 22.

152. Indeed, such a hypothesis is not borne out by the statistics analyzed by Justice Didcott in his concurring opinion.

153. Since 1991, section 64 of the *Correctional Service Act 8 of 1959* has provided that a person sentenced to life imprisonment may only be released from prison in the following circumstances: (a) the advisory release board, "with due regard to the interest of society," recommends that the prisoner be released and (b) the Minister of Correctional Services accepts that recommendation and au-

thorizes the release of the prisoner. This means that the Minister of Correctional Services must accept responsibility for the release of the prisoner, and can only do so if the advisory release board is in favour of the prisoner being released.

154. This statement is taken from the provision on National Reconciliation.

155. Sopinka J. (La Forest, Gonthier, Iacobucci and Major JJ., concurring) in *Rodriquez* v. *British Columbia*, (1994) 17 C.R.R.(2d) 193, at 218.

156. This proposition is advanced in greater detail by J. Price (1995), "De Rebus" 89.

157. Wright CJ., in *People* v. *Anderson, supra* note 62, at 897.

158. *S.* v. *P.,* 1991 (1) S.A. 517 (A), at 523D–F. See also *supra* note 74.

159. The Preamble to the Constitution records that the new order will be a "constitutional state in which . . . all citizens shall be able to enjoy and exercise their fundamental rights and freedoms." The commitment to recognition of human rights is reaffirmed in the concluding provision on National Unity and Reconciliation.

160. Brennan J., in *Furman* v. *Georgia, supra* note 34, at 305.

161. Currie, *supra* note 139, refers to an analysis of the "remarkable variety of views" on the meaning of 'essence.' *Ibid.,* at 178 (citing 2 Maunz/Durig, Art. 19, Abs. II, Rdnr. 16).

162. Grimm, *supra* note 138, at page 276, states, "operating at an earlier stage than the essential content limit in Article 19(2), the proportionality principle has rendered the former almost insignificant." Currie, *supra* note 139, notes that the German Federal Constitutional Court has remarked in at least one case that dealt with the 'essential content' question that the Court "state[d] an alternative ground that, because of its greater stringency [the proportionality test], has made it unnecessary in most cases to inquire whether a restriction invades the 'essential content' of a basic right." Currie, *supra* note 139, at 306–307 (citing 22 BVerfGE 180, 220 (1967))

163. *R.* v. *Oakes, supra* note 132, at 337 (citing *R.* v. *Big M Drug Mart Ltd.,* [1985] 1 S.C.R. 295, at 352).

164. See Kommers, *supra* note 89.

165. Sections 8(2), 9, 10 and 11(2) are in fact non-derogable rights and in terms of section 34(5)(c) cannot be suspended during an emergency.

166. Self-defense is treated in our law as a species of private defense. It is not necessary for the purposes of this judgment to examine the limits of private defense. Until now, our law has allowed killing in defense of life, but also has allowed killing in defense of property, or other legitimate interest, in circumstances where it is reasonable and necessary to do so. *S.* v. *Van Wyk,* 1967 (1) S.A. 488 (A). Whether this is consistent with the values of our new legal order is not a matter which arises for consideration in the present case. What is material is that the law applies a proportionality test, weighing the interest protected against the interest of the wrongdoer. These interests must now be weighed in the light of the *Constitution.*

167. "The inherent right of the State to assume extraordinary powers and to use all means at its disposal in order to defend itself when its existence is at stake is recognized by our common law as an exceptional and extreme constitutional tool." Per Selikowitz J. in *End Conscription Campaign* v. *Minister of Defence,* 1989 (2) S.A. 180(C), at 199H. Here too it is not necessary to examine the limits of this "inherent right," or the limitations (if any) imposed on it by the *Constitution.* All that need be said is that it is of an entirely different character than the alleged "right" of the State to execute murderers, and subject to different considerations.

168. Innes J. in *Whittaker* v. *Roos and Bateman,* 1912 AD 92, at 122–123. See also *Goldberg and Others* v. *Minister of Prisons and Others,* 1979 (1) S.A. 14 (A), at 39H–40C; *Nestor and Others* v. *Minister of Police and Others,* 1984 (4) S.A. 230 (SWA), at 250F–251D.

169. See also *Woods* v. *Minister of Justice, Legal and Parliamentary Affairs and Others,* 1995 B.C.L.R. 56 (ZSC), at 58F–G; *Turner* v. *Safley,* 482 U.S. 78, 84–85 (1987).

Judicial Committee of the
Privy Council: Guerra v. Baptiste

[Note: On November 2, 1993, the Judicial Committee of the Privy Council declared that prolonged detention on death row constituted inhuman and degrading treatment: Pratt et al. v. Attorney General for Jamaica et al., [1993] 4 All.E.R. 769, [1993] 2 L.R.C. 349, [1994] 2 A.C. 1, [1993] 3 W.L.R. 995, 43 W.I.R. 340, 14 H.R.L.J. 338, 33 I.L.M. 364 (J.C.P.C.). In reasons released on November 6, 1995, it revisited the question of the "death row phenomenon" in Guerra v. Baptiste et al., [1995] J.C.J. No. 43. *Note that a communication by Lincoln Guerra and Brian Wallen to the Human Rights Committee was declared inadmissible on April 4, 1995:* Guerra and Wallen v. Trinidad and Tobago, (1995) 16 H.R.L.J. 400.]*

From the Court of Appeal of Trinidad and Tobago

Lord Goff of Chieveley:—On 18th May 1989 the appellant, Lincoln Guerra, together with Brian Wallen, was convicted of the murder of Leslie Ann Girod and her baby son, Gregg, and was sentenced to death. The crime was one of shocking brutality. Their Lordships quote from the judgment of the Court of Appeal delivered by Justice Hamel-Smith on 27th July 1994, at page 8:—

> The murders for which Guerra and Wallen were convicted were heinous and abominable in the extreme. Quite apart from the fact that violent robberies and kidnapping were committed in the course of these murders, Leslie was raped and afterwards bludgeoned. Her infant baby, Gregg, was decapitated and her husband who was with them had his throat slit.

Following their conviction and sentence the two men were placed in cells on death row in the State Prison at Port of Spain. On 7th April

1990 the appellant, together with other prisoners on death row, escaped from prison. After the escape a prison guard then on duty was
found strangled to death. However on 25th June 1990 the appellant
was recaptured and returned to death row. On 29th July 1994 Brian
Wallen died in prison of natural causes. It is for that reason that Lincoln Guerra alone is the appellant in the present proceedings. Meanwhile, on 7th June 1989, the two men gave notice of application for
leave to appeal against their convictions. But it was not until 12th October 1993 that their appeals were heard by the Court of Appeal—
nearly four and a half years after their conviction and sentence. Their
Lordships will return later to the cause of this delay. The hearing was
concluded on 2nd November, when the appeals were dismissed. The
Court handed down reasons for the decision on 25th November
1993. A petition by the two men for leave to appeal to the Privy
Council was dismissed on 21st March 1994, the formal order being
drawn up on 30th March. On 21st March attorneys acting for the
two men wrote to the United Nations Human Rights Committee and
to the Inter-American Commission on Human Rights, seeking a determination that their constitutional rights had been violated by reason of the delay which had elapsed since their conviction and sentence to death on 18th May 1989, four years and ten months before.
The Attorney General of Trinidad and Tobago was duly informed of
these applications.

After the dismissal on 21st March of the petition of the two men
for leave to appeal to the Privy Council, the authorities moved with
great speed. Two days later, on 23rd March, the Advisory Committee on the Power of Pardon (with whom, pursuant to section 89(1)
of the Constitution, the designated Minister consulted before advising the President whether to reprieve the two men) met to consider
the question of commutation of their death sentences. Following
the consultation, the Minister must have recommended that the law
should take its course. The warrants for their execution were read to
them at 1440 hours on the next day, 24th March, for execution at
0700 hours on the following morning, 25th March. It follows that
less than 17 hours' notice was given to them of their impending execution.

Even so, following the reading of the warrants of execution, those advising the two men succeeded in filing a constitutional motion on the same evening on behalf of the two men alleging that their execution pursuant to the warrants would constitute a violation of their constitutional rights.

A summons was immediately issued for a stay of execution pending the determination of the constitutional motion. Justice Lucky dismissed the application at 2200 hours that evening. Very early the following morning a single judge of the Court of Appeal, Justice Hosein, also dismissed the application for a stay, but granted leave to appeal to the Privy Council from his order and further granted a stay of execution for 48 hours pending an appeal to the Privy Council. Their Lordships find it unnecessary to recount in detail the events of the next few days, which were largely concerned with steps taken with a view to obtaining stays of execution pending the hearing of the constitutional motion or of any appeal from an order dismissing the motion. It is enough to record that, pursuant to the leave to appeal granted by Justice Hosein, a stay was granted, and continued, by the Privy Council until 25th April 1994. On 18th April 1994 Justice Jones heard and dismissed the constitutional motion, and refused a stay of execution pending an appeal; but on 29th April Justice Sharma, by consent, granted a stay of execution until after the determination of the appeal from Justice Jones to the Court of Appeal, the intervening period since 25th April having been covered by an undertaking by the Attorney-General that no execution would take place. On 9th June the Court of Appeal, having heard the appeal, reserved judgment. On 25th July, following the execution of Glen Ashby during the hearing by the Court of Appeal of his appeal from the dismissal of a constitutional motion, no stay of execution being then in place, the Privy Council, in order to preserve its jurisdiction as the final Court of Appeal for Trinidad and Tobago, granted a stay of execution of the appellant and Brian Wallen in the event of the Court of Appeal dismissing their appeal from the decision of Justice Jones. On 27th July 1994 the Court of Appeal dismissed their appeal from Justice Jones but, since the stay granted by the Privy Council then took effect, they themselves found it unnecessary to order a stay. Two days later, as already recorded, Brian Wallen died in prison.

On 6th September 1994 the State of Trinidad and Tobago submitted to the United Nations Human Rights Committee that the appellant's communication to the Committee was inadmissible for non-exhaustion of domestic remedies. On 4th April 1995 the Committee accepted that submission but stated that they would reconsider the appellant's communication after the appeal on his constitutional motion had been disposed of. That appeal came before their Lordships' Board on 27th June 1995.

The following issues were the subject of submissions to their Lordships:

(1) Whether the lapse of 4 years and 10 months between 18th May 1989 (when the appellant was convicted and sentenced) and 21st March 1994 (when the appellant's petition for leave to appeal to the Privy Council was dismissed) had the effect that the execution of the appellant would have been in breach of his constitutional rights, on the principle established in *Pratt*.

(2) Whether the very short notice (17 hours) given to the appellant of his impending execution was in breach of his constitutional rights.

(3) Whether there was a breach of the appellant's constitutional rights in failing to allow him an opportunity to make representations to the Advisory Committee.

(4) Whether the failure of the State to adopt a procedure which permitted the appellant to make representations to the United Nations Human Rights Committee or the State to take into account the advice of the United Nations Human Rights Committee, constituted a breach of the appellant's constitutional rights.

(5) Whether the courts below erred in failing to grant a stay of execution pending the hearing and determination of the appellant's constitutional motion.

Of the above issues, that arising from the decision in *Pratt et al.* v. *Attorney General for Jamaica et al.*, [1993] 4 All.E.R. 769, [1993] 2 L.R.C. 349, [1994] 2 A.C. 1, [1993] 3 W.L.R. 995, 43 W.I.R. 340, 14 *H.R.L.J.* 338, 33 I.L.M. 364 (J.C.P.C.), was plainly the central issue in the case. At the close of argument, their Lordships concluded that the appellant's appeal on this issue was well-founded; and they therefore announced immediately that the appeal would be allowed and the appellant's sentence of death commuted to a sentence of life imprisonment. Their Lordships' reasons for reaching this conclusion are set out below.

Their Lordships are however faced with the situation that four other issues were raised before them. The second issue (relating to notice of execution) is a discrete issue within a comparatively narrow compass, on which there are conflicting decisions of the Courts of Trinidad and Tobago. Their Lordships have accordingly concluded that they should decide that issue. The fifth issue (concerned with failure to grant a stay of execution) is academic in the sense that a stay of execution was eventually granted; and in any event the point is now covered by the decision of the Privy Council in *Reckley* v. *Minister of Public Safety and Immigration*, [1995] 3 W.L.R. 390, which the respondents accept is applicable in Trinidad and Tobago. It is therefore unnecessary for their Lordships to deal with this issue.

There remain the issues relating to the Advisory Committee and the United Nations Human Rights Committee. Each of these issues raises a fundamental question of great importance; indeed the former involves a challenge to the decision of the Privy Council in *de Freitas* v. *Benny*, [1976] A.C. 239, [1975] 3 W.L.R. 388 (J.C.P.C.). Moreover, having regard to the decision that the appellant's death sentence should be commuted to a sentence of life imprisonment on the principle in *Pratt*, the issue relating to the Advisory Committee does not arise for decision, since even if it was decided in favor of the appellant it could lead to no more than a direction that the matter should be reconsidered by the Committee; and the issue relating to the United Nations Human Rights Committee too does not arise for decision, because the United Nations Human Rights Committee determined that the appellant's communication to the Committee on 21st March 1994 was, inadmissible for non-exhaustion of domestic remedies, *i.e.* until after the determination of the present appeal. In all the circumstances, their Lordships do not consider that it would be appropriate for them to deal with either of these issues in the present case.

I. DELAY

Their Lordships turn first to the issue of delay. It has been urged on behalf of the appellant that such delay occurred in the appellate process, between the date of his conviction and sentence on 18th May 1989, and the date when his petition for leave to appeal was dismissed by the Privy Council on 21st March 1994, that to execute him after the period of time spent by the appellant on death row would constitute a breach of his rights under the *Constitution of Trinidad and Tobago*, on the principles established by the Privy Council in *Pratt*.

The constitutional position

Under section 17(1) of the *Constitution of Jamaica*, it is provided that "No person shall be subjected to torture or to inhuman or degrading punishment or other treatment." It was held in *Pratt* that to execute a man after a prolonged period of delay could constitute inhuman punishment contrary to that provision. There is no exact parallel to that provision in the *Constitution of Trinidad and Tobago* of 1976. However, sections 4 and 5 of the Constitution provide as follows:—

> 4. It is hereby recognized and declared that in Trinidad and Tobago there have existed and shall continue to exist . . . the following fundamental human rights and freedoms, namely:
>
> (a) the right of the individual to life, liberty, security of the person and enjoyment of property and the right not to be deprived thereof except by due process of law; [. . .]
>
> 5.(1) Except as is otherwise expressly provided in this Chapter and in section 54, no law may abrogate, abridge or infringe or authorize the abrogation, abridgement or infringement of any of the rights and freedoms hereinbefore recognized and declared.
>
> (2) Without prejudice to subsection (1), but subject to this Chapter and to section 54, Parliament may not—[. . .]
>
> (b) impose or authorize the imposition of cruel and unusual treatment or punishment. . . ;

Before the coming into force of the *Constitution of Trinidad and Tobago* of 1976 (and indeed the *Constitution* of 1982) capital punishment was accepted as a punishment which could lawfully be imposed, so that execution pursuant to a lawful sentence of death could amount to depriving a person of his life by due process of law, and could not of itself amount to a cruel and unusual punishment contrary to section 5(2)(b). However, as was recognized by the Privy Council in *Pratt,* at page 19C (following a suggestion of Lord Diplock in *Abbott* v. *A.-G. of Trinidad and Tobago,* [1979] 1 W.L.R. 1342, 32W.I.R. 347 (J.C.P.C.), at 1348 (W.L.R.)), applying the common law the judges of Jamaica would have had power to stay a long delayed execution as not being in accordance with the due process of law. Their Lordships have no doubt that the same is true of the judges of Trinidad and Tobago, and that such execution, if not stayed, would constitute cruel and unusual punishment with the effect that not only would any attempt by Parliament to authorize it be contrary to section 5(2)(b) of the Constitution, but also that, on the principles stated by Lord Diplock in *Thornbill* v. *Attorney-General for Trinidad and Tobago,* [1981] A.C. 61 (to which their Lordships will refer in more detail in the next section of this judgment), such execution would not be in accordance with the due process of law under section 4(a) of the *Constitution* which recognizes the right of the individual to life and the right not to be deprived thereof except by the due process of law. For these reasons, their Lordships conclude that the principles stated in *Pratt* are applicable in Trinidad and Tobago as they are in Jamaica, the only difference (which is of no importance) being that in Jamaica such execution would constitute inhuman punishment, whereas in Trinidad and Tobago it would constitute cruel and unusual punishment.

The facts

The following account of the relevant events occurring after the conviction and sentence of the appellant is taken from the chronology supplied by the respondents, and evidence submitted by the respondents before the courts below.

The appellant (with Brian Wallen) was convicted and sentenced to death on 18th May 1989. He and Wallen gave notice of application for leave to appeal to the Court of Appeal, which was filed with the Court on 7th June 1989. As already recorded, the appellant was at large between 7th April and 25th June 1990.

In November 1990 the appellant applied for legal aid for his appeal. On 20th March 1991 a judge granted a certificate for legal aid for the appellant. On 15th April 1991 the Legal Aid and Advisory Authority (L.A.A.A.) asked Mr. B. Dolsingh to appear for the appellant on legal aid; though it appears that it was not until 10th May 1993 that the L.A.A.A. received the judge's certificate for the appellant's legal aid.

The transcript of the summing-up was available on 13th February 1990, but the notes of evidence were not. Mr. Gonsalves, the Clerk of Appeals who has been attached to the Appeal Division since January 1993, has stated that there is no evidence when the notes of evidence became available. At all events, on 10th May 1993 Mr. Gonsalves notified Mr. Dolsingh and the attorney for Wallen that the notes of evidence and the summing-up were available, and that the date for the hearing of the appeals of the appellant and Wallen was fixed for 25th May 1993. Mr. Gonsalves has also stated that a copy of the summing- up was sent to Mr. Dolsingh on 13th May, and that on 21st May Mr. Dolsingh informed Mr. Gonsalves that he had received the notes of evidence but that, as he had only received them that day, an adjournment of the hearing would be necessary. The hearing was in fact adjourned first to 21st July, and again over the long vacation to 5th October, on each occasion on the application of Wallen's attorney. With the date fixed for October, Mr. Dolsingh filed the appellant's grounds of appeal on 24th August, and amended grounds of appeal on 10th September. It appears that Wallen's grounds of appeal were not filed until 4th October and for that reason the hearing was adjourned for one more week. The appeal began on 12th October and continued until 2nd November, when the Court of Appeal announced that the appeals would be dismissed. The reasons for their decision were handed down on 25th November. As is plain both from the length of the hearing and the reasons of the Court, the issues raised were of some complexity. On 5th November 1993 the appellant gave notice of his intention to petition the Privy Council for leave to appeal, his application for leave being dismissed on 21st March 1994.

The cause of the delay

From the foregoing chronology of events, it is plain that the principal cause of delay was the lapse of time between the end of the trial on 18th May 1989 and the furnishing to the appellant's attorney on

21st May 1993 of the notes of the evidence at the trial—a lapse of time of four years. However, their Lordships think it right to mention at this stage that, in their judgment on the appellant's constitutional motion, the Court of Appeal stated that in their view "the period between sentence and final appeal must be discounted by some five months to take into account the delay occasioned by the appellants in prosecuting their appeals. The Court of Appeal, in what can be considered a departure from its normal practice, highlighted the delay in its judgment . . . as it was quite evident that an attempt was being made to deliberately postpone the hearing." Their Lordships confess that they have found this statement rather puzzling. The only statement made in the earlier judgment of the Court of Appeal is that the appeals began on 12th October 1993 "after a number of adjournments made for one reason or another at the request of attorneys and stretching from 25th May 1993." Moreover it is difficult to see what blame could attach to the first adjournment (from 25th May to 21st July) which, on the respondents' evidence, resulted from the late furnishing of the notes of evidence. The only adjournments which could possibly be criticized were those from 21st July over the long vacation to 5th October, and from 5th October to 12th October—a total period of two and a half months. However, as will appear hereafter, this comparatively short period of delay is not, in their Lordships' view of the case, relevant to the outcome on the issue of delay.

The judgments of Justice Jones and the Court of Appeal
Justice Jones set out the facts of the present case, and then turned to the problems involved in Trinidad in preparing notes of evidence. Here he referred to an affidavit of Mr. Gonsalves, who described the difficulties involved in the following passage:—

> The Notes of Evidence taken at such trials are recorded in long hand by the Trial Judge in a note book. These notes are then given to the Judge's secretary to be deciphered, sometimes with extreme difficulty, since the Trial Judge usually writes at a rapid pace which inevitably results in a deterioration of his handwriting. The Judge's secretary then produces a typescript of the Notes of Evidence which is then submitted to the Judge for checking during the Judge's busy

High Court schedule. Judges sit in court continuously during the Court term and may even sit as vacation judges during the Court vacation. Apart from the main seat of the High Court in Port of Spain, High Court Judges are also assigned to the Courts in San Fernando and in the island of Tobago and while so assigned it is difficult for them to give the necessary assistance in checking the transcripts. Having regard to the factors stated herein and the resources available generally, there is usually a lapse of time before the Notes of Evidence become available.

Mr. Gonsalves went on to describe the efforts being made to introduce a more efficient system based on computer aided transcription.

Justice Jones also cited passages from judgments of Chief Justice Bernard, in which he described the problems facing the judiciary, and especially the Court of Appeal, in Trinidad, having regard to the small number of judges and their lack of administrative support staff and the increasing workload which they have to bear, especially in criminal appeals as a result of the spate of violent crime, including murders, in the country. Their Lordships have of course studied this material with great care, and with sympathy and understanding for the great difficulties which face the judges of Trinidad and Tobago. Justice Jones stated that it was against this background that delays in the jurisdiction must be viewed. He also accepted an argument that while the appeal is pending the condemned man could entertain no fear of execution. He concluded that the period between conviction and reading of the death warrants was not unreasonable or such as to amount to cruel or unusual treatment or punishment, and in any event was within the five year period considered by the Privy Council in *Pratt*.

The Court of Appeal, whose judgment was delivered by Justice Hamel-Smith, set out the reasoning of Justice Jones, and proceeded to reinforce it by observations of their own. They indicated that, in their opinion, the five-year "time limit" laid down in *Pratt* was inappropriate for Trinidad and Tobago because it was too short. Furthermore, it could not be said that the appellants' case was simply shelved and forgotten as appears to have been the case in *Pratt*. They stressed the increased workload which has resulted from the crime wave in Trinidad, and maintained that, although the condemned prisoner may expect a certain amount of expedition in the hearing of his appeals, he must recognize that his appeal is not the only one and that a balance must be maintained. They continued:—

> But this Court is not blind nor is it blinkered to the cries of the law abiding citizens . . . that the laws of this country must be enforced. They perceive the scales of justice not simply to have tipped but overbalanced in favour of the criminal element in this country. When due process has run its course they expect that the penalty prescribed by law will be enforced and enforced with despatch. . . .
>
> For the appellants to complain that the period in question is sufficient to constitute the imposition of cruel and unusual punishment on them is to ignore reality, more so when there has been no delay whatsoever between final appeal and the reading of the death warrant, that time period which all other jurisdictions which maintain the death penalty recognize to be the most critical in determining whether there has been a breach of the right in question.

They concluded by stating that, in the final analysis, the period in question had not exceeded the time limit imposed in *Pratt* and as a result the appeal must fail on the ground of delay.

The approach of the Judicial Committee
Their Lordships turn first to the principles established in *Pratt*. The fundamental principle is to be found at pages 33B–D of the judgment of the Judicial Committee in that case, as follows:—

> In their Lordships' view a state that wishes to retain capital punishment must accept the responsibility of ensuring that execution follows as swiftly as practicable after sentence, allowing a reasonable time for appeal and consideration of reprieve. It is part of the human condition that a condemned man will take every opportunity to save his life through use of the appellate procedure. If the appellate procedure enables the prisoner to prolong the appellate hearings over a period of years, the fault is to be attributed to the appellate system that permits such delay and not to the prisoner who takes advantage of it. Appellate procedures that echo down the years are not compatible with capital punishment. The death row phenomenon must not become established as a part of our jurisprudence.
>
> It follows that the mere fact that the appellant takes advantage of the appellate procedures open to him will not of itself debar him from claiming that the delay involved has contributed to the breach of his constitutional rights. But if the delay has occurred as a result

of exploiting the available procedures in a manner which can be described as frivolous or an abuse of the court's process, the delay incurred cannot be attributed to the appellate process and is to be disregarded.

It also follows that no fixed time is specified for the period within which execution should take place after conviction and sentence. On the contrary, the period is to be ascertained by reference to the requirement that execution should follow as swiftly as practicable after sentence, allowing a reasonable time for appeal and consideration of reprieve.

In the judgments delivered by the courts below in the present case, much emphasis was placed on the problems created for the courts by the shortage of resources available to them, especially in the difficult conditions now prevailing in Trinidad and Tobago. Their Lordships were already aware of the difficulties facing those who administer justice in Trinidad and Tobago, and of the very serious wave of violent crime which now afflicts the country. They have been much assisted by the authoritative account of the present position set out in the judgments of Justice Jones and of the Court of Appeal, and also in passages from the judgments of Chief Justice Bernard quoted by them. Their Lordships have also been impressed by the steps which have already been taken to tackle the present problems, and in particular, following *Pratt*, to reduce the backlog of cases and to curtail the long delays which have occurred in the past between sentence of death and completion of the appellate process. Indeed their Lordships were informed by leading counsel for the respondents in the present appeal that the backlog had been almost overcome. Even so, when considering to what extent regard may be had to problems facing the judicial system in assessing a reasonable time for appeal for present purposes, it is necessary to refer to the following passage in the judgment of the Board in *Pratt* at pp. 34F–35A:—

> Their Lordships are very conscious that the Jamaican Government faces great difficulties with a disturbing murder rate and limited financial resources at their disposal to administer the legal system. Nevertheless, if capital punishment is to be retained it must be carried out with all possible expedition. Capital appeals must be expedited and legal aid allocated to an appellant at an early stage. The

aim should be to hear a capital appeal within 12 months of conviction. . . . [If] there is to be an application to the Judicial Committee of the Privy Council it must be made as soon as possible. . . . In this way it should be possible to complete the entire domestic appeal process within approximately two years. Their Lordships do not purport to set down any rigid timetable but to indicate what appear to them to be realistic targets. . . .

This passage is, in their Lordships' opinion, as applicable to Trinidad and Tobago as it is to Jamaica, and demonstrates the limited extent to which regard can be had in the present context to problems facing the judicial system. It follows that such problems cannot be allowed to excuse long delays. If capital punishment is to be carried out it must be carried out "with all possible expedition." It is in this sense that a "reasonable time" for appeal is to be understood. In the assessment of such reasonable time, great importance must be attached to ensuring that, consonant with the tradition of the common law and the recognition of the inhumanity involved in prolonging the period awaiting execution in a condemned cell on death row, such delay will not occur and any delay which does occur will be curtailed.

In *Pratt* at page 35G, the Board also concluded that:—

. . . in any case in which execution is to take place more than five years after sentence there will be strong grounds for believing that the delay is such as to constitute "inhuman or degrading punishment or other treatment."

It is to be observed that this period was not specified as a time limit. Its function was to enable the Jamaican authorities to deal expeditiously with the substantial number of prisoners who had spent many years on death row, without having to deal with all such prisoners individually following constitutional proceedings. It follows that the period of five years was not intended to provide a limit, or a yardstick, by reference to which individual cases should be considered in constitutional proceedings. With great respect to the Court of Appeal in the present case, they erred in so regarding it.

Having regard to the foregoing considerations, their Lordships approach the present case as follows. They start with the fact that the time which had elapsed between sentence of death and completion of the hearing by the Court of Appeal was four and a half years, and that the time which elapsed between sentence and the completion of the entire domestic appellate process (i.e. until after dismissal of the appellant's petition for leave to appeal to the Privy Council) was four years and ten months. These figures are to be compared with realistic targets of approximately twelve months and two years respectively. The result of that comparison is that each of the target periods was very substantially exceeded. Furthermore examination of the facts reveals that the overwhelming reason for this excess was the failure to make available the judge's notes of the evidence at the trial until four years after the trial was over. The respondents submitted that this was a not unreasonable time having regard to the conditions prevailing in Trinidad as described by Mr. Gonsalves in his affidavit. Their Lordships feel driven to state that they do not see how it could be said that an appellate process is being carried out with all possible expedition if it takes four years to produce the notes of the evidence at the trial. In any event, any such contention is impossible to sustain in the present case, because nobody appears to know why it took so long to produce the notes. No doubt the trial judge, like all trial judges in Trinidad, was very fully occupied; but that of itself cannot explain why this relatively humdrum though laborious task should take such a very long time, especially as the judge had the assistance of a secretary. In all the circumstances, their Lordships are bound to conclude that there has been a substantial and unjustifiable period of delay in the disposal of the appellant's appeal, a period which in all probability exceeds three years. The fact that the appellant was at large for about two months, during which time he was spared the anguish of mind suffered by those on death row, has no significant bearing on this long period of delay, nor has the similar period arising from the adjournment of the hearing of the appeal over the long vacation in 1993, assuming (which their Lordships respectfully doubt) that it is of any relevance.

Brief reference was made in the respondent's written case to the moratorium on the reading of death warrants pending the Prescott Commission's Report on the death penalty. The Report, which recommended that the death penalty should be retained, was made available on 27th September 1990, and was accepted by the Cabinet and laid before Parliament on 20th October 1990. However, the point was not pursued in argument, presumably because the period of the moratorium fell within the two year target period for consideration of appeals by the appellant, and so does not appear to have been of any relevance.

Bearing in mind that the unjustified period of delay runs into a period of years, and has led to a lapse of time since sentence of death was imposed far in excess of the target periods of twelve months and two years and indeed close to the period (five years) from which it may be inferred, without detailed examination of the particular case, that there has been such delay as will render the condemned man's execution thereafter unlawful, their Lordships have no doubt that to execute the appellant after such a lapse of time would constitute cruel and unusual punishment contrary to his rights under sections 4(a) and 5(2)(b) of the *Constitution*.

It follows that their Lordships are unable to accept the reasoning of the courts below on this aspect of the case. It was for the above reasons that their Lordships came to the conclusion, announced at the conclusion of the hearing, that the appeal must be allowed and the appellant's death sentence commuted to a sentence of life imprisonment.

Finally on this aspect of the case their Lordships wish to refer to the view expressed both by Justice Jones and by the Court of Appeal that little if any regard should be paid to the period spent by a condemned man on death row before his final appeal has been dismissed. Their Lordships do not feel able to subscribe to this philosophy which, if accepted, would inevitably lead to toleration of the death row phenomenon in circumstances where a number of avenues of appeal can be pursued by an appellant. The simple fact is that, following conviction and sentence to death, the condemned man is placed on death row and has there to contemplate the prospect of execution even though, in some cases but not in others, he may have a real hope of a successful appeal. This fact alone is enough to justify the conclusion that the period before the appellate process has been finally exhausted must be taken into account in deciding whether there has been such delay since the death sentence was imposed as to render execution thereafter cruel and unusual punishment.

2. FAILURE TO GIVE SUFFICIENT NOTICE OF EXECUTION

The warrant for the appellant's execution was read to him at 1440 hours on Thursday 24th March 1994, for his execution at 0700 hours on the following day, 25th March. This gave him less than 17 hours' notice of his execution. It was submitted that so short a notice of execution constituted a breach of the appellant's constitutional rights. This submission was rejected by the courts below.

In considering this aspect of the present appeal, their Lordships are guided by the authoritative exposition of the principles embodied in chapter 1 of the *Constitution* of Trinidad and Tobago (concerned with the recognition and protection of fundamental human rights and freedoms) in the judgments of the Judicial Committee in *de Freitas* v. *Benny, supra,* and *Thornbill* v. *Attorney-General for Trinidad and Tobago, supra,* the judgment in each case being delivered by Lord Diplock. In those cases, the judgments were given with reference to the *Constitution* of 1962; but the same principles apply to the *Constitution* of 1976 which is applicable in the present case, and their Lordships will refer to the relevant sections in chapter 1 of the latter *Constitution*.

Chapter 1, and sections 4 to 6 in particular, proceed on the presumption that the rights and freedoms referred to in sections 4 and 5 are already secured to the people of Trinidad and Tobago by the law in force at the commencement of the *Constitution* of 1976. Consistently with that presumption, section 6(1) (a) has the effect of debarring a citizen from asserting that anything done to him which was authorized by the law in force immediately before the coming into effect of that *Constitution* infringes any of the rights and freedoms recognized in section 4 or which are the subject of section 5(2). The operative effect of section 4 for the future is that the rights and freedoms there recognized and declared to have existed before the coming into effect of the *Constitution* shall continue to exist as provided in the section; and section 5(1) outlaws the future abrogation, abridgement or infringement of those rights and freedoms by laws made thereafter.

In *Thornbill* at page 70, Lord Diplock drew a distinction between the rights and freedoms recognized and protected under subsections (a) to (k) of section 4 (section 1 of the 1962 *Constitution*), and the types of conduct specified in subsections (a) to (h) of section 5(2) (section 2 of the 1962 *Constitution*). The former are in general terms, and it may sometimes be necessary to have regard to the law in force when the *Constitution* came into force to determine the limits of the rights and freedoms there set out. The latter however are particularized in greater detail, their function being to spell out (though not necessarily exhaustively) what is included in the due process of law and the protection of the law in section 4(a) and (b) (section 1(a) and (b) of the 1962 *Constitution*) respectively.

The question at issue in *Thornbill* was whether the appellant, who for three days after his arrest was refused the opportunity of communicating with his lawyer, could complain of a breach of his rights under section 2(c) (ii) of the 1962 *Constitution* (section 5(2) (c) (ii) of the present *Constitution*). The Judicial Committee, restoring the decision of Justice Georges, held that there was such a breach since, having regard to section 2(c) (ii), the appellant was deprived of his rights to the due process of law and the protection of the law. However, Lord Diplock went on to state (at pp. 71A–D) that, even if the treatment complained of had not been specifically described in section 2, nevertheless:—

> "In the context of section 1, the declaration that rights and freedoms
> of the kinds described in the section have existed in Trinidad and
> Tobago, in their Lordships' view, means that they have in fact been
> enjoyed by the individual citizen, whether their enjoyment by him
> has been *de jure* as a legal right or *de facto* as the result of a settled
> executive policy of abstention from interference or a settled practice
> as to the way in which an administrative or judicial discretion has
> been exercised."

The *de facto* enjoyment of the right in question as a matter of settled practice could in that case be derived from the adoption by the Judges of Trinidad and Tobago of the English Judges' Rules 1964. In the result, the respondent could only succeed if he was able, invoking section 3, to show that the practice of allowing an arrested person to consult a lawyer of his choice at the earliest opportunity was contrary to law at the time of commencement of the *Constitution*. Obviously he was unable to discharge that burden.

Their Lordships turn to the facts of the present case. Here they are concerned with the period of notice given to the appellant of his impending execution. The essential submissions advanced on behalf of the appellant were that the period of notice was so short that execution in such circumstances would constitute cruel and unusual punishment contrary to section 5(2)(b), or that it would deprive him of his life otherwise than by due process of law or deprive him of the protection of the law contrary to section 4(a) or (b) respectively. In relation to the latter submission it must be borne in mind that, as Lord Diplock stated in *Abbott* v. *Attorney-General of Trinidad and Tobago, supra*, at 1347F–G, the due process of law must continue to be observed in the case of a condemned man after sentence of death has been passed upon him, and indeed embraces the carrying out of the sentence itself.

Their Lordships are of the opinion that justice and humanity require that a man under sentence of death should be given reasonable notice of the time of his execution. Such notice is required to enable a man to arrange his affairs, to be visited by members of his intimate family before he dies, and to receive spiritual advice and comfort to enable him to compose himself, as best he can, to face his ultimate ordeal. Their Lordships understand that this principle was long recognized in England in the days when capital punishment was still in force; and, for reasons which will shortly appear, the like principle appears to have long been accepted in Trinidad and Tobago. In these circumstances they are satisfied that to execute a condemned man without first giving him such notice of his execution would constitute cruel and unusual punishment contrary to section 5(2)(b) of the *Constitution*.

The matter can however be taken further because in *Thomas (Andy)* v. *The State* (unreported) 29th July 1987, Nos. 6346 and 6347 of 1985, it was held by Justice Davis that there was a settled practice in Trinidad and Tobago for a condemned man to be advised of the time and date of his execution by the reading of a death warrant to him on a Thursday for execution on the following Tuesday. This practice amounted, in his opinion, to an established custom which was well known, so much so that he would, if invited to do so, have held that he had judicial notice of that custom. It is plain that, on the evidence before him, he must have been satisfied that the custom extended back long before the coming into effect of the *Constitution* of 1976, and indeed the *Constitution* of 1962.

In the present case, however, Justice Jones declined to follow the decision of Justice Davis on this point. He referred to section 57 of the *Criminal Procedure Act* (ch. 12:02), which provides as follows:

(1) Every warrant for the execution of any prisoner under sentence of death shall be under the hand and Seal of the President, and shall be directed to the Marshal, and shall be carried into execution by such Marshal or his assistant at such time and place as mentioned in the warrant.

(2) The President may, by warrant under his hand and seal directed to the Marshal . . . order such execution to be carried into effect at such time and place as shall be appointed and specified in the warrant, in which case the execution shall be done at such time and place as shall be so appointed.

He commented that nowhere in this or any other law is it laid down that a death warrant is to be read on a Thursday for execution the following Tuesday, and that the time and place for execution falls squarely within the province of the executive. He further understood the effect of Lord Diplock's judgment in *Thornbill* to be that, for a custom to be elevated to a right under the *Constitution*, that custom must be described and declared in the *Constitution*.

The Court of Appeal found it difficult to follow the reasoning of Justice Davis in holding that there was a settled practice, forming part of the due process of law, that warrants for execution should be read on a Thursday for execution the following Tuesday. But in any event they considered that to hold that any such practice formed part of the due process of law would be inconsistent with section 57 of the *Criminal Procedure Act*, under which the fixing of the time for execution was purely within the discretion of the President. To hold otherwise would be an interference with executive powers conferred upon the President by law.

With all respect, their Lordships are unable to accept the reasoning of Justice Jones and the Court of Appeal. First, in their opinion, Justice Jones erred in his interpretation of the judgment of Lord Diplock in *Thornbill*. Indeed, it appears from Lord Diplock's judgment in that case (at pp. 71B–E) that if, at the time when the *Constitution* came into force, citizens have de facto enjoyed a right or freedom as a matter of settled practice, such a right or freedom may be recognized and protected under chapter 1 of the *Constitution* as forming part of the due process of law, even if it is not specified as such in section 5(2) of the *Constitution*. Second, their Lordships do not accept that section 57 of the *Criminal Procedure Act* has the effect attributed to it by Justice Jones and the Court of Appeal. No doubt under section 57 a warrant of execution under the hand and seal of the President constitutes the manner authorized by law for fixing the date of execution. But their Lordships are unable to see how the provisions of section 57 are inconsistent with the existence of a settled practice relating to the period of notice to be given to a condemned man of his execution, or with the proposition that de facto enjoyment of such settled practice at the time when the *Constitution* came into effect led to its forming part of the due process of law recognized and protected under chapter 1 of the *Constitution*. Such a conclusion does not, in their Lordships' opinion, amount to a fetter upon administrative discretion any more objectionable than any other settled practice which may be given effect to upon the principle stated by Lord Diplock in *Thornbill*.

It follows that their Lordships accept the reasoning of Justice Davis on this point. Even so, they doubt if the settled practice found by him to exist goes so far as to require the warrant to be read on any particular day of the week, or to prevent the warrant from being read on a day more than four clear days before the date of execution specified in the warrant. In their Lordships' opinion the effect of the settled practice as found by Justice Davis is that the warrant of execution must be read at a date which gives the condemned man the benefit of at least four clear days between the reading of the death warrant and his execution, and that those four clear days should include a weekend, no doubt to ensure that, so far as is reasonably practicable, the condemned man's family should be free to visit him; and the effect is that the reasonable time referred to by their Lordships in relation to the prohibition against cruel and unusual punishment should be so interpreted. Customarily, as appears from the evidence before Justice Davis, this requirement is fulfilled by reading the warrant on a Thursday for execution on the following Tuesday; and, in the absence of any evidence to the contrary, there seems to be no reason why, as a matter of practice, that custom should not continue to be observed in Trinidad and Tobago.

The giving of reasonable notice to a condemned man of his impending execution has another distinct purpose to perform, which is to provide him with a reasonable opportunity to obtain legal advice and to have resort to the courts for such relief as may at that time be open to him. The most important form which such relief may take in the circumstances is an order staying his execution. If the condemned man is not given reasonable notice of his execution, he may be deprived of the opportunity to seek such relief, with the effect that his right not to be deprived of his life except by due process of law may be infringed, contrary to section 4(a) of the *Constitution*. In this connection it must not be forgotten that, by virtue of section 5(2)(h), the right to the due process of law includes the right not to be deprived of "such procedural provisions as are necessary for the purpose of giving effect and protection to the aforesaid rights and freedoms." It follows that, in their Lordships' opinion, the due process of law requires that a reasonable time should be allowed to elapse between the reading of a warrant of execution and the execution itself, not only for the humanitarian purposes which their Lordships have previously described, but also to provide a reasonable opportunity for the condemned man to take advice and if necessary seek relief from the courts. The settled practice that a period of at least four clear days (including a weekend) will be necessary to constitute such reasonable time should be regarded as applicable as much to the latter purpose as to the former.

Fortunately, in the present case, those acting for the appellant succeeded in filing the necessary proceedings later in the evening of 24th March, and in obtaining a stay of his execution early the following morning. Even so, the giving of less than 17 hours' notice to the appellant of his execution constituted a breach of his constitutional rights, under sections 4(a), 5(2)(b) and 5(2)(h) of the *Constitution*. However, since their Lordships have already concluded that the appellant's sentence of death must be commuted to a sentence of life imprisonment on other grounds, it is unnecessary that any further relief should be granted by reason of the above breaches of his constitutional rights.

United States Ratification of the International Covenant on Civil and Political Rights, and Reservations on the Death Penalty

[Note: In 1992 the United States of America ratified the International Covenant on Civil and Political Rights, but at the same time it formulated reservations to articles 6 and 7 concerning the death penalty. The reservations read as follows.]

The United States reserves the right, subject to its Constitutional constraints, to impose capital punishment on any person (other than a pregnant woman) duly convicted under existing or future laws permitting the imposition of capital punishment, including such punishment for crimes committed by persons below eighteen years of age.

The United States considers itself bound by Article 7 to the extent that "cruel, inhuman or degrading treatment or punishment" means the cruel and unusual treatment or punishment prohibited by the Fifth, Eighth or Fourteenth Amendments to the Constitution of the United States.

[Eleven European states formulated objections to the reservations.]

Belgium: "The Government of Belgium wishes to raise an objection to the reservation made by the United States of America regarding article 6, paragraph 5, of the Covenant, which prohibits the imposition of the sentence of death for crimes committed by persons below

18 years of age. The Government of Belgium considers the reservation to be incompatible with the provisions and intent of article 6 of the Covenant which, as is made clear by article 4, paragraph 2, of the Covenant, establishes minimum measures to protect the right to life. The expression of this objection does not constitute an obstacle to the entry into force of the Covenant between Belgium and the United States of America."

Denmark: *With regard to the reservations made by the United States of America*:
"Having examined the contents of the reservation made by the United States of America, Denmark would like to recall article 4, para 2, of the Covenant according to which no derogation from a number of fundamental articles, *inter alia* 6 and 7, may be made by a State Party even in time of public emergency which threatens the life of the nation. In the opinion of Denmark, reservation (2) of the United States with respect to capital punishment for crimes committed by persons below eighteen years of age as well as reservation (3) with respect to article 7 constitute general derogations from articles 6 and 7, while according to article 4, para 2, of the Covenant such derogations are not permitted. Therefore, and taking into account that articles 6 and 7 are protecting two of the most basic rights contained in the Covenant, the Government of Denmark regards the said reservations incompatible with the object and purpose of the Covenant, and consequent [*sic*] Denmark objects to the reservations. These objections do not constitute an obstacle to the entry into force of the Covenant between Denmark and the United States."

Finland: "The Government of Finland has taken note of the reservations, understandings and declarations made by the United States of America upon ratification of the Covenant. It is recalled that under international treaty law, the name assigned to a statement whereby the legal effect of certain provisions of a treaty is excluded or modified, does not determine its status as a reservation to the treaty. Understanding (1) pertaining to articles 2, 4 and 26 of the Covenant is therefore considered to constitute in substance a reservation to the Covenant, directed at some of its most essential provisions, namely those concerning the prohibition of discrimination. In the view of the Government of Finland, reservation of this kind is contrary to the object and purpose of the Covenant, as specified in article 19(c) of the Vienna Convention on the Law of Treaties.

"As regards reservation (2) concerning article 6 of the Covenant, it is recalled that according to article 4(2), no restrictions of articles 6 and 7 of the Covenant are allowed for. In the view of the Government of Finland, the right to life is of fundamental importance in the Covenant and the said reservation therefore is incompatible with the object and purpose of the Covenant.

"As regards reservation (3), it is in the view of the Government of Finland subject to the general principle of treaty interpretation according to which a party may not invoke the provisions of its internal law a justification for failure to perform a treaty.

"For the above reasons the Government of Finland objects to reservations made by the United States to article 2, 4 and 26 (cf. Understanding (1)), to article 6 (cf. Reservation (2)) and to article 7 (cf. Reservation (3)). However, the Government of Finland does not consider that this objection constitutes an obstacle to the entry into force of the Covenant between Finland and the United States of America."

France: "At the time of the ratification of [the said Covenant], the United States of America expressed a reservation relating to article 6, paragraph 5, of the Covenant, which prohibits the imposition of the death penalty for crimes committed by persons below 18 years of age. France considers that this United States reservation is not valid, inasmuch as it is incompatible with the object and purpose of the Convention [*sic*]. Such objection does not constitute an obstacle to the entry into force of the Covenant between France and the United States."

Germany: "The Government of the Federal Republic of Germany objects to the United States' reservation referring to article 6, paragraph 5, of the Covenant, which prohibits capital punishment for crimes committed by persons below eighteen years of age. The reservation referring to this provision is incompatible with the text as well as the object and purpose of article 6, which, as made clear by paragraph 2 of article 4, lays down the minimum standard for the protection of the right to life. The Government of the Federal Republic of Germany interprets the United States' 'reservation' with regard to article 7 of the Covenant as a reference to article 2 of the Covenant, thus not in any way affecting the obligations of the United States of America as a state party to the Covenant."

Italy: "The Government of Italy . . . objects to the reservation to art. 6, paragraph 5, which the United States of America included in its instrument of ratification. In the opinion of Italy reservations to the provisions contained in art. 6 are not permitted, as specified in art. 4, para 2, of the Covenant. Therefore this reservation is null and void since it is incompatible with the object and purpose of art. 6 of the Covenant. Furthermore in the interpretation of the Government of Italy, the reservation to art. 7 of the Covenant does not affect obligations assumed by States that are parties to the Covenant on the basis of article 2 of the same Covenant. These objections do not constitute an obstacle to the entry into force of the Covenant between Italy and the United States."

Netherlands: *With regard to the reservations to articles 6 and 7 made by the United States of America:*
"The Government of the Kingdom of the Netherlands objects to the reservations with respect to capital punishment for crimes committed by persons below eighteen years of age, since it follows from the text and history of the Covenant that the said reservation is incompatible with the text, the object and purpose of article 6 of the Covenant, which according to article 4 lays down the minimum standard for the protection of the right to life. The Government of the Kingdom of the Netherlands objects to the reservation with respect to article 7 of the Covenant, since it follows from the text and the interpretation of this article that the said reservation is incompatible with the object and purpose of the Covenant. In the opinion of the Government of the Kingdom of the Netherlands this reservation has

the same effect as a general derogation from this article, while according to article 4 of the Covenant, no derogations, not even in times of public emergency, are permitted. It is the understanding of the Government of the Kingdom of the Netherlands that the understandings and declarations of the United States do not exclude or modify the legal effect of provisions of the Covenant in their application to the United States, and do not in any way limit the competence of the Human Rights Committee to interpret these provisions in their application to the United States. Subject to the proviso of article 21, paragraph 3, of the Vienna Convention of the Law of Treaties, these objections do not constitute an obstacle to the entry into force of the Covenant between the Kingdom of the Netherlands and the United States."

Portugal: *With regard to the reservations made by the United States of America:*
"The Government of Portugal considers that the reservation made by the United States of America referring to article 6, paragraph 5 of the Covenant which prohibits capital punishment for crimes committed by persons below eighteen years of age is incompatible with article 6 which, as made clear by paragraph 2 of article 4, lays down the minimum standard for the protection of the right to life. The Government of Portugal also considers that the reservation with regard to article 7 in which a State limits its responsibilities under the Covenant by invoking general principles of National Law may create doubt on the commitments of the Reserving State to the object and purpose of the Covenant and, moreover, contribute to undermining the basis of International Law. The Government of Portugal therefore objects to the reservations made by the United States of America. These objections shall not constitute an obstacle to the entry into force of the Covenant between Portugal and the United States of America."

Spain: *With regard to the reservations made by the United States of America:*
". . . After careful consideration of the reservations made by the United States of America, Spain wishes to point out that pursuant to

article 4, paragraph 2, of the Covenant, a State Party may not derogate from several basic articles, among them articles 6 and 7, including in time of public emergency which threatens the life of the nation. The Government of Spain takes the view that reservation (2) of the United States having regard to capital punishment for crimes committed by individuals under 18 years of age, in addition to reservation (3) having regard to article 7, constitute general derogations from articles 6 and 7, whereas, according to article 4, paragraph 2, of the Covenant, such derogations are not to be permitted. Therefore, and bearing in mind that articles 6 and 7 protect two of the most fundamental rights embodied in the Covenant, the Government of Spain considers that these reservations are incompatible with the object and purpose of the Covenant and, consequently, objects to them. This position does not constitute an obstacle to the entry into force of the Covenant between the Kingdom of Spain and the United States of America."

Sweden: "The Government of Sweden has examined the content of the reservations and understandings made by the United States of America. In this context the Government recalls that under international treaty law, the name assigned to a statement whereby the legal effect of certain provisions of a treaty is excluded or modified, does not determine its status as a reservation to the treaty. Thus, the Government considers that some of the understandings made by the United States in substance constitute reservations to the Covenant.

"A reservation by which a State modifies or excludes the application of the most fundamental provisions of the Covenant or limits its responsibilities under that treaty by invoking general principles of national law, may cast doubts upon the commitment of the reserving State to the object and purpose of the Covenant. The reservations made by the United States of America include both reservations to essential and non-derogable provisions, and general references to national legislation. Reservations of this nature contribute to undermining the basis of international treaty law. All States Parties share a common interest in the respect for the object and purpose of the treaty to which they have chosen to become parties.

"Sweden therefore objects to the reservations made by the United States to:

- article 2; cf. Understanding (1)
- article 4; cf. Understanding (1)
- article 6; cf. Reservation (2)
- article 7; cf. Reservation (3)
- article 15; cf. Reservation (4)
- article 26; cf. Understanding (1).

"This objection does not constitute an obstacle to the entry into force of the Covenant between Sweden and the United States of America."

[In March–April 1995 the United States presented its initial report to the Human Rights Committee, in compliance with article 40 of the International Covenant on Civil and Political Rights. The report discussed the death penalty in some detail, an indication that despite the reservations, the United States considers itself to be subject to many of the norms contained in articles 6 and 7 of the Covenant. The report is cited as U.N. Doc. CCPR/C/81/Add.4.]

139. Death penalty. The sanction of capital punishment continues to be the subject of strongly held and publicly debated views in the United States. The majority of citizens through their freely elected officials have chosen to represent the majority sentiment of the country. In addition, federal law provides for capital punishment for certain very serious federal crimes. Capital punishment is only carried out under laws in effect at the time of the offense and after exhaustive appeals. The U.S. Supreme Court has held that the Eighth Amendment to the U.S. Constitution (which proscribes cruel and unusual punishment) does not prohibit capital punishment. *Gregg* v. *Georgia*, 428 U.S. 153 (1976) (plurality opinion). However, the death penalty is available for only the most egregious crimes and, because of its severity, warrants unique treatment that other criminal sentences do not require.

140. First, it cannot be imposed even for serious crimes—such as rape, kidnapping, or robbery—unless they result in the death of the

victim. *Coker* v. *Georgia*, 433 U.S. 584 (1977); *Enmund* v. *Florida*, 458 U.S. 782, 797 (1982); *Eberheart* v. *Georgia*, 433 U.S. 917 (1988); *Hooks* v. *Georgia*, 433 U.S. 917 (1977). Moreover, it is not enough for imposition of capital punishment that the crime resulted in death; the crime must also have attendant aggravating circumstances. In other words, restrictions on imposition of the death penalty are tied to a constitutional requirement that the punishment not be disproportionate to the personal culpability of the wrongdoer, *Tison* v. *Arizona*, 481 U.S. 137, 149 (1987), and the severity of the offense, *Coker* v. *Georgia*, 433 U.S. 584, 592 (1977) (death penalty is disproportionate punishment for crime of rape).

141. Thus, offenses set forth in several federal statutes (e.g., first degree murder) that were enacted before 1968, the date of the decision in *United States* v. *Jackson*, 390 U.S. 570, in theory carry a death penalty, but because the crimes are not narrowed sufficiently by statutorily required aggravating circumstances, the death penalty in fact may not be imposed for those crimes.

142. As noted elsewhere, the *ex post facto* clause of the Constitution bars the retroactive increase in penalties available in criminal cases. In operation, it thus forbids the Government from imposing a death penalty on an offender for a crime that, at the time of its commission, was not subject to capital punishment.

143. The death penalty cannot be carried out unless imposed in a judgment issued by a competent court and subject to appellate review. Of the thirty-six states with capital punishment statutes at the end of 1991, thirty-four provided for an automatic review of each death sentence and thirty-one provided also for automatic review of the conviction. Those that do not mandate automatic review authorize review when the defendant wishes to appeal. The fact that a state appellate court reviews each death sentence to determine whether it is proportionate to other sentences imposed for similar crimes reduces the likelihood that the death penalty will be inflicted arbitrarily and capriciously so as to constitute cruel and unusual punishment. *Gregg* v. *Georgia*, 428 U.S. 153 (1976). Typically the review is undertaken regardless of the defendant's wishes and is conducted by the state's highest appellate court. In the states not providing auto-

matic review, the defendant can appeal the sentence, the conviction, or both. If an appellate court vacates either the sentence or the conviction, it may remand the case to the trial court for additional proceedings or for retrial. As a result of resentencing or retrial, it is possible for the death sentence to be reimposed.

144. Finally, the U.S. Supreme Court has found that where a sentencing jury may impose capital punishment, the jury must be informed if the defendant is parole ineligible, in other words where a life prison sentence could not result in parole. *Simmons* v. *South Carolina*, 114 S.Ct. 2187 (1994) (plurality).

145. Right to seek pardon or commutation. Under the U.S. system, no state may prohibit acts of executive clemency, including amnesty, pardon, and commutation of sentence. *Gregg* v. *Georgia*, 428 U.S. 153, 199 (1976). Indeed, in a recent Supreme Court decision, *Herrera* v. *Collins*, 113 S.Ct. 853 (1993), the Court recognized the availability of executive clemency for persons facing the death penalty whose convictions have been affirmed, whose collateral appeal rights have been exercised and exhausted, and who thereafter present a newly articulated claim of factual innocence. . . .

146. U.S. reservation. The application of the death penalty to those who commit capital offences at ages sixteen and seventeen continues to be subject to an open debate in the United States. In the United States the death penalty may be imposed on wrongdoers who were sixteen or seventeen years of age at the time of the offense. The Supreme Court ruled that it is unconstitutional to impose a death penalty upon a person who was fifteen years of age when he committed the offense (*Thompson* v. *Oklahoma*, 487 U.S. 815 (1988) (plurality opinion)), but it has approved under the Eighth Amendment the imposition of a death penalty on a wrongdoer who was sixteen years of age at the time of the murder (*Stanford* v. *Kentucky*, 492 U.S. 361 (1989)). Four of the nine Justices dissented in the latter case, contending that execution of an offender under eighteen years of age is disproportionate and unconstitutional. Id. at 403. A more recent Supreme Court decision addressing the issue noted that of thirty-six states whose laws permitted capital punishment at the time of the decision, twelve declined to impose it on persons seventeen

years of age or younger, and fifteen declined to impose it on sixteen-year-olds. *Stanford* v. *Kentucky*, 492 U.S. 361 (1989).

148. Because approximately half the states have adopted legislation permitting juveniles aged sixteen and older to be prosecuted as adults when they commit the most egregious offenses, and because the Supreme Court has upheld the constitutionality of such laws, the United States took the following reservation to the Covenant:

> The United States reserves the right, subject to its Constitutional constraints, to impose capital punishment on any person (other than a pregnant woman) duly convicted under existing or future laws permitting the imposition of capital punishment, including such punishment for crimes committed by persons below eighteen years of age. . . .

166. Death row. As discussed under article 6, the U.S. Supreme Court has ruled that the death penalty is not in and of itself cruel and unusual punishment. For many years, the Court set aside sentences of death that were imposed under a procedure that allowed prejudice and discrimination to be factors in determining the sentence. *Furman* v. *Georgia*, 408 U.S. 238 (1972). Since that decision, many states and the federal government have created new death penalty laws that have withstood Supreme Court scrutiny. As of 20 April 1994, there were approximately 2,848 prisoners on death row, all of whom had been convicted of murder. In 1993, thirty-eight prisoners were executed, bringing to 240 the total of all prisoners executed since 1976, the year the Supreme Court reinstated the death penalty. See *Gregg* v. *Georgia*, 428 U.S. 153 (1976).

167. In the states that have prisoners under sentence of death, various protections are afforded to ensure that their treatment is neither cruel, unusual, nor inhumane. The living conditions and treatment of such prisoners are guided by department of corrections' regulations unique to each state, but there are some general principles that apply universally. Most departments of corrections house death penalty prisoners in a separate wing of a maximum security prison to ensure that these prisoners do not mingle with prisoners in the general population. Death row inmates spend a great majority of time in their cells. In some states they are permitted to work and to attend

programs and activities, and in all states they are given time for recreation. Most death row inmates have access to educational programs though in many cases they are self-study programs. All death row inmates are given access to library books, legal resources and other resources. They are also permitted to make purchases from the commissary. Inmates under sentence of death spend a great deal of time pursuing hobbies such as arts and crafts, drafting, and bible study. They are permitted to visit with family members and friends as well as attorneys. In some states the visits are non-contact, and in many states the visits take place in an area removed from the general population visits. Finally, death row inmates are permitted to correspond with persons outside the institution and to make telephone calls.

168. Currently, in nearly every state death row inmates live in single-person cells, though population pressures may cause this to change. There is always concern regarding the mental health and psychological state of death row inmates. Accordingly, in many states these inmates are reviewed by a psychologist or psychiatrist on a regular basis, and in all states inmates have access to such professionals upon request. Death row inmates have access to religious services and activities, though generally such activities take place in the individual's cell or in an area separated from the general population. Staff selected to work with death row inmates are generally very experienced; a 1991 study by the American Corrections Association and the National Institute of Justice revealed that staff working these position had, on average, seven years' experience. Only a few states provide specialized training for staff who work with death-sentenced inmates, though most correctional administrators specially select staff who are particularly professional and mature.

169. Death row inmates have access to the same types of recourse available to other inmates to redress grievances. They can file a formal grievance through the internal administrative remedy process, they can file suit in court, and they can write to the news media and legislators.

[On March 29, 30 and 31, 1995, the United States of America presented its report to the fifty-third session of the Human Rights Committee. In response to questions from members of the committee, the

United States provided supplementary comments concerning implementation of the death penalty.]

U.N. Doc. CCPR/C/SR.1401

15. Mr. HARPER (United States of America). The most significant reservation concerning the criminal justice system related to article 6, paragraph 5 of the Covenant. United States law authorized capital punishment for crimes committed by juvenile offenders who were sixteen or seventeen years of age, although the execution of juveniles below the age of sixteen years was unconstitutional. His Government did not endorse the recent ruling by the European Court of Human Rights that capital punishment was "cruel, unusual or degrading treatment or punishment" and had entered a reservation to article 7 of the Covenant. In the United States, the issues of capital punishment and of whether juveniles should be treated as adults in certain situation were still being debated. Current United States law reflected the will of the American people, upheld by the Supreme Court. He noted that capital punishment was not prohibited by the Covenant or by international law. . . .

52. Mrs. MEDINA QUIROGA. Referring to a recent press report in which it had been alleged that experiments had been carried out on children and psychiatric patients in New York State, she asked what steps would be taken to end such practices. She also wondered what progress had been made in the debate in Congress on the issue of race and the death penalty, as discussed in paragraph 86(c) of the report. Recalling that the United States had reserved the right to impose the death penalty on persons under eighteen years of age in certain cases, she suggested that the reservation might, in fact, be unacceptable because of the consensus in international law against capital punishment of juveniles.

U.N. Doc. CCPR/C/SR.1402

12. Mr. FRANCIS. He noted that in *Stanford* v. *Kentucky* the four dissenting Supreme Court Justices had deemed the execution of an offender under eighteen years of age to be disproportionate and un-

constitutional, that twenty-seven states did not favor the application of the death penalty to juveniles under the age of seventeen years, that its application to those committing capital offenses at ages sixteen and seventeen was the subject of continuing debate in the United States, and that the voting age in the United States was eighteen years. Bearing all of that in mind, he wished to know whether the existing situation offered favorable prospects for a joint initiative by the states and the federal government to establish eighteen years as the minimum age at which the death penalty would be applicable....

20. Mr. BRUNO CELLI. With reference to the section of the report on the right to life (art. 6 of the Covenant), he said it was surprising that the report had devoted only a few paragraphs to the question of the death penalty, whereas paragraph 139 clearly stated that the sanction of capital punishment continued to be strongly debated in the United States. The question of the death penalty was one of the most delicate and controversial human rights issues and a subject which, in the past, had had very negative effects on the enjoyment of fundamental rights and freedoms in the United States as well as in other multiracial societies. In that regard, the reporting State should clarify the grounds on which the report had asserted that the policy to retain the death penalty for the most serious crimes appeared to represent the majority sentiment of the country. To his knowledge, public opinion had not been directly consulted on the subject, by means of a referendum for instance, nor had that issue been the focus of recent electoral campaigns, with a few exceptions. He questioned whether there was not an obvious contradiction between the abolitionist trend which was gaining ground in democratic societies around the world and the restoration of the death penalty, normatively and practically, in the United States of America, which had placed civil and political rights at the center of its existence and which protected human rights in its domestic policy and proclaimed them in its foreign policy. He asked the reporting State to explain that paradox to the Committee. More specifically, he wished to know what legal premises had prompted the Supreme Court of the United States in 1976 to revise its previous interpretation that the death penalty violated the Constitution and to permit its re-establishment. Additional

information on the social, ethical and other foundations that were thought to justify the application of the death penalty, especially with regard to minors, should be provided. . . .

21. Mr. BHAGWATI. The reservation which the United States had made to the death penalty for minors between the ages of sixteen and eighteen was justified in the report on the grounds that the Supreme Court had held that it was not unconstitutional to impose the death penalty on persons over the age of sixteen. The real issue at stake, however, was not whether that penalty was unconstitutional, but whether it was right for any Government to impose the death penalty on a minor aged sixteen or seventeen on the grounds that law and order necessitated such a measure. He hoped that the United States would reconsider its position on that matter and asked the reporting State to clarify how many minors between the ages of sixteen and eighteen had been sentenced to death and how many had been executed since 1976. The Committee would also appreciate the same data with regard to mentally retarded persons. . . .

34. Mr. POCAR. The imposition of the death penalty in cases involving persons under eighteen years of age was not in conformity with international standards, which could be considered part of international customary law. Accordingly, he appealed to the United States Government to withdraw its reservation relating to the death penalty in the near future. It would be interesting to learn what the Government's position was in the national debate on the subject.

35. [. . .] Lastly, he had doubts concerning the compatibility of the reservation to article 7 of the Covenant if the protection afforded by the Constitution was less than that provided by the Covenant, which relected international customary law in that area. . . .

38. Mr. LALLAH. With regard to the right of life, protected under article 6 of the Covenant, he saluted the new United States commitment to outlawing the execution of pregnant women (para. 148); the laws in that respect must now be changed. Yet the United States currently led the world in the execution of juveniles. The Government must take into account the ethos evolving throughout the world away from the death penalty. That was espcially important in a country like

the United States, with its checkered history of bias against certain minorities. Before the New York State Legislature had reached its final decision to reinstate the death penalty, for instance, it might have made a difference if the federal Government had made those lawmakers aware of the Government's new commitments under the Covenant, even taking into account the reservations. . . .

44. Mr. PRADO VALLEJO expressed concern that one United States reservation (para. 148) reserved the right to impose capital punishment under future as well as existing laws, and on persons below eighteen years of age. That reservation could run counter to articles 6 and 7 of the Covenant. . . .

51. Mr. FRANCIS, noting that apparently only thirteen or fourteen persons were executed each year out of the approximately 2,500 on death row in the United States, asked whether that slow pace was determined by the appeals process or by a reluctance to execute. . . .

53. The CHAIRMAN, speaking in his personal capacity, . . . opposed the imposition of the death penalty on minors.

U.N. Doc. CCPR/C/SR.1405

12. Turning to the issue of the death penalty, [Mr. Harper] said that the decision to retain it reflected a serious and considered democratic choice of the American public. Elected officials were keenly aware of the views of their constituents on that issue and it was not appropriate in that democratic system to dismiss considered public opinion and impose by fiat a different view. It was important to note, moreover, that the Covenant clearly did not prohibit the death penalty; on the contrary, article 6 expressly contemplated that States might impose that penalty, but provided a number of requirements for when it could be imposed, which the United States fully accepted. The sometimes lengthy delay between conviction and punishment was due in large part to the extensive possibilities of seeking review and enforcement of constitutional guarantees of the right of appeal. The reference to future laws in the reservation clarified the fact that the possibility of imposing the death penalty was not limited to the precise laws existing at the time the Covenant was ratified, but

could cover laws or amendments enacted in the future by which the penalty was imposed. It was not aimed specifically at types of punishments, but rather at particular types of crimes.

13. On the issue of the juvenile death penalty, he assured the Committee that the matter was being debated and that changes had not been ruled out. Nevertheless, United States laws currently favored applying the death penalty in limited cases. A large majority of states permitted juveniles to be tried as adults in grave cases involving capital offenses at the age of either sixteen or seventeen. While it was legally possible to impose a higher limit at the federal level, it was a question of democratic decision-making and not legal possibilities.

14. It was generally accepted that children below a certain age should not suffer the death penalty no matter how terrible the crime. In the United States that age had been set at sixteen. The United States disagreed that customary international law established a clear prohibition at the age of eighteen. The only authority cited was the Convention on the Rights of the Child, which adopted eighteen as the age of majority for all purposes, not specifically for the criminal area. Furthermore, widespread adherence to a treaty did not create customary international law. That was especially true for the Convention on the Rights of the Child, a major purpose of which was to create new obligations not already provided for by existing law. It was a matter of record that the drafters of the Convention actually intended to permit a reservation to that provision, as stated in documents E/CN.4/1986/39 and E/CN.4/1989/48.

15. The United States had also explained in its analysis of general comment No. 24 [for the United States analysis of the Human Rights Committee's General Comment No. 24 relating to reservations, see (1995) 16 *H.R.L.J.* 422] that there was no basis in international law for the view that a reservation could not be made to a provision of a treaty which reflected customary international law. The theory that no reservation could be taken to a non-derogable right, while popular, was also an innovative view and did not reflect existing law. . . .

45. Mr. DI GREGORY (United States of America) drew attention to a Bureau of Justice Statistics Bulletin entitled *Capital Punishment 1993*.

The report, published in December 1994, contained statistics on both adults and juveniles. It did not include a statistic requested by Mr. Bhagwati—namely, that thirty-six persons under the age of eighteen at the time of arrest had been sentenced to death. Two, both of whom had been seventeen years of age at the time they had committed the offense, had been executed. Replying to Mr. Mavrommatis, he said that thirty-one of the thirty-eight states with death penalty statutes imposed capital punishment only for murder and other serious crimes, including aggravated homicide. Seven states had extended the death penalty to certain serious non-homicidal crimes which involved grave risk of death to others or to society. Those crimes included treason, train-wrecking, aircraft hijacking, aggravated kidnapping and forcible rape of a child.

46. Replying to a question raised by Mr. Francis, he reiterated that the United States did not accept the concept of the "death row phenomenon" advanced by the European Court of Human Rights. On the contrary, it recognized that a prisoner might spend years in prison before the execution of the death sentence. The delay enabled defense lawyers to pursue every possible avenue of appeal and review. Most defendants had been tried in state courts and were eligible to appeal their sentences and convictions to the appellate court of the state in which they had been tried. In addition to the direct appeals, they could indirectly challenge their convictions by arguing that they had received ineffective assistance or counsel during the trial. They also had a limited right to have their convictions reviewed by the federal courts. While the appellate process was time consuming, it was deemed to be an important safeguard in the American legal system.

47. Replying to Mr. Lallah's question concerning the appointment of competent counsel in cases of capital punishment, he said that defendants were entitled to be represented; counsel would be appointed if a defendant could not afford to engage someone. In the federal courts, defendants accused of capital crimes, regardless of whether they were indigent, had the right to be represented by two lawyers. Where lawyers were court-appointed, one was generally experienced in capital cases. The current Administration and the Department of Justice were promoting legislation to ensure that defen-

dants accused of capital crimes in the state courts were represented by experienced and competent counsel.

48. Concerning Mr. Mavrommatis's question about approximately sixty new grounds for capital punishment contained in the *Violent Crime Control and Law Enforcement Act* of 1994, he said that constitutional and federal statutes limited the death penalty to the most egregious crimes that posed an extremely grave risk to society. Generally, capital punishment was imposed for the most aggravated offenses involving murder. It was applicable if the defendant had intentionally killed the victim, inflicted serious bodily injury that resulted in death, participated in an act knowing that death would result or had participated in an act of violence with reckless disregard for human life which had resulted in death. Federal law also authorized the death penalty for non-homicidal offenses which caused serious harm to the nation, including espionage and treason. Drug kingpins who trafficked in extremely large quantities and whose profits were twice the amount of those punishable by life imprisonment and drug kingpins who attempted to murder or order the murder of public officers, jurors, witnesses or their families in order to obstruct justice were also subject to the death penalty.

49. In 1994, the United States Congress had enacted legislation establishing constitutional procedures for the imposition of the death penalty under federal law where it had already existed under fifteen particular statutes. It had established twenty-nine new capital statutes for a combined total of approximately sixteen offenses. Fifty-six of those crimes involved aggravated homicide resulting from violent crimes, such as kidnapping, child sexual abuse and terrorist acts. Four of them involved non-homicidal offenses which caused grave harm to the nation.

50. Responding to Mr. Lallah's question about methods of execution, he said that, under the United States Constitution, no sentence, including a death sentence, could be carried out in an inhumane or barbaric manner. The five methods of execution currently employed by states which had death penalty statutes included lethal injection, electrocution, lethal gas, hanging and firing squads. Hanging and

firing squads were being phased out, however, and the trend nationally was towards lethal injection.

51. Responding to a question raised by Mr. Mavrommatis and Mr. Lallah, he said that a number of states did not have laws which affirmatively expressed a prohibition against the execution of pregnant women. With the adoption of the recently enacted *Violent Crime Control and Law Enforcement Act* of 1994, the United States congress had expressly prohibited the execution of pregnant women (United States Criminal Code, Title 18, section 3596(b)). The lack of affirmative laws in no way suggested that a death sentence would be even theoretically contemplated in such circumstances. The delegation appreciated the Committee's concern but believed that the issue did not pose a problem.

52. Responding to Mr. Bruni Celli and other Committee members who had inquired about the period 1972–1976, when the death penalty had been temporarily halted by the Supreme Court, he said that the United States Supreme Court had never held the death penalty to be unconstitutional. In 1972, the Supreme Court had held that existing death penalty sentencing procedure did not meet the constitutional requirements for reliability and individual consideration. It had not, however, held that the death penalty in and of itself was unconstitutional. In 1976, the Supreme Court had upheld revised sentencing procedures established by the State of Georgia, which required consideration of specific aggravating factors in imposing the death penalty, and of relevant mitigating factors that ensured individual treatment of each defendant. Sentencing procedures in other states which provided similar guidance to the sentencing authority had also been found to be constitutional. In the 1976 decision upholding the revised procedures, three of the Supreme Court justices had cited two centuries of precedent recognizing that capital punishment was not invalid.

53. Replying to questions raised by Mrs. Medina Quiroga and Mrs. Higgins concerning racial discrimination and capital punishment, he said that United States law expressly prohibited the imposition of the death penalty on the basis of race and required that each capital case

should be considered on an individual basis. He read out Title 18, section 3592(f) of the Federal Criminal Code, which required a jury deliberating a death sentence to be instructed not to consider the race, color, religious beliefs, national origin or sex of the defendant or of any victim and not to recommend a sentence of death unless it would have recommended that sentence for the crime in question regardless of such criteria. In returning its findings, the jury was also required to submit a certificate signed by each juror declaring that his or her decison was not based on discriminatory criteria and that he or she would have made the same recommendation regardless of the race, color, religious beliefs, national origin or sex of the defendant or victim.

54. Replying to Mrs. Higgins's question, he said that the Racial Justice Act contained two key provisions. The first prohibited the execution of any person under state or federal law if the sentence had been imposed on the basis of race; the second provided that an inference that a death sentence had been imposed on the basis of race could be etablished if there was valid evidence demonstrating that race had been a statistically significant factor in the decision, at either the state or federal level. The United States House of Representatives had adopted the Racial Justice Act as part of comprehensive anti-crime legislation referred to as the Crime Bill of 1994. The Senate had adopted a version of the Crime Bill which did not include the Racial Justice Act. The Supreme Court had held that, for purposes of constitutional analysis, statistical evidence of racial discrimination was not sufficient to support an inference of an unacceptable risk of racial discrimination in the imposition of the death sentence. Its reasoning was that the capacity of prosecutorial discretion to guarantee individualized justice was firmly entrenched in United States law. Leniency could also be considered a form of discrimination; however, ruling out leniency was alien to the United States system of justice.

55. In an effort to ensure that capital punishment imposed by federal courts would be handled in a fair and consistent manner, in early 1995 the United States Attorney-General had established aprocess for the review of each case by the Attorney-General in the light of any mitigating factors, including evidence of racial bias against the de-

fendant or evidence of discrimination by the Department of Justice. Prior to the establishment of that procedure, three United States district courts had thoroughly reviewed the files of the Department of Justice on all death penalty cases, most recently in May 1994. Each of the three courts had found no indication of racial bias in decisions to impose a sentence of capital punishment. One court had stated that, if anything, the criteria, policies and procedures of the Department of Justice demonstrated a heightened concern to ensure that the death penalty was not unfairly imposed on grounds of race or ethnic origin.

56. In response to concerns expressed by a number of Committee members concerning juveniles between sixteen and eighteen years of age, he said that federal statutes prohibited the execution of persons who had been under eighteen years of age at the time they committed a capital crime. Those statutory provisions exceeded the requirement of the Constitution, which prohibited capital punishment if persons were sixteen years of age at the time the crime had been committed. The Constitution required that, regardless of age, the relative youth or immaturity of a defendant must be considered if raised in mitigation. Addressing Mr. Bhagwati's concern about the execution of persons who were mentally retarded or disabled to a degree which prevented them from understanding the nature of the proceedings against them, the nature of the punishment and the reason for its imposition. The Constitution also required that evidence of mental retardation or mental illness must always be considered if offered in mitigation, regardless of the degree of such condition. Concerning Mr. Bhagwati's question about the number of mentally retarded persons executed since 1972, he said that the Bureau of Justice did not maintain statistics on the mental capacity of persons sentenced to death.

U.N. Doc. CCPR/C/SR.1406

2. The CHAIRMAN said that he wished to make a few comments on the overall issue of reservations, addressing in part some of the concerns of the United States about the Committee's general comment 24.

When the Vienna Convention on the Law of Treaties had been concluded, States parties, in formulating the provisions on reservations, had never had in view multilateral human rights treaties designed to create an international framework for the protection of the rights of individuals, irrespective of their nationality. Those treaties differed significantly from the traditional international agreements whose purpose was the inter-State exchange of bargained-for benefits. General comment 24 carefully explained (CCPR/C/21/Rev.1/Add.6, para. 17) the difficulties that arose in the application of the Vienna Convention provisions for the handling of reservations to the Covenant. The Committee believed that the States parties themselves, through their conduct, had affirmed a lack of interest in making the traditional Vienna Convention system work for human rights treaties.

3. The conclusions reached by the Committee were essentially the same as those acknowledged by the institutions of the inter-American and European regional human rights systems and reflected contemporary international human rights law. The Committee affirmed that it was not its position that any reservation to a substantive provision necessarily contravened the Covenant's objects and purposes. It agreed that the best guarantee of human rights was for those rights to be reflected in internal law, and its task was to ensure that they were. The Committee's interpretations as set out in its general comments were not strictly binding, although it hoped that the comments carried a certain weight and authority. In the Committee's experience, States parties often wished to give careful consideration to them for that reason. . . .

11. Mr. POCAR. A reservation should not concern a Covenant right that was protected under peremptory rules of customary law. Referring to the death penalty for juveniles, he stressed the need to take into consideration the current practice in most States and the fact that the execution of juveniles might be considered to be in contradiction to such rules. In addition, article 6 of the Covenant must be viewed within the context of the other articles, particularly article 24, which stated that every child should have the right to such measures of protection as required by his status as a minor. Accordingly, a

reservation to article 6 without a reservation to article 24 was contradictory. The reporting State should take that into account when considering the possible withdrawal of its reservation. . . .

14. Mr. MAVROMATTIS. Particular attention should be given to the right to life, especially with regard to methods of execution. . . . With regard to the long periods of time spent on death row, the reporting State should consider improving the situation by means of shorter and stricter limits for the lodging of appeals. . . .

21. Mr. BRUNI CELLI observed that it was still difficult to accept what he saw as the subjective affirmations in paragraph 139 of the report that the majority of citizens through their freely elected officials had chosen to retain the death penalty and that such a policy represented the majority sentiment of the country. There had been no real debate on that issue during electoral campaigns and no true measurement of the electorate had been taken. Yet even if those affirmations were accurate, should such a sensitive issue be decided by majority rule? Certainly the majority of non-governmental organizations in the country, and the American Bar Association itself, had come out against the death penalty, and the international community and international treaties were all moving in the direction of its abolition. The execution of minors, to which the United States reserved the right in its second reservation, was particularly troubling, both in itself and because it violated article 37(a) of the Convention on the Rights of the Child, to which the United States was a signatory even if it had not yet ratified it. Its position on that issue would also make it the only country in the hemisphere prevented from acceding to the American Convention on Human Rights. . . .

28. Mr. EL-SHAFEL. The United States must repeal its legislation permitting the execution of juveniles under eighteen. Such a practice would prevent the United States from ultimately ratifying the Convention on the Rights of the Child. . . .

33. Mr. KLEIN. . . . [T]he imposition of the death penalty on minors perhaps did not deserve the unyielding defense it was being given, and certain methods of execution that no longer seemed humane should perhaps be reconsidered. . . .

35. Mr. FRANCIS said that although all articles of the Covenant were equally important, those relating to life and death had a particular urgency. He reiterated his firm belief that there was a sufficient consensus within the reporting State to establish eighteen years as the minimum age for the imposition of the death penalty. That the way was clear for it to take that step was evident from pages 3 and 4 of its report. The United States should assume a leadership role in the field of human rights. . . .

39. Mr. BHAGWATI. He remained unconvinced of the validity of the United States reservation to article 6 of the Covenant and recalled that the Committee had stated in general comment 24 that reservations that offended peremptory norms were incompatible with the object and purpose of the Covenant. Article 6 established standards which were peremptory in nature, and the right to life was the most precious right protected by the Covenant. He hoped that the reservation would be withdrawn by the time the reporting State submitted its second periodic report. He agreed with Mrs. Medina Quiroga that a defense of the reservation which relied on the democratic choice of the people could not be a justification, but was at best an explanation. The United States government should take the lead in educating the public regarding the importance of honoring the commitments assumed upon ratification of the Covenant. . . .

44. Mr. ANDO. . . .He had taken note of the fact that the question of the continued imposition of the death penalty on minors under eighteen years of age was not yet settled and that discussion of the issue would continue. He agreed with Mr. Pocar that article 24, paragraph 1, of the Covenant, on special measures of protection for minors, was relevant in that regard. . . .

50. Mrs. EVATT. The Covenant was a living document that must be able to meet the needs of a changing world, just as the United States Bill of Rights had proved to be. While the Committee respected and supported the democratic process in the reporting State and elsewhere, it must consistently apply basic human rights standards to all States, and those standards could not be subverted, even by the democratic process. She agreed with Mrs. Medina Quiroga and Mr.

Bhagwati in that regard, and referred in particular to the reporting State's reservation to article 6 of the Covenant with respect to the imposition of capital punishment on minors.

[At the conclusion of the presentation of the initial report, on April 6, 1995, the Human Rights Committee adopted its "comments" (U.N. Doc. CCPR/C/79/Add.47).]

C. Principal Subjects of Concern

13. The Committee has taken note of the concerns addressed by the delegation in writing to its Chairman about the Committee's General Comment No. 24(52) on issues relating to reservations made upon ratification or accession to the Covenant or the Optional Protocols thereto (CCPR/C/21/Rev.1/Add.6). Attention is drawn to the observations made by the Chairman of the Committee at the 1406th meeting, on 31 March 1995 (CCPR/C/SR.1406).

14. The Committee regrets the extent of the State party's reservations, declarations and understandings to the Covenant. It believes that, taken together, they intended to ensure that the United States has accepted what is already the law of the United States. The Committee is also particularly concerned at reservations to article 6, paragraph 5, and article 7 of the Covenant, which it believes to be incompatible with the object and purpose of the Covenant. . . .

16. The Committee is concerned about the excessive number of offenses punishable by the death penalty in a number of States, the number of death sentences handed down by courts, and the long stay on death row which, in specific instances, may amount to a breach of article 7 of the Covenant. It deplores the recent expansion of the death penalty under federal law and the re-establishment of the death penalty in certain States. It also deplores provisions in the legislation of a number of States which allow the death penalty to be pronounced for crimes committed by persons under eighteen and the actual instances where such sentences have been pronounced and executed. It also regrets that, in some cases, there appears to have

been lack of protection from the death penalty of those mentally retarded. . . .

D. Suggestions and recommendations

27. The Committee recommends that the State party review its reservations, declarations and understandings with a view to withdrawing them, in particular reservations to articles 6 paragraph 5, and 7 of the Covenant. . . .

31. The Committee urges the State party to revise the federal and State legislation with a view to restricting the number of offenses carrying the death penalty strictly to the most serious crimes, in conformity with article 6 of the Covenant and with view eventually to abolishing it. It exhorts the authorities to take appropriate steps to ensure that persons are not sentenced to death for crimes committed before they were eighteen.

[In November 1994 the United States ratified the Convention Against Torture and Other Cruel, Inhuman and Degrading Treatment or Punishment. Reservations concerning the death penalty were also formulated.]

I. The Senate's advice and consent is subject to the following reservations:

(1) That the United States considers itself bound by the obligation under article 16 to prevent "cruel, inhuman or degrading treatment or punishment," only insofar as the term "cruel, inhuman or degrading treatment or punishment" means the cruel, unusual and inhumane treatment or punishment prohibited by the Fifth, Eighth and/or Fourteenth Amendments to the Constitution of the United States. . . .

II. The Senate's advice and consent is subject to the following understandings, which shall apply to the obligations of the United States under the Convention:

[. . .]

(4) That the United States understands that international law does

not prohibit the death penalty, and does not consider this convention to restrict or prohibit the United States from applying the death penalty consistent with the Fifth, Eighth and/or Fourteenth Amendments to the Constitution of the United States, including any constitutional period of confinement prior to the imposition of the death penalty.

[There have been no objections to these reservations.]

Tunis Conference Declaration on the Death Penalty in the Legislation of Arab States

[A joint initiative of the Arab Institute for Human Rights and the Citizens and Parliamentarians' League for the Abolition of the Death Penalty "Hands Off Cain," with the support of the European Community, a scientific conference, "Death Penalty in International law and Arab Legislations," was held in Tunis October 14–15, 1995. The conference was attended by several Arab and international researchers and experts in legal, religious, social, and media matters, members of Parliaments, and representatives of non-governmental organizations.]

The initiative is of vital importance as this Conference is the first to address the death penalty at the Arab level. It is also timely as it fits into the recently launched world campaign against the death penalty.

The conference dealt with three basic issues:

1. The death penalty in monotheistic religions;
2. The death penalty in international law and Arab legislations;
3. Impediments to and prospects for the abolition of the death penalty in Arab legislations.

The participants first stressed the fact that the conference objectives were:

• raising awareness about the crucial issue of the death penalty;
• the need for a thorough research in the strategic significance of the death penalty;
• identifying the impediments to placing the death penalty within the points of reference for the Arab legislator.

In this respect, the participants share a commitment to certain principles and an agreement on the following:

• a commitment to the abolition of the death penalty as a strategic move;

• that the characterizing utter cruelty of the death penalty is such that it deprives one's right to live, is an irreversible sentence, and once given effect there is no way to correct any errors once sentences are pronounced;

• that the so-called preventive effect of capital punishment is doubtful;

• that marginalized groups are more likely to be the victims of capital punishment in comparison with the remaining social groups;

• that the scientific study of the deep reasons behind criminality is rather superficial and radical solutions to criminal tendencies are yet to be found;

• that within the Arab civilizational and cultural background, no real impediments exist and obstruct the evolution of secular legislations in the process of setting up limits to the death penalty and abolishing it.

The participants firmly believe that dividing the world between "the civilized" who abolished the death penalty and "the backward" who still apply it is irrelevant. However, this should not minimize the importance of the awareness about the necessity of striving towards reaching higher levels in the field of respecting the human essence, so as to enrich the *Universal Declaration on Human Rights* by adding a new basic principle which consists in the fact that States cannot dispose freely of their citizens' right to live. Humanity has already proved such attainments to be within reach when it abolished slavery and banned torture.

The participants underlined the outstanding role of this historical period in the progress of the international movement for the abolition of the death penalty: a movement drawing on international agreements, and especially on the third article of the *Universal Declaration of Human Rights*, article 6 of the *International Covenant on*

Civil and Political Rights and the *Second Optional Protocol* appended to the *Covenant* and related to the abolition of the death penalty. They also reaffirmed the wholeness and indivisibility of human rights, and their universal dimension.

The participants pointed to the necessity of analysis and a critique of some readings and views which take cultural, religious and social particularities as an excuse to impeding the progress of the human rights movement in general, and the call for the abolition of the death penalty, in particular. They also warned against the tendencies of outbidding and "at-takfir" (accusing people of apostasy) which poison and threaten the cultural and political atmosphere in a number of Arab countries and cause assassinations and terrorizing of thinkers in the name of the sacred. They further denounced political tyranny in the Arab region and the recourse to the death penalty as a means of eliminating political opponents.

The discussions noted the dynamism of religions, including Islam, their texts and their points of reference as well as the wide range of readings they offer which differ from the traditionalist and the narrow interpretations, readings that would bring out a completely different view of several legislative aspects. This is reckoned to form a significant step in their appraisal of the human essence and to ensure the right to live.

And in the light of the need of cultural, religious and social data for the setting up of a theoretical and scientific methodology in order to tackle some of their problems, the participants expressed their belief and commitment to the necessity for the abolition of the death penalty as a strategic move while adopting the step-by-step strategy. They suggested several means to overcome the circumstantial obstacles and achieve the proposed objective in the most efficient manner. In this respect, the participants strongly stigmatized summary death sentences as illegal no matter who their doers were, be they the governments or armed groups, and expressed their full support to the world campaign to postpone executions for a specific period of time which will in turn enable the focus on the following complementary dispositions:

• the reinforcing of guaranteeing just trials and necessity for unanimous approval on the part of the members of a court when pronouncing the death penalty sentence.

• the necessity for the setting up of automatic appeal procedures (without the sentenced application) in order to re-examine cases where the death sentence was pronounced.

• the abolition of emergency courts.

• the abolition of all legal articles which require the death penalty in political, opinion and religious freedom cases.

• the consolidation of opportunities to seek reprieve.

• the backing-up of the independence of the judicial system.

• stimulating discussion of religious matters having a direct incidence on human rights, and backing up the trend calling for a re-reading of the cultural and heritage reference points which will argue for serving humanity and emphasizing human rights.

• working towards creating and improving democratic environments as one of the requirements for protecting human rights and raising public awareness about all vital causes. The right to life rated first.

• affirming the outstanding role of education in the awareness about the fundamental rights and the preservation of human life.

• calling on all countries including the Arab ones to adopt the international texts in general and the *Second Optional Protocol*, in particular

• calling on the participants to start sensitizing and developing public awareness on the need to abolish the death penalty in their respective countries through meetings and discussions at the level of universities and cultural associations.

STATISTICS ON
CAPITAL PUNISHMENT

Status of the death penalty internationally (Countries and territories whose laws do not provide for the death penalty for any crime)

	Number of States
Abolitionist for all crimes	60
Abolitionist for ordinary crimes only	14
Abolitionist de facto	35
Total abolitionist in law or practice	109
Retentionist	82

Sources: Amnesty International, The Death Penalty, List of Abolitionist and Retentionist Countries, September 1995, AI Index: ACT 50/06/95; "Capital punishment and implementation of the safeguards guaranteeing the protection of the rights of those facing the death penalty, Report of the Secretary-General," U.N. Doc. E/1995/78 (1995).

States that are abolitionist for all crimes (Countries and territories whose laws do not provide for the death penalty for any crime)

State	Date of Abolition	Date of Abolition for Ordinary Crimes	Date of Last Execution
Andorra	1990		1943
Angola	1992		
Australia	1985	1984	1967
Austria	1968	1950	1950
Bolivia			1974
Bosnia and Herzegovina	1995		[1]
Cambodia	1989		
Cape Verde	1981		1835
Colombia	1910		1909
Costa Rica	1877		
Croatia	1990		[1]
Czech Republic	1990[2]		
Denmark	1978	1933	1950
Dominican Republic	1966		
Ecuador	1906		
Finland	1972	1949	1944
France	1981		1977

(continued)

States that are abolitionist for all crimes (continued)

State	Date of Abolition	Date of Abolition for Ordinary Crimes	Date of Last Execution
Germany	1949/1987[3]		1949[3]
Greece	1993		1972
Guinea-Bissau	1993		1986[4]
Haiti	1987		1972[4]
Honduras	1956		1940
Hong Kong	1993		1966
Hungary	1990		1988
Iceland	1928		1830
Ireland	1990		1954
Italy	1994	1947	1947
Kiribati			
Liechtenstein	1987		1785
Luxembourg	1979		1949
Macedonia	1991		[1]
Marshall Islands			[1]
Micronesia (Federated States)			[1]
Moldova	1995		1989
Monaco	1962		1847
Mozambique	1990		1986
Namibia	1990		1988[4]
Netherlands	1982	1870	1952
New Zealand	1989	1961	1957
Nicaragua	1979		1930
Norway	1979	1905	1948
Palau			[1]
Panama			1903[4]
Paraguay	1992		1928
Portugal	1976	1867	1849[4]
Romania	1989		1989
San Marino	1865	1848	1468[4]
São Tomé and Principe	1990		[1]
Slovakia	1990[2]		
Slovenia	1991		[1]
Solomon Islands		1966	[1]
South Africa	1995		1989
Spain	1995	1978	1975
Sweden	1972	1921	1910
Switzerland	1992	1942	1944
Tuvalu			[1]
Uruguay	1907		

		[1]
Vanuatu		
Vatican City State	1969	
Venezuela	1863	

Sources: Amnesty International, The Death Penalty, List of Abolitionist and Retentionist Countries, September 1995, AI Index: ACT 50/06/95; "Capital punishment and implementation of the safeguards guaranteeing the protection of the rights of those facing the death penalty, Report of the Secretary-General," U.N. Doc. E/1995/78 (1995).

1. No executions since independence.
2. The death penalty was abolished in the Czech and Slovak Federal Republic in 1990. On January 1, 1993, the Czech and Slovak Federal Republic divided into two states, the Czech Republic and the Slovak Republic. The last execution in the Czech and Slovak Federal Republic was in 1988.
3. The death penalty was abolished in the Federal Republic of Germany (FRG) in 1949 and in the German Democratic Republic (GDR) in 1987. The last execution in the FRG was in 1949; the date of the last execution in the GDR is not known. The FRG and the GDR were unified in October 1990.
4. Date of last known execution.

States that are abolitionist for ordinary crimes only *(Countries whose laws provide for the death penalty only for exceptional crimes such as crimes under military law or crimes committed in exceptional circumstances such as wartime)*

Country	Date of Abolition	Date of Last Execution
Argentina	1984	
Brazil	1979	1855
Canada	1976	1962
Cyprus	1983	1962
El Salvador	1983	1973[1]
Fiji	1979	1964
Israel	1954	1962
Malta	1971	1943
Mauritius		
Mexico		1937
Nepal	1990	1979
Peru	1979	1979
Seychelles		[2]
United Kingdom	1973	1964

Sources: Amnesty International, The Death Penalty, List of Abolitionist and Retentionist Countries, September 1995, AI Index: ACT 50/06/95; "Capital punishment and implementation of the safeguards guaranteeing the protection of the rights of those facing the death penalty, Report of the Secretary-General," U.N. Doc. E/1995/78 (1995).

1. Date of last known execution.
2. No executions since independence.

States that are abolitionist de facto (*Countries and territories which retain the death penalty for ordinary crimes but can be considered abolitionist in practice in that they have not executed anyone during the past ten years or more, or in that they have made an international commitment not to carry out executions*)

Country	Date of Last Execution
Albania[1]	
Bahrain	1977
Belgium	1950
Bermuda	1977
Bhutan	1964[2]
Brunei Darussalam	1957
Burundi	1982
Central African Republic	1981
Chile	1985
Congo	1982
Comoros	[2]
Djibouti	[2]
Gambia	1981
Guatemala	1983
Guinea	1983
Ivory Coast	1960[3]
Lesotho	
Madagascar	1958[2]
Maldives	1952[2]
Mali	1980
Nauru	
Niger	1976[2]
Papua New Guinea	1950
Philippines	1976
Russia[4]	
Rwanda	1982
Senegal	1967
Sri Lanka	1976
Suriname	1982
Swaziland	1983
Togo	
Tonga	1982
Turkey	1984

Ukraine[5]
Western Samoa   3

Sources: Amnesty International, The Death Penalty, List of Abolitionist and Retentionist
Countries, September 1995, AI Index: ACT 50/06/95; "Capital punishment and implementation of the safeguards guaranteeing the protection of the rights of those facing the
death penalty, Report of the Secretary-General," U.N. Doc. E/1995/78 (1995).

1. Preparatory to Albania's joining the Council of Europe, in a declaration signed on
June 29, 1995, Pjeter Arbnori, president of the Albanian Parliament, said he was willing
to commit his country "to put into place a moratorium on executions until [the] total
abolition of capital punishment."

2. Date of last known execution.

3. No executions since independence.

4. Undertaking by the government upon joining the Council of Europe in January
1996.

5. During a meeting between delegates of the Parliamentary Assembly of the Council
of Europe and Ukrainian government officials on October 17, 1995, in Kiev, the Minister of Justice, Serhiy Holovatiy, confirmed the government's commitment to abolish the
death penalty and institute an immediate moratorium an executions.

States that retain the death penalty (*States that retain and use the death penalty for ordinary crimes*)[1]

Afghanistan	Dominica	Kazakhstan
Algeria	Egypt	Kenya
Antigua and Barbuda	Equatorial Guinea	Korea (DPR)
Armenia	Eritrea	Korea, Republic of
Azerbaydzhan	Estonia	Kuwait
Bahamas	Ethiopia	Kyrgyzstan
Bangladesh	Gabon	Laos
Barbados	Georgia	Latvia
Belarus	Ghana	Lebanon
Belize	Grenada	Liberia
Benin	Guyana	Libya
Botswana	India	Lithuania
Bulgaria	Indonesia	Malawi
Burkina Faso	Iran	Malaysia
Cameroon	Iraq	Mauritania
Chad	Jamaica	Morocco
China	Japan	Myanmar
Cuba	Jordan	Nigeria

(continued)

States that retain the death penalty *(continued)*[1]

Oman	Sierra Leone	Uganda
Pakistan	Singapore	United Arab Emirates
Poland	Somalia	United States of America
Qatar	Sudan	Uzbekistan
Saint Christopher and	Syria	Viet Nam
Nevis	Tadzhikistan	Yemen
Saint Lucia	Taiwan	Yugoslavia
Saint Vincent and the	Tanzania	Zaire
Grenadines	Thailand	Zambia
Saudi Arabia	Trinidad and Tobago	Zimbabwe

Sources: Amnesty International, The Death Penalty, List of Abolitionist and Retentionist Countries, September 1995, AI Index: ACT 50/06/95; "Capital punishment and implementation of the safeguards guaranteeing the protection of the rights of those facing the death penalty, Report of the Secretary-General," U.N. Doc. E/1995/78 (1995).

1. Most of these countries and territories are known to have carried out executions during the past ten years. For some states, Amnesty International has no record of executions and is unable to ascertain whether executions have in fact been carried out. Several states have carried out executions in the past ten years but have since instituted national moratoria on executions.

Number of abolitionist countries at year-end, 1980–1995

Year	Abolitionist for All Crimes	Abolitionist in Law or Practice
1980	25	62
1981	27	63
1982	28	63
1983	28	64
1984	28	64
1985	29	64
1986	31	66
1987	35	69
1988	35	80
1989	39	84
1990	46	88
1991	46	83
1992	49	84
1993	53	90
1994	55	97
1995	59	105

Source: Amnesty International.

Recorded worldwide executions by year, 1980–1995

Year	Countries Carrying out Executions	Executions Recorded	Countries with over 100 Executions	Percent of Recorded Executions in Countries with over 100 Executions
1980	29	1,229		
1981	34	3,278		
1982	42	1,609		
1983	39	1,399		
1984	40	1,513	4	78
1985	44	1,125	3	66
1986	39	743	3	56
1987	39	769	3	59
1988	35	1,903	3	83
1989	34	2,229	3	85
1990	26	2,029	4	84
1991	32	2,086	2	89
1992	35	1,708	2	82
1993	32	1,831	1	77
1994	37	2,331	3	87
1995	41	2,931	3	85

Source: Amnesty International.

States Parties to the Second Optional Protocol to the International Covenant on Civil and Political Rights
(as of January 1, 1996)

Australia	Iceland	Namibia	Seychelles
Austria	Ireland	Netherlands	Slovenia
Croatia	Italy	New Zealand	Spain[1]
Denmark	Luxembourg	Norway	Sweden
Ecuador	Macedonia	Panama	Switzerland
Finland	Malta	Portugal	Uruguay
Germany	Mozambique	Romania	Venezuela
Hungary			

Source: "State of Ratifications of Major Human Rights Conventions" (1995), 13 *Netherlands Quarterly of Human Rights* 491.

1. At the time of ratification, Spain made the following reservation: "Pursuant to article 2, Spain reserves the right to apply the death penalty in the exceptional and extremely serious cases provided for in Fundamental Act No. 13/1985 of December 9, 1985, regulating the Military Criminal Code, in wartime as defined in article 25 of that Act" (U.N. Doc. CCPR/C/2/Rev.3, p. 101).

States Parties to the Sixth Protocol to the European Convention on Human Rights (as of January 1, 1996)

Austria	Hungary	Malta	Slovakia
Czech Republic	Iceland	Netherlands	Slovenia
Denmark	Ireland	Norway	Spain
Finland	Italy	Portugal	Sweden
France	Liechtenstein	Romania	Switzerland
Germany	Luxembourg	San Marino	

Source: "State of Ratifications of Major Human Rights Conventions" (1995), 13 *Netherlands Quarterly of Human Rights* 491.

States Parties to the American Convention on Human Rights That Have Abolished the Death Penalty[1]

Argentina[2]	Costa Rica	Haiti	Paraguay
Bolivia	Dominican Republic	Honduras	Peru[2]
Brazil[2]	Ecuador	Mexico[2]	Suriname[3]
Chile[3]	El Salvador[2]	Nicaragua	Uruguay
Colombia	Guatemala[3]	Panama	Venezuela

Source: "State of Ratifications of Major Human Rights Conventions" (1995), 13 *Netherlands Quarterly of Human Rights* 491.

1. Pursuant to article 4§2 of the Convention, "The death penalty shall not be reestablished in states that have abolished it." Consequently, states parties to the Convention that have abolished the death penalty are abolitionist from the standpoint of international law.

2. Abolitionist for ordinary crimes.

3. De facto abolitionist.

States Parties to the Protocol to the American Convention on Human Rights to Abolish the Death Penalty

Panama
Uruguay
Venezuela

Source: "Annual Report of the Inter-American Commission on Human Rights 1994," O.A.S. Doc. OEA/SER.L.V/II.88 Doc. 9 rev., p. 246.

United States of America: Minimum age authorized for capital punishment (*According to date of infraction*)

Age Less than 18	Age 18	No Age Specified
Alabama (16)	California	Arizona
Arkansas (14)[1]	Colorado	Florida
Delaware (16)	Connecticut[2]	Idaho
Georgia (17)	Federal system	Montana
Indiana (16)	Illinois	Pennsylvania
Kentucky (16)	Maryland	South Carolina
Louisiana (16)	Nebraska	South Dakota[5]
Mississippi (16)[3]	New Jersey	Utah
Missouri (16)	New Mexico	Washington
Nevada (16)	Ohio	
New Hampshire (17)	Oregon	
North Carolina (17)[4]	Tennessee	
Oklahoma (16)		
Texas (17)		
Utah (14)		
Virginia (15)		
Wyoming (16)		

Source: United States, Capital Punishment 1993, NCJ-145031.
    1. Arkansas Code Ann. 9-27-318(b)(1)(Repl. 1991).
    2. Conn. Gen. Stat. 53a–46a(g)(1).
    3. Minimum age defined by statute is 13, but effective age is 16 based on an interpretation of U.S. Supreme Court decisions by the state attorney general's office.
    4. Age required is 17 unless the murderer was incarcerated for murder when a subsequent murder occurred; the age then may be 14.
    5. Juveniles may be transferred to adult court. Age may be a mitigating circumstance.

United States of America: Number of executions, 1977–1995

Year	Number
1977	1
1979	2
1981	1
1982	2
1983	5
1984	21
1985	18

(continued)

United States of America: Number of executions, 1977–1995 (continued)

Year	Number
1986	18
1987	25
1988	11
1989	16
1990	23
1991	14
1992	31
1993	38
1994	31
1995	56

Sources: United States, Capital Punishment 1993, NCJ-150042; Agence France-Presse.

United States of America: Method of execution

Lethal Injection	Electrocution	Lethal Gas	Hanging	Firing Squad
Arizona[1,6]	Alabama	Arizona[1]	Montana[1]	Idaho[1]
Arkansas[1,2]	Arkansas[1,2]	California[1]	New Hampshire[1,4]	Utah[1]
California[1]	Connecticut	Colorado[1,3]	Washington[1]	
Colorado[1,3]	Florida	Maryland		
Delaware	Georgia	Mississippi[1,5]		
Federal	Indiana	Missouri[1]		
Idaho[1]	Kentucky	North Carolina[1]		
Illinois	Nebraska	Wyoming[1,7]		
Louisiana	Ohio[1]			
Mississippi[1,5]	South Carolina			
Missouri[1]	Tennessee			
Montana[1]	Virginia			
Nevada				
New Hampshire[1,4]				
New Jersey				
New Mexico				
New York				
North Carolina[1]				
Ohio[1]				
Oklahoma				
Oregon				

Pennsylvania
South Dakota
Texas
Utah[1]
Washington[1]
Wyoming[1,7]

Source: United States, Capital Punishment 1993, NCJ-150042.
   1. Authorizes two methods of execution.
   2. Arkansas authorizes lethal injection for those whose capital offense occurred after 7/4/83; for those whose offense occurred before that date, the condemned prisoner may select lethal injection or electrocution.
   3. Colorado authorizes lethal gas for those whose crimes occurred before 7/1/88 and lethal injection for those whose crimes occurred on or after 7/1/88.
   4. New Hampshire authorizes hanging only if lethal injection cannot be given.
   5. Mississippi authorizes lethal injection for those convicted after 7/1/84; execution of those convicted prior to that date is to be carried out with lethal gas.
   6. Arizona authorizes lethal injection for those sentenced to death after 11/15/92. Those sentenced before may choose between lethal injection and lethal gas.
   7. Wyoming authorizes lethal gas, if lethal injection is ever held unconstitutional.

United States of America: Time between imposition of death sentence and execution, by race, 1977–1993

Year of Execution	Number Executed			Average Time from Sentence to Execution (Months)[1]		
	All Races[2]	White	Black	All Races[2]	White	Black
1977–1983	11	9	2	51	49	58
1984	21	13	8	74	76	71
1985	18	11	7	71	65	80
1986	18	11	7	87	78	102
1987	25	13	12	86	78	96
1988	11	6	5	80	72	89
1989	16	8	8	95	78	112
1990	23	16	7	95	97	91
1991	14	7	7	116	124	107
1992	31	19	11	114	104	135
1993	38	23	14	113	112	121
Total	226	136	88	94	89	102

Source: United States, Capital Punishment 1993, NCJ-150042.
   1. Average time was calculated from the most recent sentencing date. The range for elapsed time of the 226 executions was from 3 months to 212 months.
   2. Includes two aboriginals.

United States of America: Number sentenced to death and executed, and average time on death row

State	Number under Sentence of Death	Average Time on Death Row (Years)	Number Executed Since 1977	Number Executed Since 1930
Alabama	120	6.4	12	145
Arizona	112	6.4	—	41
Arkansas	33	5.6	10	122
California	363	6.2	2	294
Colorado	3	N/A[1]	—	47
Connecticut	5	N/A[1]	—	21
Delaware	15	4.2	5	15
District of Columbia	—	—	—	40
Federal	6	N/A[1]	—	33
Florida	324	6.3	33	202
Georgia	96	6.9	20	383
Idaho	22	6.7	1	3
Illinois	152	6.5	5	91
Indiana	47	7.4	3	43
Iowa	—	—	—	18
Kansas	—	—	—	15
Kentucky	30	7.2	—	103
Louisiana	45	5.4	22	154
Maryland	15	5.5	1	68
Massachusetts	—	—	—	27
Mississippi	50	5.1	4	158
Missouri	80	5.7	13	73
Montana	8	N/A[1]	1	6
Nebraska	11	12.4	1	4
Nevada	65	6.7	5	34
New Hampshire	—	—	—	1
New Jersey	7	N/A[1]	—	74
New Mexico	1	N/A[1]	—	8
New York	—	—	—	329
North Carolina	99	3.5	7	268
Ohio	129	5.5	—	172
Oklahoma	122	6.1	5	63
Oregon	13	1.6	—	19
Pennsylvania	169	5.6	1	152
South Carolina	47	6.3	4	166
South Dakota	2	N/A[1]	—	1

Tennessee	98	7.4	—	93
Texas	357	6.3	97	368
Utah	11	N/A[1]	4	17
Vermont	—	—	—	4
Virginia	49	4.4	26	114
Washington	10	5.6	2	48
West Virginia	—	—	—	40
Wyoming	—	—	1	8
Total	2,716	6.1	285	4,085

Source: United States, Capital Punishment 1993, NCJ-150042; Amnesty International—USA, Death Penalty Newsletter, July–September 1995.

1. Averages not calculated on fewer than ten inmates.

Index